Innocent until Nominated

G. Calvin Mackenzie
Editor

Innocent until Nominated

The Breakdown of the Presidential Appointments Process

Brookings Institution Press
Washington, D.C.

ABOUT BROOKINGS

The Brookings Institution is a private nonprofit organization devoted to research, education, and publication on important issues of domestic and foreign policy. Its principal purpose is to bring knowledge to bear on current and emerging policy problems. The Institution maintains a position of neutrality on issues of public policy. Interpretations or conclusions in Brookings publications should be understood to be solely those of the authors.

THE BROOKINGS INSTITUTION
1775 Massachusetts Avenue, N.W., Washington, D.C. 20036
www.brookings.edu

Library of Congress Cataloging-in-Publication data

Innocent until nominated : the breakdown of the presidential appointments process / G. Calvin Mackenzie, editor.
p. cm.
Includes bibliographical references and index.
ISBN 0-8157-5401-9 (pbk. : alk. paper)
1. United States—Officials and employees—Selection and appointment.
2. Cabinet officers—Selection and appointment—United States.
3. Government executives—Selection and appointment—United States.
4. Judges—Selection and appointment—United States.
5. Presidents—United States. I. Mackenzie, G. Calvin.
JK731 .I56 2001
352.3'265'0973—dc21 2001004191

9 8 7 6 5 4 3 2 1

The paper used in this publication meets minimum requirements of the American National Standard for Information Sciences—Permanence of Paper for Printed Library Materials: ANSI Z39.48-1992.

Typeset in Sabon

Composition by R. Lynn Rivenbark
Macon, Georgia

Printed by R. R. Donnelley and Sons
Harrisonburg, Virginia

THE BROOKINGS INSTITUTION

The Brookings Institution is an independent organization devoted to nonpartisan research, education, and publication in economics, government, foreign policy, and the social sciences generally. Its principal purposes are to aid in the development of sound public policies and to promote public understanding of issues of national importance. The Institution was founded on December 8, 1927, to merge the activities of the Institute for Government Research, founded in 1916, the Institute of Economics, founded in 1922, and the Robert Brookings Graduate School of Economics and Government, founded in 1924. The Institution maintains a position of neutrality on issues of public policy to safeguard the intellectual freedom of the staff.

Foreword

AS THIS BOOK goes to press, the administration of George W. Bush is entering its seventh month in office. One would expect that by now the hundreds of people who compose the new administration would be hard at work defining and implementing the president's agenda. That, after all, is the way our democratic process is supposed to work: the people choose a new president, who then fills the top offices of the government with his own appointees, who then shape public policy in accord with electoral directives.

The contemporary reality, however, is far different. As of July 2001, with nearly an eighth of his term behind him, President Bush has few of his key players on the field. Barely half of his top 500 executive branch appointees have been nominated, and fewer than a quarter of the total have been confirmed by the Senate. It now seems likely that the administration will be well into its second year before all of these key positions are filled.

None of this is unique to the current president. The presidential appointments process has been slowing for years. The average appointee of President Kennedy was confirmed in 2.4 months, but the average for appointees of both Presidents George H. W. Bush and Bill Clinton was more than eight months.

The appointments process has become coarser, as well as longer. Nominees are subjected to more intrusive investigations, more scathing criticism, and more frequent twisting by the political winds than ever before. One consequence is that too many talented Americans are now reluctant to accept the call to public service—not because the challenge and opportunity lack appeal, but because they do not want to endure the uncertainties and the ordeal of the appointments process.

In this book, scholars with wide-ranging acquaintance with the presidential appointments process examine its history and recent evolution. They explore the problems faced by presidents in recruiting presidential appointees; the special burdens of presidential transitions; and the ever-expanding array of forms, questionnaires, and background checks that nominees now face. They examine the Senate's increasingly aggressive exercise of the confirmation power and the special attention that it pays to judicial appointments. The book also reports the findings of two original surveys of the attitudes and experiences of past presidential appointees and potential candidates for appointment.

The essays in this volume were commissioned by the Presidential Appointee Initiative, a project of the Brookings Institution, funded by The Pew Charitable Trusts, that has used the insights of scholarship and analysis to raise national consciousness about the failings of the presidential appointments process and the resulting costs to the quality of government performance. Working with leaders in the executive and legislative branches, the Presidential Appointee Initiative has sought to encourage thoughtful responses and solutions to these problems.

Edited by G. Calvin Mackenzie, the Goldfarb Family Distinguished Professor of American Government at Colby College and a visiting fellow at Brookings, this book presents a powerful problem statement for the nation. The American approach to filling the top offices of the federal government is unique. The belief has long prevailed that government ought to draw on the very best of its citizens, from all walks of life, to contribute their skills and acumen as leaders. For much of our history, America has been well served by this "in-and-outer" system—but now reform is urgently needed. And intelligent reform must begin with accurate analysis of the problems and their causes. The insights of the contributors help to explain what ails the presidential appointments process and what must be done to restore its traditional role as an efficient and hospitable gateway to the able and creative leaders so desperately needed by the national government in Washington.

Brookings is grateful to The Pew Charitable Trusts for its financial support of the Presidential Appointee Initiative. The project has been led by Paul C. Light, vice president and director of the Governmental Studies program at Brookings, and by Sandra Stencel, executive director of the project, and Carole Plowfield, the associate director.

At the Brookings Institution Press, Katherine Kimball ably edited the manuscript, Barbara Malczak proofread the pages, and Deborah Patton provided the index.

The views expressed here are solely those of the authors and should not be attributed to any person or organization acknowledged above or to the trustees, officers, or other staff members of the Brookings Institution.

MICHAEL H. ARMACOST
President, Brookings Institution

Washington, D.C.
July 2001

Contents

Innocent until Nominated

CHAPTER ONE

The State of the Presidential Appointments Process

G. CALVIN MACKENZIE

AMERICANS HAVE ALWAYS had the peculiar idea that amateurs could govern. In no other country have citizens been so devoted to the idea. In the parliamentary democracies, political leaders emerge from years of partisan legislative activity. No one gets to be prime minister without first serving as a backbencher, then a junior minister or shadow spokesperson, then perhaps a more senior minister, and then—usually after successfully fending off furious leadership challenges—as party leader. Amateurs do not govern in the parliamentary democracies.

When a new prime minister takes office, it is not to the thundering accompaniment of thousands of his or her predecessor's lieutenants departing and a similar number from the winning side moving in to replace them. A few score, maybe a hundred or so, slide in as cabinet ministers and their deputies—nearly all of them parliamentary veterans like their leaders—but most of the management of government remains in the reliable hands of senior civil servants. The ship of state may turn, perhaps even dramatically, but the crew remains largely the same.

In the presidential democracies of the Western Hemisphere, a candidate may occasionally come to power directly from the private sector, as did Vicente Fox in Mexico recently or Alberto Fujimori in Peru in 1990. In those cases, too, the election of an outsider did not bring any sweeping changes—and certainly no great influx of the inexperienced—to the top levels of administration. So it is throughout nearly all the world, in democracies parliamentary and presidential, in monarchies and autocracies.

Government is the business of professionals, and access to leadership must usually follow a long apprenticeship.

Not, however, in America. Here we freely and regularly place our trust in presidents who are strangers to the capital city, its political folkways, and its administrative routines. Four of the past five American presidents had never held any position in the federal government in Washington before their inaugurations. When a new American president takes office, he is permitted to fill thousands of executive branch positions with people whose only necessary qualification is their ability to endure and survive the Senate confirmation process. Like him, they need bring no experience in national government nor even any demonstrable acquaintance with the department or agency in which they will serve. No permanent secretary, no lion of the civil service, stands ready to guide these new appointees, to protect them from missteps and misjudgments. There are civil servants aplenty in all the departments and agencies, many of them truly talented and experienced; but most are buried under many layers of political appointments and rarely have any significant direct contact with the political appointees at the top of the administrative structure.

If this is a management model that few other countries have adopted, so is it a model to which few other organizations in American society subscribe. One searches in vain for a sizable American corporation in which top management is drawn from people with no experience in the company or at least in the business it conducts. Hospitals, universities, other nonprofit organizations all stick closely to the tried-and-true approach of relying on leaders who know the ropes before they are asked to pull them.

The national government stands alone in trusting top leadership roles to outsiders and amateurs. Why? The historical record yields few answers. The framers of the Constitution considered several models of appointment but never discussed in any depth the question of leadership development for the executive branch. Nor did the question much inspire other Americans in the years that followed. It would be more than a century before the national government created a civil service, and the Pendleton Act of 1883 was never a measure intended to improve the top leadership of the executive branch.

Over the course of the twentieth century, as the number of top-level political appointees steadily expanded, no significant discussion of alternative approaches to filling those positions ever took place. Even the expansion itself was sporadic and ad hoc; it was never driven by the adoption of any theory or philosophy suggesting that multiplying the number of positions filled by political appointment was a key to better government. It happened instead by incidental accumulation, the product of dozens of unrelated decisions about the shape and structure of individual agencies or departments.

The contemporary approach to leadership development and selection draws most of its defenders from among its political beneficiaries or those who despair of the prospect of change and search for benefits in an unchosen inheritance. The presidential appointments system, they argue, is an effective device for letting the president "take control" of hostile bureaucracies. Arthur Schlesinger Jr., in his history of the John F. Kennedy presidency, drew a typical image of the fair prince leading his valiant transients against the dark forces of permanence.

> The permanent government [had] developed its own stubborn vested interests in policy and procedure, its own cozy alliances with the committees of Congress, its own ties to the press, its own national constituencies. It began to exude the feeling that Presidents would come and Presidents go but it went on forever. The permanent government was, as such, politically neutral; its essential commitment was to doing things as they had been done before. This frustrated the enthusiasts who came to Washington with Eisenhower in 1953 zealous to dismantle the New Deal, and it frustrated the enthusiasts who came to Washington with Kennedy in 1961 zealous to get the country moving again.[1]

Others argue that, whatever its imperfections, the appointments system provides periodic infusions of fresh ideas and fresh blood to the tired government in Washington. From Bozeman and Boston, from Sacramento and Atlanta come the new faces every four years, ready to show the nation's government how things are done in the countryside—a necessary corrective, the defenders argue, to the "inside-the-beltway mentality" that inhabits and debilitates the Washington crowd.

Some even hold to the ancient argument that filling the top levels of an administration with political appointees is essential to motivating participation in politics. Citizens will be more likely to contribute time and money in behalf of their preferred presidential candidate, the argument goes, if the prospect of some reward, in the form of a job in Washington, looms ahead.

The reality is that the current system of presidential appointments has few defenders—and few attackers. It is widely accepted as a fact of life, unlikely soon to change. Politicians may bemoan its frailties and burdens, but there has never been a significant effort to redesign or replace the appointments process. Scholars of public management may recognize its uniqueness and its costs, but few of them invest their energies in developing and advocating alternatives. The appointments process is just there, like the Washington Monument, the cherry blossoms, and annual battles over the budget—a feature of Washington life. All political calculations assume it; all strategies for changing the direction of public policy must confront it.

This begs a question, however, a terribly important question. If we rely so heavily on the presidential appointments process to staff the highest levels of government, to ensure a president's ability to act on the directions that voters endorse in our elections, to replenish the government with new ideas and energy, shouldn't we at least ask how good a job it does of performing these tasks? That is to say, simply, does the contemporary presidential appointments process work?

The Changing Context

The words mean what they say: political appointments are political. Whatever else it may have been over the past two centuries, the appointments process has vibrated to political rhythms. When changes take place in American society and politics, they inevitably, and usually quickly, find their way into the appointments process. It has always been a clear and revealing mirror of our politics.

In the years since World War II, and in the past three decades especially, American politics has undergone several profound changes. Each of those has affected the operations of the presidential appointments process, yielding today a process that differs in important ways from the one that Harry S Truman and Dwight D. Eisenhower superintended a half century ago. We cannot begin to explain the character of the contemporary appointments process without some understanding of the profound political changes that transfigured it.

The Expanding Role of Government

The work done by the New Dealers and the leaders who managed the war effort against the Axis powers set in motion a series of changes that would radically and permanently transform the relationship between the American people and their government. In response to the Great Depression, federal spending tripled in the 1930s, from $3 billion in 1930 to $9 billion in 1939. New agencies and departments sprang up everywhere. World War II required more federal spending from 1940 through 1945 than the United States had expended in all the previous years of the century.

During its heyday, the New Deal was characterized by its leaders as a response to an emergency. Most of those leaders genuinely believed that much of their work was temporary. They would get the economy back on track and then close up shop and go home. World War II was viewed in the same way. The American tradition had been to mobilize for wars and then to demobilize again as soon as the war was over. After 1945, however, neither the New Deal nor the war machine went away. What those two signal events in American history produced was a permanent and tectonic shift in the role of the federal government in American society. With that shift came a powerful redefinition of the meaning of Washington as the center of national life.

By 1950, the nation's eyes had formed the habit of focusing on Washington. We looked there for leadership and representation—for the assistance that government could provide us. In the second half of the twentieth century, as the stakes of government decisions grew, Washington became the principal battleground for all the competing forces in American life.

Deterioration of Political Parties

As government expanded, ironically, the single device best suited to ensuring the coherence of its actions declined. Political parties, the glue that had bonded our separated institutions together for more than a century and a half, started to deteriorate in the middle of the twentieth century, and by the century's end they had fallen into an acute state of disrepair.

All of the important roles that political parties had played in American public life—in the nomination of candidates, as intermediaries with voters, as financiers and managers of campaigns, as repositories of political skills—had evolved to others by century's end. Direct primaries and caucuses chose the candidates, and the candidates then did their own fundraising and hired expert consultants to manage their campaigns. Television, not the local ward boss, became the primary medium of communication between elected officials and the people they represented.

Parties lost their grip on politics and became irrelevant to much of what happened in legislatures and executive offices.

In the early 1960s, the most important studies of voting behavior pointed to partisan identification as the strongest factor in determining how a citizen would vote. By 2000, a third of the potential electorate called themselves independents, 50 percent more than at mid-century. Martin Wattenberg, one of the most incisive chroniclers of the decline of political parties, writes that

> for over four decades the American public has been drifting away from the two major political parties. Once central guiding forces in American electoral behavior, the parties are currently perceived with almost complete indifference by a large portion of the population. Public affection for the parties has declined not because of greater negative feelings about the Democrats and Republicans, but rather because of an increasing sense that parties are no longer crucial to the governmental process.[2]

The central role that the Democratic and Republican Party organizations had once played as employment agencies for the worker bees of politics deteriorated almost completely—a victim of the twin scourges of an expanding civil service and declining control over the electoral nominating process. When executives no longer had to rely on parties for their own nominations and elections, they were no longer obligated to rely on them as sources of their appointees, either; and so they halted, rather abruptly in most places, a practice that had prevailed in America for more than a century: deference to political parties in choosing political appointees.

The News Explosion

As the role of the national government grew, Washington became the source of more news, and the organizations that reported the news expanded as well. The press became a pervasive presence. As the boundaries of what constituted news began to expand, the press also became a more invasive presence.

At the beginning of Franklin D. Roosevelt's second term, there were more reporters in Washington than ever before, but the total was still small. Leo Rosten's pathbreaking 1937 study of the Washington press corps identified only 504 accredited correspondents covering all the political news in the city.[3] By comparison, in 1996 the White House had more than two thousand accredited reporters, and the Congress nearly five thousand.[4]

Rosten also uncovered a set of norms among Washington reporters of the time very different from those that prevail today. Reporters were reluctant to write stories that would anger their sources and cause them to dry up. Rosten quotes as emblematic one reporter's description of this relationship:

> The Washington correspondent . . . wants to hold friendships, and he believes that if he prints all the news and the truth he cannot do this. Friendship means news. So the reporter becomes something of a servitor, a satellite—unknowingly. His truth is not his own; and, therefore, not the public's. The Washington correspondent today does his work as a business proposition. . . . If by printing a fact he will arouse the anger of a good news-source his decision is easy and immediate. For an angry friend means less news, more work, and a poorer record of stories.[5]

Another notable difference in Washington press coverage before World War II was the paucity of stories about the activities of presidential appointees in the departments and agencies. Careful coverage of the work of the departments required time and expertise that few reporters possessed. As one of the leading histories of Washington press coverage notes, that pattern has altered significantly in the past half century.

> The perspective of more than one hundred and fifty years points up several shifts in the emphasis and volume of Washington news found in the newspaper files. . . . A very marked change in the twentieth century has been the increased attention given to the executive departments. There are two reasons for that increase. One is the mere fact that the importance of the departments, the number of workers employed in them, the volume of work they do, and its effects on the lives of Americans has very greatly expanded. The second reason is that those departments employ information specialists.[6]

In the last decade of this century, the Washington press corps has become the elite of American journalism. Nearly all Washington reporters are college graduates, and many have graduate degrees. More than 40 percent consider themselves specialists and spend most of their careers covering one institution or policy area.[7] The best reporters now tend to gravitate to Washington and to bring the best skills in American journalism to coverage of the actions of federal officials.

Moreover, the agencies of the government are more vigorous than ever before in inviting, encouraging, and facilitating coverage of their activities. Every agency of the federal government has an active public information operation trying to tell its story and shape the way that story is reported. Stephen Hess describes the State Department's operation in the Reagan years:

> The State Department had forty-two full-time press officers in Washington. . . . Pressroom facilities had twenty-nine partitioned working spaces, spacious offices for the AP [Associated Press] and UPI [United Press International], and six radio-TV booths. A wire service room allowed reporters access to the flowing tickers of AP, UPI, Reuters, and the CIA's Foreign Broadcast Information Service. . . . The State Department issued 441 press releases in 1981.[8]

News output has grown because news consumption has grown. The second half of the twentieth century saw a rapid rise in the number of news outlets in the United States and in the choices available to consumers of news. More than 100 million Americans (80 percent of the adult population) read a newspaper daily. The average household owns 5.6 radios. Nearly two-thirds of all households subscribe to cable TV. Each night, about 30 million Americans tune in to the evening news broadcasts of one of the three national TV networks. With the proliferation of cable and satellite TV options and the rapid emergence of the Internet as a major news source, the opportunities for news consumption continue the pattern of expansion that began when KDKA in Pittsburgh produced the first broadcast news in 1920.[9]

Modern Washington is not like its earlier permutations. It is much more open to public view, and its officials are much larger targets of public attention, than ever before. The news in Washington is big business, and the competition for stories—particularly for stories with mass consumer appeal—is more ferocious than it has ever been.

In the Garden of the Special Interests: Let a Thousand Flowers Bloom

The press constitutes only one growth sector in postwar Washington. The other major element of change has been the expansion in the number, size, and sophistication of the special interest groups located or represented in Washington. As decisions made in Washington came to affect a wider number of Americans, the recipients of government benefits and services—and the pursuers of those—made tracks to the capital. They hired professional counsel and public relations specialists and lobbyists. They often set up their own offices and employed their own staffs of analysts and lobbyists. Every measure of growth of special interest representation in Washington inclines sharply upward over the past three decades.

The growth in the journalism community and in special interest representation are among the most important forces shaping modern Washington. Their occurrence also produced a new dynamic in the capital, a kind of political jujitsu. As the forces swirling around government grew, government expanded to deal with them—and to deal with itself. With more to do, Congress spent more days in session. Executive branch officials were called to testify more often, were required to submit more reports, were expected to be available on little notice to any member of Congress and, increasingly, to powerful congressional staffers.

To handle the demands of managing more programs, relating more often to more constituencies, and satisfying more persistent congressional interest, the leadership cadres of all federal agencies thickened. As table 1-1 indicates, the White House staff, congressional staffs, and the senior levels of the executive branch all experienced significant growth in the postwar period, just as the nongovernment elements of the Washington community were also expanding.

Diminishing Trust in Government

From 1967 through 1974, another tectonic shift occurred. The Vietnam War brought down more than the Johnson administration: it sealed the fate of the durable New Deal political coalition, and it signaled the end of the great liberal hour in twentieth-century American politics. The momentum for a more active federal government—a momentum that began with the Populists and Progressives nearly three-quarters of a century earlier—was spent, and Vietnam was its final, tragic act. The country scoffed at Barry Goldwater's ideas in 1964; in 1980 his principal political heir was elected president.

In those same few years in the early 1970s, two dogged young investigative reporters brought down another administration, and with it fell the last remnants of public faith in the good intentions and moral character of public servants. When Ronald Reagan said in his first inaugural

Table 1-1. *Growth in Government Employment, Selected Elements, Selected Years, 1935–92*

Number

Year	*Executive branch positions, EL-1 to EL-5*	*White House office employees*	*Senate and House employees (total)*
1935	56	44	1,284
1952	81	245	2,800[a]
1960	451	446	4,000[a]
1964	600	349	4,900[a]
1968	719	273	5,800[a]
1972	845	596	7,706
1976	979	541	10,190
1980	1,579	406	11,116
1984	1,693	374	11,334
1988	1,752	362	11,546
1992	2,393	400	11,846

Source: Paul C. Light, *Thickening Government* (Brookings, 1995), pp. 190–92; Lyn Ragsdale, *Vital Statistics on the Presidency* (CQ Press, 1996), pp. 258–61.

a. Estimates based on data for nearby years.

address that "government is the problem, not the solution," he was simply reporting the emergent consensus of the American people. Trust and confidence in government turned dramatically downward after the mid-1960s (figure 1-1).

A clamor grew for more constraints on public officials as venality and self-dealing became prominent features in the prevailing caricature of public servants. In 1978, the Congress passed and President Jimmy Carter signed the Ethics in Government Act of 1978. This and several subsequent elaborations created the most tightly woven fabric of ethical and financial constraints imposed by any national government on its top officials.

New rules needed new enforcers, and up they cropped everywhere: inspectors general, designated agency ethics officers, independent counsels, an Office of Government Ethics, a Merit Systems Protection Board, and a Public Integrity Section of the Justice Department's Criminal Division to prosecute violators. The effort to protect the public from its own leaders became one of the fastest-growing sectors of government in the years after Vietnam and Watergate. For those who entered government service as presidential appointees, ethics regulation became a unique and distasteful occupational hazard.

Figure 1-1. *Trust in Government, 1958–96*

Source: Data from American National Election Studies.

Note: The figure shows the percentage of respondents who answered, "Just about always" or "Most of the time," when asked, "Do you trust the government in Washington to do what is right?"

A History in Five Acts: The Appointments Process Evolves

It is no surprise that the presidential appointments process was transformed in the last three decades of the twentieth century. The rapid alterations in its political context made those transformations difficult to resist, perhaps even inevitable. To understand the character of the modern appointments process, and especially the new politics that now drive it, it is helpful to look at how that process has evolved over the course of American history—and how at every stage the appointments process has been shaped by the politics of its time.

The Governing Elite, 1789–1800

Although it lacked a king and a royal family, the government of the United States in its early years rather closely resembled the government of the country from which Americans had revolted. Political leadership was the province of the upper class—the wealthy, the landed, the educated. These were the men who had made the Revolution, and they were its primary beneficiaries. They saw politics and government as their heritage and responsibility and were proprietary in their approach toward it.

In the nation's early years, a small group of men flowed through the top levels of government, moving freely from Congress to cabinet to courts. They tended to know one another well, and constructing an administration was not unlike preparing a seating plan for a fancy dinner: invite the best people, then distribute and balance them appropriately. George Washington's first cabinet is emblematic. Treasury Secretary Alexander Hamilton was a leader in New York politics and had been Washington's aide during the war for independence. Thomas Jefferson, the secretary of state, was a scion of Virginia and had already served as governor and ambassador. Henry Knox, the secretary of war, had commanded the artillery under General Washington. Another Virginia governor and delegate to the Constitutional Convention, Edmund Randolph, was attorney general.

Through the first three presidential administrations, this remained a government that few but the privileged could penetrate. Opposing sides emerged and began to compete for control of the offices of government, but on all sides it remained an essentially elite competition. Whether Federalist or Democratic Republican, the presidents of the first two decades of experience under the new Constitution drew their appointees from a small and largely familiar circle of eminent men. Most Americans merely watched from a distance a government that was closed to them and dominated by their betters.

Patronage, 1800–1950s

When political parties began to emerge and the Congress started to mature at the beginning of the nineteenth century, presidential appointments became more contentious. Senators asserted their control over appointments in their own states—customs collectors, port officers, district judges, and the like—and presidents more often found themselves forced to make personnel choices that would avoid the increasingly rocky shoals of Senate confirmation.

In 1820, Congress passed the Four Years Act, limiting the terms of most federal officers, including collectors of customs and U.S. attorneys, to four years. Under the new law, an administration could make its own appointment upon the expiration of an appointee's term without going through the often brutal process of removal. Some advocates of the law argued that it would improve accountability, but John Quincy Adams saw the matter more clearly:

> The Senate was conciliated by the permanent increase of their power, which was the principal ultimate effect of the Act, and every Senator was flattered by the power conferred upon him of multiplying chances to provide for his friends and dependents. . . . The result of the Act has been to increase the power of patronage exercised by the President, and still more that of the Senate and of every individual Senator.[10]

Intense politicization of appointments had already begun before Andrew Jackson became president, but his election in 1828 marked the beginning of a significant redefinition of American democracy. Jackson believed that government had become the vested interest of a governing class, serving "rather as a means of promoting individual interests than as an interest created solely for the service of the people." His solution was the first significant reform of the appointments process: a policy of rotation in office. Official duties, Jackson believed, could be made "so plain and simple that men of intelligence can readily qualify themselves for their performance."[11]

Recent studies suggest that the new patronage system that Jackson launched actually yielded less turnover than promised, with probably fewer than a quarter of all federal appointees being dismissed to make way for Jacksonian spoilsmen. The principle quickly took hold, however, and as Jackson's leading biographer has noted, "whatever evils it brought into American life, its historical function was to narrow the gap between the people and the government—to expand popular participation in the workings of democracy. For Jackson it was an essential step in the gradual formulation of a program for a democratic America."[12]

As the country spread rapidly beyond its original boundaries, the task of winning elections became more complex and daunting. A new tactic of political mobilization was introduced: the exchange of rewards for votes and the delivery of votes. To the successful political operative, election day brought more than just a moment of celebration; it now brought also the promise of a job in government.

The political process opened to a much wider range of participants, and many of them were motivated by its practical consequences. Spoilsmen began to replace the gentry in Washington and in government offices everywhere, and soon the task of selecting presidential appointees changed dramatically. No longer a juggling of elites, it became instead a vast patronage operation into which political party leaders soon inserted themselves. The concept of a governing class had begun to take hold in the early years, but Jackson's victory dashed that notion and replaced it with one quite opposite: that anyone could govern as long as he were skilled enough to be active in the party that won the last election—or resourceful enough to find his own patron. Advertisements like the following appeared regularly in Washington newspapers in the years after the Civil War: "Wanted—A government clerkship at a salary of not less than one thousand dollars per annum. Will give one hundred dollars to any one securing me such a position."

Save for changes in its dimensions, this system remained in place for more than a century. Positions in government were filled by the hand of the victorious president and his party. Routine procedures for accomplishing this began to emerge, so that by the middle of the twentieth century parties dominated all but the highest-level personnel selections, and the leader of the president's party—to remain a constant voice in the president's ear—was usually seated in the cabinet, often as postmaster general (where, not coincidentally, he presided over the department with the largest number of patronage appointments). The civil service system appeared as a minor distraction with the passage of the Pendleton Act in 1883, but it was a long time before any substantial number of federal jobs were brought under civil service coverage, and most of those of greatest consequence to the president never were (see table 1-2).

Long after Andrew Jackson's disappearance from public life, another general, this one named Eisenhower—perhaps the least devoutly partisan president of the century—came to the White House. He intended to staff his administration as he had staffed his army commands, by handpicking the best people available. He soon learned, however, that the patronage era was not yet dead, despite the spreading signs of affliction. He wrote in his diary on January 5, 1953, "My experience in this case has generated in me the profound hope that I will be compelled to have little to do, during the next four years, with the distribution of federal patronage. Having been fairly successful in late years in learning to keep a rigid check on my temper, I do not want to encounter complete defeat at this late date"[13]

Table 1-2. *Growth of the Civil Service, by Decade, 1881–1971*
Percent

Year	*Federal positions*	*Year*	*Federal positions*
1881	0	1931	76.8
1891	21.5	1941	68.9
1901	44.3	1951	86.4
1911	57.5	1961	86.1
1921	79.9	1971	84.1

Source: Data from Harold W. Stanley and Richard G. Niemi, *Vital Statistics on American Politics, 1997–1998* (Brookings, 1998), p. 255.

During all the decades that patronage reigned as the vital principle of personnel selection in the national government, presidents were rarely free to choose their own subordinates. Presidents varied in their willingness to stand up to demanding party leaders or senators, but none had a completely free hand, and as a practical matter, none had an effective alternative for finding and recruiting people for federal service. As the size of the government began to swell with the Depression and World War II, the task of choosing people to staff its highest levels became more daunting, and the capacity of the patronage system to produce the skilled and experienced people needed to lead the new agencies more wanting. Another turning point was at hand.

Nascent Corporatism, 1958–74

President Eisenhower had no investment in the old ways of staffing presidential administrations and little obligation to the leaders of his newly adopted party. Nor did he find much to admire in the decentralized, inefficient messiness of the traditional patronage process. It was, said his chief of staff Sherman Adams, a "constant annoyance."[14]

It is not mere coincidence that the efforts of Eisenhower's administration to reshape the appointments process reflected the emerging corporatism of the time. The man in the gray flannel suit seemed to be taking charge of all aspects of American life, and it was no surprise that the business leaders who surrounded Eisenhower should seek to impose fixed routines, clear hierarchies of authority, and a crystallization of objectives on the presidential appointments process.

They started late and never fully succeeded in what often resembled an endless wrestling match between the Republican National Committee and the White House. It was not until 1957 that an effort led by businessman and White House aide Rocco C. Siciliano yielded the first significant restructuring of the appointments process in modern times. President Truman had been the first president to designate a single aide to manage his appointments; but that person, Donald Dawson, was part liaison with the patronage apparatus of the Democratic Party and part firefighter for many of Truman's appointment scraps with the Senate. Dawson had little time or inclination to try to centralize full control over the appointment power in the White House. The initial effort to accomplish that task came from an Eisenhower White House exasperated with personnel selection procedures they could not control and could not connect to Eisenhower's management and policy objectives.

In September 1957, Eisenhower issued an executive order creating the position of special assistant to the president for personnel management and appointed Siciliano to that post. This was a new front in the continuing battle by the Eisenhower White House to wrest control of the appointments process from the Republican Party. More than that, it was an effort to bring some sense of order and rationality to the broader personnel activities of government—to tie personnel decisions to management and policy decisions. For most of the preceding century, all but a minority of personnel choices had served no purpose larger than feeding the appetites of loyal party workers for jobs between elections. Now in the late 1950s, a new sense of personnel as part of a corporate enterprise, the business of governing, was beginning to take hold.

The Siciliano initiative came late in Eisenhower's presidency. Typically, little of it survived the transition to Kennedy, and the new president began to staff his administration without any clear structure or set of procedures in place. Multiple power centers within the White House competed for control of his appointments and often duplicated effort. By this time, the Democratic Party was nearly exhausted as a patronage source. Kennedy's problem was less the consequence of conflict with his party leaders or other Democrats in Congress than it was the need to find a large number of technically qualified appointees for an increasingly complex government and confronting the reality that he and the politicians around him simply did not know enough of the kinds of people they needed. "I thought I knew everybody," Kennedy said, "and it turned out I only knew a few politicians."[15]

The realization thus dawned that a modern government required a much more sophisticated mechanism for identifying and recruiting leadership than had previously existed. In pursuit of this end, Dan Fenn Jr. was brought to the White House from the Harvard Business School and assigned the task of developing a more appropriate set of appointment procedures. What he recommended, and later implemented, built on and extended the work that Rocco Siciliano had done in the previous administration.

The personnel operation in the Kennedy White House began to take on features not seen before in the appointments process: increased and more professional staffing, creation of reference networks, divisions of labor, active recruiting beyond the usual party and political sources. For the first time, a White House had the capacity to reach out beyond the usual suspects in filling administration jobs. By contemporary standards, it was small and primitive. Compared with anything that preceded it, however, the Kennedy personnel operation was a modern wonder—and a watershed.

The Kennedy efforts carried over into the Johnson administration and became more firmly institutionalized. Although invariably active in making final personnel choices, Johnson was comfortable deferring to a personnel staff the identification and recruitment of strong candidates. He further helped to solidify the role of a White House personnel office by requiring those who had appointment recommendations to take them to John Macy, his chief personnel aide. This protection of the process gave it status and became habit forming. The Washington community was learning that the personnel office now superintended the appointments process and was the primary contact point on all appointment matters. Macy later recalled that "a number of times it was reported back to me that somebody would come in and complain about a particular appointment that the President had made and he was quoted as having said, 'Well, don't blame me. It's that God damn Macy. He insists on having merit.' And that tended to terminate the conversation as far as the complainant was concerned."[16]

Richard Nixon stumbled into the staffing business, as most of his predecessors had. One of his aides inadvertently flooded the transition offices with recommendations and resumés when he invited just about everyone listed in *Who's Who in America* to suggest potential nominees. Several groups within the transition staff operated independently of one another in the search for administration personnel. The president himself made the biggest gaffe of all when he told his assembled cabinet at an early meeting that the secretaries should take primary responsibility for filling the positions in their departments and that they should base their selections on ability first and loyalty second.

By the middle of Nixon's first term, it became apparent to him and senior members of his staff that they had failed to use the appointment lever to impose the president's priorities on the executive branch. A young management expert then working at the Department of Health, Education, and Welfare was brought to the White House to study the problem and make recommendations.

This expert was Fred Malek, and in December 1970 he delivered a report full of suggestions on ways to better tie the White House personnel process to the president's management needs and policy priorities.

> In the two years of the Nixon Administration, the difficulty in effectively managing the federal Government has become increasingly apparent. The Executive Branch has not galvanized sufficiently as a team implementing Presidential policy. . . . While the causes of this problem are varied and complex, the President can do much to solve it by increasing his direct management control over appointees to noncareer positions in the Executive Branch.[17]

What followed was a sweeping revitalization of the presidential personnel effort. Some of that drew on themes and practices that had emerged in the Democratic administrations of the 1960s; but the Nixon effort, which Malek was appointed to lead, went much further. A centralized office called the White House Personnel Operation was established to manage all personnel selection efforts. Malek hired professional executive recruiters and gave them specific portfolios. Close liaison was established with the departments and agencies to ensure White House supervision of appointments to lower-level positions, and a group within the personnel office monitored the performance of Nixon appointees to identify those who were not adequately supporting the president's programs and initiatives.

What resulted was a personnel process sprung almost completely free of its patronage roots. Politics was still very much in its bloodstream, but the process aimed to treat politics as one of several factors that had to be balanced and managed to produce an administration that could serve a president's needs. The principal goal of the revitalization that occurred in the early 1970s was control—control of presidential personnel selections by the president, not by senators or party leaders or cabinet secretaries. All of the administrations that followed have eventually established a

White House personnel operation resembling the corporatist model that Nixon's administration created, one possessed of the following primary characteristics:

—a central personnel office headed, in most cases, by a senior adviser to the president

—the development and electronic management of databases of potential candidates for appointments

—adherence to routine procedures for identifying, recruiting, clearing, and approving appointees

—close liaison, often resembling dominance, with departments and agencies on all appointments to lower-level positions

Scandal-Proofing and Divided Government: New Realities, 1975–87

The Senate Commerce Committee was on the cutting edge of an important change that began to emerge on Capitol Hill in the mid-1970s. The Commerce Committee had an unusually large confirmation jurisdiction, including most of the regulatory commissions. To its chair and staff director, as to many Washingtonians, the reality was dawning that divided government was no mere aberration but rather an enduring fact of modern government. As figure 1-2 indicates, this perception was indeed prescient.

To participate influentially in policymaking, the congressional majority could no longer merely bide its time until one of its own recaptured the presidency. Instead they would have to rely on their own devices to focus more strategically on the levers of congressional power. One of those levers was the confirmation power. Warren Magnuson, then chair of the Senate Commerce Committee, threw down the gauntlet in a speech in 1973: "I must tell you that we have swallowed nominees . . . who have left a bitter aftertaste, and our tolerance for mediocracy and lack of independence from economic interests is rapidly coming to an end."[18]

For most of the Senate's history, its exercise of the confirmation power had been inconsistent and deferential. The occasional confirmation controversy could capture public attention, and one of the most popular novels of 1959, Allen Drury's *Advise and Consent*, portrays the Senate in a dither over a presidential appointment. All of that masked a much more conventional reality, however: the Senate rarely interfered in any significant way with the president's selection of people to manage the government. The Senate, it can fairly be said, was more deferential than difficult.

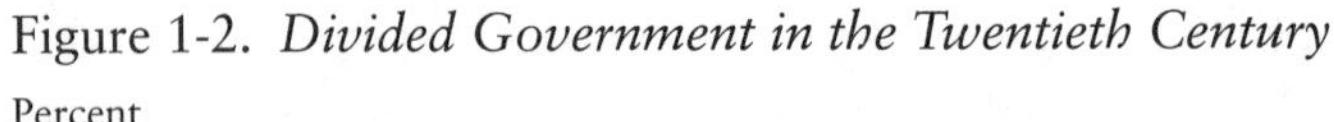

Figure 1-2. *Divided Government in the Twentieth Century*

Percent

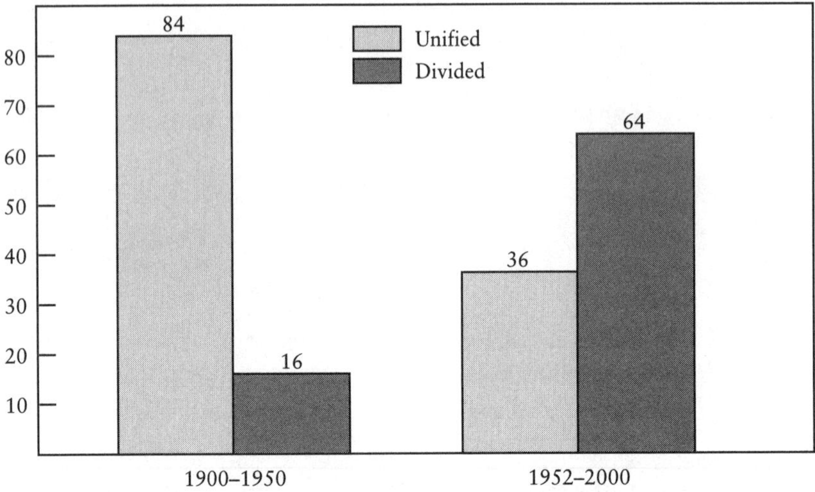

Source: Data from Harold W. Stanley and Richard G. Niemi, *Vital Statistics in American Politics, 1997–1998* (Brookings, 1998), pp. 34–35.

This bothered some outsiders who thought the Senate was failing in one of its important responsibilities. In 1977, for example, the public interest lobbying organization Common Cause published a highly critical study of the Senate's indifferent exercise of the confirmation process, titled "The Senate Rubberstamp Machine." It found that "presidential nominees are hastily considered in an extremely comfortable atmosphere without the benefit of a full record or tough scrutiny. . . . The patty-cake nature of questioning at confirmation hearings is symbolic of the fact that senators do not want to be rigorous and thorough. They want to consent, not question."[19]

The tide had already begun to turn, however. Several Senate committees had adopted questionnaires and information forms that they required nominees to complete. Senators were asking harder questions of nominees and setting clearer and higher standards for confirmation. Senate committee staffs more than doubled in size in the 1970s, from a total of 635 in 1970 to 1,269 in 1979, affording more opportunity for careful investigation of nominees by individual committees.[20]

It is not surprising that the Senate's committees, with more time and resources with which to scrutinize nominees, began to find more flaws in some of those who came before them for a confirmation recommendation. With the Senate adopting a more aggressive posture and arming itself to act on that, rejections and withdrawals of nominations became more common. President Gerald R. Ford was the first victim of this rapid change in the Senate's approach to confirmation. More than a dozen of his nominees were rejected or forced to withdraw by a newly energized Senate no longer willing to defer passively to the president's choices. At no previous time in American history had so many nominees been so vigorously—and effectively—opposed.

The background music was swelling, as well. Campaign finance irregularities in the 1972 election and the subsequent explosion of the Watergate scandal yielded a burst of reform legislation in the 1970s. The campaign finance reform acts of 1971 and 1974 opened to public view information on candidates for public office that has always been confidential. The Ethics in Government Act of 1978 imposed a wide array of new requirements on public servants in the executive branch, including a requirement for public disclosure of their personal finances and an extensive array of dos and don'ts to guide their service in government and their employment after leaving.[21]

Other, less formal changes were also occurring. On a Saturday night in October 1974, Wilbur Mills, one of the Congress's most powerful members and chair of the House Ways and Means Committee, was discovered by the Capitol Police bloodied and standing near the Tidal Basin by the Jefferson Memorial. Mills was not notably sober, and the woman who leaped from his car into the water was not notably his wife but rather a stripper named Fanne Fox.

This was a watershed incident—no pun intended—not because it was rare for a member of Congress to overimbibe or even to keep company with fast women. What was different here was the full and sensational play given the incident by the national press. Rarely in the past had such escapades made it into the papers, certainly not into the serious ones. The Mills incident, however, was a story with legs—still no pun intended—and it caused a lot of brow-furrowing introspection about the role of the press. The consensus conclusion of that seemed to be that the old constraints were gone. The press could be expected to report almost anything that would sell papers. Government officials were put on notice: the line between private and public lives was rapidly evaporating.

Into this transforming environment marched a parade of candidates for presidential appointment who had not expected the invasive scrutiny they would receive or the potential for cruel and punishing publicity that could explode around them. Even presidential personnel aides were caught off guard by the significant atmospheric changes in the appointments process. Pendleton James, who managed personnel recruitment at the outset of the Reagan administration, "found out too late about the new laws we had to live under in the appointments process. I had overlooked the [Ethics] Act, overlooked it because I frankly wasn't aware of the extent it would affect our appointments."[22]

Ronald Reagan's initial appointees had a tougher trek through the nomination and confirmation processes than those of any previous president. Many of them came from business backgrounds and quickly found themselves entangled in the new ethics laws—not because they had done anything wrong but because the burden of accounting and reporting was new and deeply vexing. Nearly a third found that they had to sell financial holdings to prevent conflicts of interest. Seventeen percent had to file recusal statements, and 13 percent established blind or diversified trusts. Forty-one percent resigned from positions on corporate and other boards.[23] A decade earlier such requirements had been largely unknown.

The collective consequence of these several developments—the dawning reality of the permanence of divided government, a spate of detailed ethics regulations, the rapid broadening of journalistic boundaries—was a significant change in the presidential appointments process. It was growing harder and taking longer for presidents to find and successfully recruit good appointees, and it was taking longer and growing harder to get them confirmed by the Senate.

And then came Bork.

Battleground, After 1987

The gloves came off in July 1987 when Ronald Reagan nominated Robert Bork to replace retiring justice Lewis Powell on the Supreme Court. On the afternoon of the nomination's announcement, Senator Edward Kennedy went to the Senate floor and made the following remark:

> Robert Bork's America is a land in which women would be forced into back-alley abortions, blacks would sit at segregated lunch counters, rogue police could break down citizens' doors in midnight raids, schoolchildren could not be taught about evolution, writers and artists would be censored at the whim of government, and the

> doors of the Federal courts would be shut on the fingers of millions of citizens for whom the judiciary is often the only protector of the individual rights that are the heart of our democracy.[24]

It was a remarkable statement. Rarely in history had a senator leapt so quickly to judgment on a nominee, and it was notable for that. It was yet more remarkable for the harshness of its tone and the clarion call it seemed to blare to all those who might wish to oppose the nominee. Let the games begin.

The president and his senior aides took little heed, however, and went off on their summer vacations. While they were away, opponents marshaled their forces and their arguments, and they did so in a way that had never been seen before in the confirmation process, in a way that redefined the strategic politics of the presidential appointments process, in a way that indelibly changed the operations of that process.

When Bork's confirmation hearings before the Senate Judiciary Committee began on September 15, 1987, a parade of witnesses appeared to challenge the nomination. There was little testimony to suggest that Bork lacked the intelligence or experience to serve on the high court. The focus instead was on his judicial philosophy, his opponents alleging that he should be denied confirmation because he was a dangerous conservative and a powerful advocate of his own views who might well dominate the Court. That was not all. Every available tactic was used to attack and discredit the nominee: television and newspaper ads, direct-mail campaigns, petitions, polling, and fund-raising. Reporters even dug up copies of Judge Bork's video rental records.

Bork was defeated 58 to 42 when the Senate finally voted on October 23rd. The assault on Bork had worked, and it left a harsh and deep legacy—the modern equivalent of General William Tecumseh Sherman's march through the South. When it was over, the earth lay scorched. Judge Bork had been dispatched, and so, too, had all pretense of civility and mutual respect in the confirmation process.

Subsequent nomination controversies revealed the lasting impact of the Bork experience. Two years later, newly elected president George Bush chose former senator John Tower to be his secretary of defense. Cabinet nominees rarely encounter great difficulty in seeking confirmation, and a long Senate tradition called for special deference to former senators taking up posts in the executive branch. Tower had left a wake of grudges and angry feelings behind him in the Senate, however; and as it turned out, his confirmation process provided a ripe opportunity for their full expression. For weeks Tower faced a steady barrage of charges about his excessive drinking, about womanizing, and about relations with clients whose interest in defense contracts might taint his objectivity in the cabinet. It was a campaign marked by innuendo, leaked documents, and salacious hints and rumors rarely tied to demonstrable evidence. Again the opponents succeeded, and on March 9, 1989, Tower's nomination was defeated by a vote of 53 to 47.

Having now observed the takedown of a Supreme Court and a cabinet nominee with tactics more brutal, intense, and comprehensive than any ever before deployed in the appointments process, Washington was beginning to realize that the old bets were off. Senate confirmation of presidential appointees was blood sport now, and so it would remain through the rest of the century.

The frustrations of divided government accounted for some of this, but in a peculiar way. It became clear in 1993, when Democrats controlled both the White House and the Congress, that appointment controversies were no longer limited to times when the branches were in opposing hands. A long parade of President Bill Clinton's nominees endured humiliation in the confirmation process—Zöe Baird, Lani Guinier, Roberta Achtenberg, Morton Halperin, and so on. Some were defeated or withdrawn. It did not require an opposition majority in the Senate to confound presidential appointment efforts. The Senate in the 1990s was the product of two converging trends that profoundly reshaped its role in the appointments process

One of those was the habit of divided government. Over the course of nearly a half century during which the Senate and the White House were controlled by different parties nearly two-thirds of the time, senators had learned to think like members of an opposition party even when they were not. New laws and practices—war powers, budget reform and impoundment control, limits on foreign military sales, expanded control over executive agreements, intelligence oversight—had deeply embedded that habit into the practice of government. After a while, it did not seem to matter much which party controlled which institution; the institutions were in a steady state of ferocious counterpoise, on war alert, regardless of party control.

Abetting this was a second trend: the deterioration, almost to the vanishing point, of any capacity in the Senate for central leadership. The

Senate in the last three decades of the twentieth century became little more than a confederation of one hundred independent fiefdoms. It departed dramatically from the institution that political scientists described in the 1950s and 1960s, a legislative body in which long periods of apprenticeship and deference eventually yielded real power to a few "whales" who dealt carefully and respectfully with one another and with the president. In those days, the president rarely needed much more than a nod of approval from the relevant committee chair for a nominee to sail through to confirmation unbowed and unbruised.

What changed in the Senate? That is a topic too complex for this chapter, but some of the causes are obvious. The weakening grip of political parties on the avenues of access to Congress forced individual senators to plot and manage their own elections, raising their own funds and in doing so incurring obligations not to party leaders but to special interests. The rapid growth of the Washington press corps and the admission of television cameras to the Senate chamber and to its committee rooms gave individual senators a stage from which they could play to particularized audiences without regard to what their leaders wanted or what good government may have required.

To assist their efforts to function independent of any resistance from party leaders, presidents, or other legislators, senators began to vote themselves new resources and opportunities for independent action. Personal and committee staffs grew. More subcommittees emerged so that every member of the majority party could chair at least one. Support agencies burgeoned on Capitol Hill—the Congressional Research Service, the Congressional Budget Office, the Office of Technology Assessment, and the General Accounting Office. For its members who wished to operate as potent princes, the Senate in the 1990s became a very hospitable royal court.

As Senate party leaders lost control of their members, they became little more than servants, vibrating to the whims and the schedules and the petty petulance of individual senators. If a member needed to be out of town for a fund-raiser on the date of the scheduled vote on a key bill, leaders rescheduled the vote. If a senator wanted to hold up a bill or a vote on a nomination because of some feud with the president or an agency head or another senator, the leaders nodded and went along. Senator Robert Byrd (D-West Virginia) came to the Senate in the days when it was run, in the old-fashioned way, by majority leader Lyndon

Johnson. When he later assumed that same position, he followed a very different leadership model, one that clearly reflected the changing character of the Senate:

> I served under both Mr. Johnson when he was Majority Leader and Mr. Mansfield. Mr. Johnson—the hard-driving type. The type who would twist arms, cajole, threaten, plead and drive. Mr. Mansfield was just the opposite. He believed in letting every Senator go his own way, make up his own mind. He didn't attempt to twist arms. . . . So they had their different styles. . . . Johnson couldn't deal with them today. I keep saying that. Johnson could not deal with them today. We have a different type Senate there today. A different type of Senator.[25]

This was the context in which the appointments process came to its current pass: a Senate of a hundred mavericks, bent above all else on self-preservation and self-promotion, for whom any opportunity to broaden a political base, dredge a new channel of campaign contributions, grab a few seconds on the evening news, or pay back a political enemy is not to be missed. That the appointments process was often a splendid opportunity to do all these things was not lost on the clever and alert members of the contemporary Senate; and, in the great tradition of American politics, they "seen their opportunities, and they took 'em."

Thus in the 1990s the appointments process became not simply a mechanism for staffing the courts and the highest levels of the executive branch. It became as well, often even primarily, a battleground in which unresolved issues of public policy were fought out and the personal vendettas of individual senators were often activated. The fiercest fights are remembered now by the names of individual appointees who were their primary victims: Bork, Tower, Guinier, Henry Foster, Anthony Lake, William Weld, William Gould, Bill Lann Lee. Some were eventually confirmed, others defeated and sent home, but all bore scars: a sullied reputation, a weakened capacity to function in government, months and money lost in the whirling, uncontrolled maelstrom of the modern appointments process. One said, "I felt it was more a mechanism to try to destroy me than anything else. I came to Washington, D.C., like prime steak and after being here a while, I feel like poor-grade hamburger."[26] To those Americans of prime quality outside of government, entering the grinder of the appointments process became a less and less appealing prospect.

Characteristics of the Contemporary Appointments Process

This historical evolution has yielded an appointments process that is different in nearly all of its characteristics—save one—from its constitutional design and earlier permutations. The one enduring characteristic of the process is that it is as deeply and intensely political now as it has always been. When I first wrote about the appointments process several decades ago, I described it in these words:

> Conflict occurs in the appointment process for a very simple reason. Appointments matter. Were that not the case, presidential administrations would not have several dozen White House aides devoting full time to appointment decisions; Senate committees would not hold hundreds of hours of confirmation hearings; interest groups, agencies, political parties, and members of the House would not spend their time or resources trying to shape appointment decisions. Yet they do all these things, and they do them because they think it makes a difference who gets appointed to serve in particular federal offices.[27]

That was the central dynamic of the appointments process then; it always has been, and it is now. In other important ways, however, the appointments process has changed.

Everybody Fights

The term *presidential appointment* is misleading. Appointments to the executive branch fall to the president only after he has fended off or negotiated agreements with many other political actors seeking or empowered to control or divert these important decisions. The appointments process is deeply contentious, and as legislative policymaking has grown more difficult in recent decades, the process has increasingly become a venue for pitched battles over the shape of public policy. The motto of participants seems to be, "If we can't change public policy with new laws because it is so hard to enact them, then, hell, we will fight to see if we can get a sympathetic appointee to make the changes we want in administering policy."

More and more, the contentiousness in the appointments process is driven not by questions about the fitness of nominees but by policy disagreements. Senators vote against nominees, and nominations fail, because the appointments process has become a policy battleground. In fact, issues of nominee fitness are close to irrelevant in the contemporary appointments process, except as wedges for those seeking to act on policy disagreements. If a senator opposes a nominee because he or she holds beliefs or supports policies a senator dislikes, it matters little how experienced or how demonstrably competent the nominee may be. If, on the other hand, a nominee's views and ideology comport with those of a senator, it matters little that he or she has little experience or demonstrated competence. A nominee's weaknesses may become a convenient peg on which to hang a policy disagreement, but it is nearly always the policy disagreement and not the questions of character or competence that stir opposition.

This is not a new phenomenon, this use of the appointments process to wage policy battles. In fact, it has always been a characteristic of the appointments process. The struggle between Andrew Jackson and the Congress over the National Bank issue was heavily played out in the appointments process and resulted in Senate rejections of four of Jackson's nominees of bank directors and the defeat of Roger Taney's nomination as secretary of the treasury. Not uncommonly in our history, the appointments process has been a convenient policy battleground. The principal historian of the appointments process, Joseph R. Harris, has noted that across its full sweep, "most contests over the President's nominations have been grounded on political considerations rather than on the qualifications of nominees."[28]

What is different now is the absence of any pretense that the appointments process is anything but a policy battleground. Most senators used to pay some lip service to the importance of freeing the president to pick his own team to run the government. It was often said in the past that the Senate's role was to review the fitness of a nominee for public service, not to second-guess ideology or policy predispositions. Senator Edward M. Kennedy—the same Senator Kennedy who excoriated Robert Bork on the day of his nomination in 1987 and who led the charge against John Ashcroft's nomination to be attorney general in 2001—said in 1969, "I think all of us would pretty much agree that we certainly do not want just to subscribe to a political test or a simplistic philosophical test in trying to reach a decision about the approval or disapproval of a candidate."[29] Senator Roman Hruska, a Nebraska Republican, remarked in 1971 that "whether the nominee is liberal or conservative should not concern this committee. Whether we agree or disagree with him is not the issue. Political questions should play no part in our decision."[30]

In the past, when senators had potential policy disagreements with a nominee, those were often a topic of individual meetings between senator and nominee or at confirmation hearings. Senators developed some tactics for narrowing or containing those disagreements. Usually those tactics were successful, and conflict was contained. In a book written twenty years ago, I described the appointments process as an accumulation of conflict avoidance mechanisms:

> Opportunities for conflict avoidance and conflict resolution are woven through the contemporary appointment process. Interested participants have several access points at which they can express their concerns. The clearance procedures employed by recent administrations provide the President with an antenna for sensing potential conflict and for addressing or avoiding it. Senate confirmation proceedings are composed of several mechanisms that permit the identification of conflicts and provide ways to whittle them down to manageable proportions. The participants in this process have established in operation what would have been difficult to design on a drawing board: a relatively open and interactive method for making hundreds of important and complex decisions with only a minimum of aggravated conflict.[31]

Much has changed since then. The familiar approach of the past no longer works; in fact, it is rarely even recalled. The past approach rested on three assumptions:

—When presidents win elections, they are entitled to choose their own team to govern.

—The Senate should not unduly deter or delay the emplacement of that team.

—Conflict over policy should be contained and whenever possible narrowed.

Today, however, the confirmation process has become conflict seeking rather than conflict avoiding, conflict magnifying rather than conflict minimizing; and the root of nearly all appointment conflict is public policy.

One of the most dramatic changes in the Congress over the past four decades is a steady and substantial decrease in the number of laws it

Figure 1-3. *Public Laws Enacted, by Congress, 1953–2000*

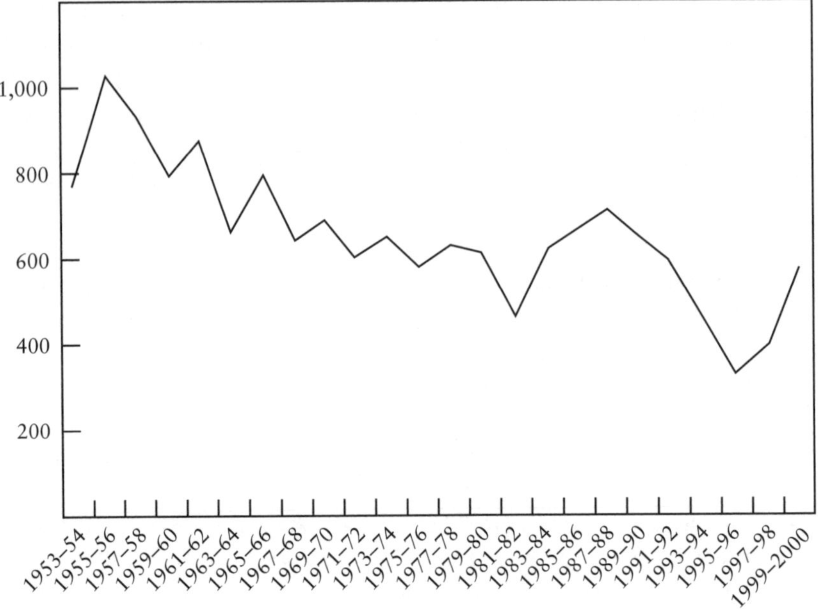

Source: *Congressional Quarterly Almanacs, 1953–2000.*

passes. Figure 1-3 illustrates this trend. To veteran Congress watchers this is the unsurprising and altogether logical consequence of divided government, deteriorated political parties, changes in congressional rules, and other developments that have made the Congress a much more hospitable place for the unfolding careers of individual members and a much less efficient lawmaking body. The agonizing difficulty of contemporary lawmaking, however, has forced policy debates into other venues, and the appointments process is a leader among those. Senators turn to the appointments process for their policy fights because they have so few alternatives. With law so hard to make and so hard to change, influencing the choice of the implementers and adjudicators of law becomes an essential strategic option.

As the desire to contest appointments has grown, the range of tactics has expanded. For most of the history of their institution, senators contested nominations in a simple way: they voted against them. They did this rarely, however, because floor votes on nominations were infrequent. Senate leaders saw little reason to have a recorded vote unless persuaded that there was significant opposition to a nomination. Until the 1950s, the president's party usually controlled the Senate and usually followed the leader. Nominations were rarely voted upon and rarely defeated.

Now, of course, there are more Senate votes and more opportunities for senators to cast votes against nominees. The commonplace of divided government accounts for some of that. So, too, does the "sunshine" movement, which opened Congress to much clearer public view and led to more recorded votes in each session.

The tactics of opposition are hardly limited now to casting a vote against a nominee. In fact, seeking to defeat a nomination by formal vote on the Senate floor remains a daunting challenge and is not the most widely used opposition tactic, nor is it the most successful. Instead, senators who oppose a nomination are much more likely to try to kill it by tactics that are not so frontal, that can be accomplished without building a sizable opposition coalition, sometimes without even drawing any dangerous enemy fire. The best friends for any opponent of a contemporary nomination are the rules of the Senate and the remarkable opportunities they provide to crusading individual senators.

FILIBUSTERS. Senate rules permit senators to hold the floor and prevent a vote on a nomination for as long as they are able. Teams of senators, joined together in a filibuster, can prevent a vote indefinitely. The only recourse under Senate Rule 22 is a cloture vote, which requires approval by 60 percent of those senators voting. If every senator votes, then sixty votes are required to end debate. Looked at more strategically, this means that forty-one senators can prevent a vote on any nomination and thus defeat it with a filibuster.

That is precisely what happened in 1995 when Dr. Henry Foster's nomination as surgeon general was under consideration in the Senate. Fifty-seven senators were on record in support of the Foster nomination, more than enough to confirm him in a straightforward vote. However, his opponents, fired by their distaste for his pro-choice views and evidence that he had performed a few legal abortions earlier in his career, had strength enough to sustain a filibuster that forced the withdrawal of the Foster nomination. A cloture vote on June 22, 1995, failed when Foster's supporters fell three votes short of the sixty needed to end the filibuster.

The filibuster tactic is not simple to implement and is used infrequently; but the threat of a filibuster is a club that lurks behind the door in many confirmation controversies. Senators can count, and when proponents of a nomination realize that the opposition approximates forty-one senators, they know that the jig is up, that they cannot overcome a filibuster and must either seek some compromise or contemplate the failure of the nomination they support.

HOLDS. Far more common than filibusters in the arsenal of opposition are Senate holds. The hold is a mysterious tactic that seems to have emerged out of the thin air of Senate practice. Any senator may impose a hold on a floor vote on a nomination simply by communicating that desire to his or her party leader.

Holds developed as little more than a way for a senator to delay action briefly in order to gather more information before acting on a bill or nomination. They were a courtesy tolerated in the individualized and deferential atmosphere of the Senate because they helped senators make better-informed decisions. They have become much more than that in recent years, however, and their effect is especially prominent now in the confirmation process. Any senator may place a hold on a nomination, delaying a confirmation vote indefinitely. Individual senators could, of course, proceed in spite of the hold, if they so chose, but they are strongly disinclined to do that, wanting to preserve the freedom to place future holds of their own.

In 1999 two senators, Charles Grassley and Ron Wyden, sought to open up this tactic slightly by convincing their colleagues that a senator who places a hold should at least be identified. That has happened inconsistently since, however, and the hold remains a murky tactic. An appointee whose nomination is caught in a hold often does not know who has placed the hold, nor the reasons for it, nor the likelihood that it will be lifted.

A hold is almost never about the qualifications or competence of the nominee upon whom it is placed. It is nearly always about some side issue of policy or administration in which the senator placing the hold has a deep interest. Senator Jesse Helms placed holds in 1995 on more than a dozen ambassadorial nominees in an effort to bring about a reorganization of the State Department that the Clinton administration did not support. Senator James Inhofe (R-Oklahoma) placed holds in 1998 on three Environmental Protection Agency nominees to protest the agency's transfer of an employee (not one of the nominees) from one position to another without consulting the Senate. Senator Rod Grams placed holds in 2000 on seven ambassadorial nominees until the State Department tightened up its disciplinary procedures for security violations. A hold is thus a form of hostage-taking. A senator holds a nomination hostage while seeking to get some information or policy concession or management change from the administration.

PACKAGING. An increasingly common device for containing conflict in the appointments process is the packaging together of several nominations. This happens especially for nominations to regulatory commissions and other multimember bodies and more commonly, as well, with judicial nominations. In such arrangements, the Senate agrees to confirm the president's choice for one position in exchange for the president's nomination of a candidate favored by a senator for another position.

A particularly visible example of this kind of packaging occurred in the fall of 1997, after nearly two years in which no appointments had been confirmed and vacancies were looming in four of the five seats on the Federal Communications Commission. Painstaking negotiations between the White House and Senate stakeholders produced a package of two Democrats, William Kennard and Gloria Tristani, and two Republicans, Michael Powell and Harold Furchtgott-Roth, that, once constructed, moved smoothly to confirmation.

Senators Trent Lott and Mitch McConnell demonstrated another variant of this tactic in 1999. Lott and McConnell placed a hold on the nomination of Richard Holbrooke to be ambassador to the United Nations but said they would lift the hold on Holbrooke if President Clinton agreed to appoint Bradley A. Smith, an avowed opponent of most campaign finance laws, to the Federal Elections Commission. Clinton ultimately agreed to the package deal.

Packaging is little more than bald politics: if you will hold your nose and approve my candidate, I will hold my nose and approve yours. When such packages are constructed, presidents essentially surrender the appointment power for some appointees in order to gain certain confirmation for others. In the impasse that the modern appointments process has come to resemble, however, packaging—whatever its defects as a form of good government—is now a common tactic. Presidents and their personnel offices now have to think of their selections not just in terms of their individual qualifications but also in terms of how they might fit into broader arrangements with nominees recommended by the opposition for other vacancies.

DELAY. No tactic of appointment combat has grown more rapidly in recent years than the simplest one of all: no action. There is nothing inherent in the appointments process that forces action, as there is, for example, in the budget process. If the Congress fails to act on the budget, the unpleasant prospect of a government shutdown looms. This usually inspires action, even if it is not always completed by the first day of the new fiscal year.

An appointment carries no similar sense of urgency. Senators who oppose a nomination may try to construct a coalition to defeat it, but that is never easy, even when the opposition party controls the Senate. Failing that, an equally effective technique is simply to delay a vote on confirmation. In the procedurally amorphous Senate, there are several ways to accomplish this. One is to encourage an extensive and detailed investigation of the nominee by the staff of the committee with jurisdiction over the nomination. Ask the nominee for more information about his or her background. Ask the White House for more material. When one request is satisfied, issue another. Seek "further clarification," a "missing file," a "redo of an incomplete form." Nominations can be strung out for months in the to-and-fro of such committee investigations. Richard Holbrooke's nomination as UN ambassador, for example, was not confirmed by the Senate until more than a year after President Clinton announced his intention to make it and nearly six months after the Senate received it.

Another variation of this is the "search until you find something" tactic. In 1997, this tactic was used to its desired effect against Anthony Lake, whom President Clinton had nominated to head the Central Intelligence Agency. Here the committee chair, Senator Richard Shelby, was determined to torpedo the Lake nomination, and the difficulty in constructing a record that justified Lake's defeat did not deter Shelby from continuing the search for damning evidence. Finally Lake, in great frustration, simply threw in the towel, saying he had become convinced that the committee would "nibble him to death rather than deal with the nomination straight-up anytime soon."[32]

Another form of delay is the simple refusal, without substantive rationale or apology, to act on a nomination. When President Clinton nominated Republican governor William Weld of Massachusetts to be ambassador to Mexico, the chair of the Foreign Relations Committee, Senator Helms, refused to hold a hearing on the nomination, declaring that Weld "was not his kind of ambassador." A majority of the committee could have overruled him, but senators are always skittish about trampling on one another's individual prerogatives, and Helms's stand stood.

Finally there is the most common form of delay—a conscious and stated intention to kill a nomination by failing to bring it to a confirmation vote. That occurred in a very visible way in 1968 when the Republican minority in the Senate prevented confirmation of Abe Fortas's nomination to be Chief Justice of the United States. Since then, both parties have practiced the tactic. It becomes especially prominent near the end of the congressional session that precedes a presidential election. Senators decide to let nominations expire without action in the hope that their party will be successful in the election and the new president will send up nominees more to their liking. Well before the 2000 presidential election, Senator Phil Gramm, chair of the Senate Banking Committee, announced that the committee would not consider two of President Clinton's nominees to the board of governors of the Federal Reserve System because he believed those nominations should be left to the new president.

RECESS AND ACTING APPOINTMENTS. Presidents have felt they have had little choice but to respond to Senate tactics with new approaches of their own, but these only contribute to an escalation of the contentiousness in the appointments process. The most visible of the presidential responses to the growing difficulty in getting appointees confirmed is to avoid the Senate completely. Presidents do this by allowing positions to be filled by acting appointees, often for long periods of time, or by making recess appointments.

There are few practical limits on acting appointments. The Vacancies Act now limits such appointees to 210 days on the job, but these limits are difficult to enforce and are often violated. In February 1998, for example, "acting" officials held 20 percent of the cabinet department jobs that require Senate confirmation—64 out of 320 slots. For a majority of those 64 posts, the administration had not even sent a nomination to Capitol Hill. Of the 64 acting officials, 43 had served beyond the 120-day limit then imposed by the Vacancies Act.

The president's authority to make recess appointments is vested in Article II, Section 2, of the Constitution. A recess appointee may serve until the end of the following session of Congress. Recent administrations have used recess appointments with some frequency: Carter 68 times, Reagan 239, Bush 78, and Clinton 140.

Typically when a president fills a position with a recess appointment, the opposing party in the Senate complains that he is making an end run around the Constitution. This may be true, but the play calling has been bipartisan; and when recess appointments are deployed, the Senate has little recourse beyond complaints or largely empty threats. In the most publicized use of this device—President Clinton's recess appointment of Bill Lann Lee as assistant attorney general for civil rights after the Senate refused to act on his nomination in late 1997—Republican senators complained vociferously. Lee served as an acting or recess appointee for the remainder of the Clinton administration, however, and the opposition of the Senate had little noticeable effect on his opportunities or capacities in office.

As the foregoing suggests, far more effort and creativity have been invested by both the Senate and the executive branch in finding more effective ways to fight over appointments than in making peace. Conflict is accepted as a fact of life, and the pursuit of advantage, of leverage, in this conflictual environment greatly exceeds any attempt to make this a more cooperative and less brutal relationship.

The Process Keeps Growing and Growing

When Franklin Roosevelt came to Washington on the heels of the 1932 presidential election, he was accompanied then, or shortly thereafter, by hundreds of men and women from across the country who reshaped American democracy. Many of them thought themselves to be at the center of a whirlwind. Many had a direct hand in writing and implementing legislation by which we continue to govern ourselves nearly three-quarters of a century later. Few of them were what we would today call presidential appointees, however. Only a relative handful held the few dozen executive branch appointments that then required confirmation by the Senate.

It is instructive to look at how things have changed, at how much wider and deeper the requirement of Senate confirmation has become. The number of so-called PAS appointees (those that require Senate confirmation) grew relatively slowly until the 1960s. Then, fueled by many of the political and structural changes noted earlier in this chapter, particularly the growing chasm of distrust between the legislative and executive branches, departments expanded vertically and horizontally, and the Congress became much more aggressive in requiring Senate confirmation for appointees to newly created positions and in expanding that requirement to existing positions to which it had not previously been attached. Table 1-3 clearly illustrates the changes that have occurred over the past forty years.

Whatever this change may have accomplished in affording the Senate a larger role in the appointments process, it has dramatically altered the

Table 1-3. *Growth in Executive-Level Appointees, Selected Years, 1935–98*

Number

Position	*1935*	*1960*	*1980*	*1998*
Secretary	10	10	13	14
Deputy Secretary	0	6	14	23
Under Secretary	3	15	28	41
Assistant Secretary	38	87	159	212
Deputy Assistant Secretary	0	78	364	484

Source: Data from Light, *Thickening Government* (Brookings, 1995), pp. 190–91; and Paul C. Light, *The True Size of Government* (Brookings, 1999), pp. 170–72.

scope and size of the task of staffing a presidential administration. A newly elected American president today faces a set of personnel replacement burdens that have no equal in any other national government nor in any other major institution in American society. Imagine how peculiar it would seem if a newly selected corporate chief executive officer were told that she had to fill all the top management positions in her company—hundreds of them—at the very outset of her tenure. Imagine a new university president on the first day of work confronting vacancies in every deanship, every vice presidency, the chair of every department. Imagine a new hospital president having immediately to appoint every administrator and the head of every medical department as the first task of running a complex, ongoing operation.

Yet that is precisely the assignment that faces a new president of the United States in our time. It is not simply the very top positions, the cabinet secretaries and a few senior subordinates, that must be filled. There are thousands of vacancies, and many hundreds of them are consequential to the success of a presidential administration: under secretaries, deputy secretaries, and assistant secretaries, agency heads and their deputies, regulatory commissioners, ambassadors, U.S. attorneys, and many more.

Presidential appointments now reach deeper into the top levels of government departments and agencies than ever before; in 2000 there were more than four times as many as there were in 1960. Moreover, the task now is not simply to find appointees who meet the president's criteria, who fit into the president's sense of what his administrative team should be. Virtually all of these important positions are now filled by appointees who must meet the different and often more distracting standard of

Senate confirmation. The size and scope of the presidential appointments process have never been greater.

The Process Is Visible, Transparent, and Permeable

For much of its history the appointments process was barely visible to public view. Even those who cared deeply about particular appointments and lobbied hard to influence them often had little idea of whom the president was considering or what was happening in the Senate's confirmation reviews. There was little that resembled the more formal and systematic selection process in the White House, and the bulk of the confirmation process was conducted beyond public view. The first public confirmation hearing was held in 1916, and public hearings remained a rarity for many years thereafter. None was televised until 1969. Until 1929 most confirmation debates were held in executive session, and most votes on confirmation were not recorded.

In the White House a personnel selection was often as much a surprise to the staff as to the public. Dan Fenn of the Kennedy personnel staff tells this story: "I remember we did an awful lot of work on Abe Ribicoff's successor at HEW [the Department of Health, Education, and Welfare]—turned out to be [Anthony J.] Celebreze. Ralph [Dungan] and I were working on this and we had a marvelous list of people. I went to bring it in to the President one day. I got there a little bit late. Ralph had gone in already and I said, 'Kenny, can I go in?' He said, 'What have you got?' I said, 'HEW.' He said, 'Oh, we settled that two months ago.'"[33]

Such invisibility and secrecy are a distant memory today. Appointments are hard news, and in the supercharged news environment of contemporary Washington, reporters are constantly digging for stories about potential appointees or appointees under consideration. When facts are scarce, rumors will do. The *Washington Post* and several other Washington publications now treat those rumors as news items and report them routinely in columns like Al Kamen's "In the Loop."

Because it is composed of many more stages than in the past, the newly elongated appointee selection process makes secrecy nearly impossible. By the time a nomination is ready to go to the Senate, dozens of people know about it, have reviewed it or vetted it, have been asked to assess it. Inside information rarely stays inside in Washington, and small leaks quickly become rivers in which all secrecy drowns.

In the Senate, all the old privacy protections have evaporated as well. Hearings are held on virtually all nominations, even those of scant impor-

Table 1-4. *Parties to Decision on Presidential Appointments Requiring Senate Confirmation*

Stage in appointments process	*Parties to process*
Recruitment and decision on candidate	President Office of Presidential Personnel Chief of staff and other White House staff Members of Congress Trade associations and lobbying organizations
Vetting process	Office of White House Counsel Federal Bureau of Investigation Internal Revenue Service Office of Government Ethics
Senate confirmation	White House Office of Legislative Affairs Cabinet, agency, board, or commission Senate committee staff Senators Candidate

Source: Material provided by White House Office of Presidential Personnel, July 10, 2000.

tance to the operations of the government. Nominees are expected to appear and answer questions at these hearings; any boundaries on such questions have long since been trespassed. Senate debate on nominations is open and televised, and Senate votes on any contested nominations are routinely recorded.

The modern appointments process is not only more visible and more transparent than ever before, it is also more permeable. Once limited to a handful of participants in the White House and the senior members of a relevant Senate committee, the appointments process today is open and hospitable to wide participation from many members of the White House staff and officials in the executive agencies, every member of the Senate, a wide array of well-informed and passionate interest groups, and individual citizens. Who is party to the appointments process these days? Nearly everyone, as the listing in table 1-4, provided by the White House Office of Presidential Personnel, indicates.

The selection of a presidential nominee now often follows delicate negotiations within the White House, often involving agency heads or department secretaries and a half dozen or more members of the White House staff. The individual who is advertised as "the president's nominee" is often a stranger to the president who has survived these intense, internal shoot-outs within the president's staff and administration. The vetting that occurs at the end of that process is often an invitation for many of the interests affected by the appointment to express their opinions about—and their opposition to or support for—the candidate under consideration.

When the nomination goes to the Senate, it is now routinely expected that a nominee will make the rounds of committee members for personal meetings. These are most often opportunities for senators to begin the process of cultivating the nominee's support for a pet program or project or encouraging him or her to undertake some action the senator favors, even if it is counter to administration policy. Any senator, not merely one on the committee with confirmation jurisdiction, can place a hold on a nomination that brings the process to a halt for as long as the senator insists on retaining the hold. When a hearing is scheduled, interest groups often request the opportunity to testify, a request that is rarely denied. In the eighty-eight hearings on cabinet nominees that occurred between 1977 and 1998, for example, interest groups appeared to testify 73 percent of the time.[34] This is a far cry from the days when such hearings were always held in executive session.

These days, interest groups do not merely testify and go away. They recognize the critical role an appointment can play in shaping public policy, and the occasion of a crucial appointment often raises the temperature of affected interests to white heat. Interest groups mobilize their members to contact their senators. They prepare and publicize their own briefing papers on the nominee's strengths or flaws. They provide spokespersons to appear on the all-news channels. They advertise in newspapers and on television. When the appointments process, in the 1980s, became one of the key public policy battlegrounds, new armies began to march across it from every point on the political compass. Now they know the way and the order of battle, and neither truce nor disarmament is in sight.

The Process Is Thick and Slow

Every change that has occurred in the appointments process over the past three decades has thickened it, adding more layers of people involved, more hurdles to be cleared, more forms to be completed. The contemporary appointments process is the red-tape hall of fame. It is hard to imagine a set of personnel processes anywhere else in America so heavily compounded of questions and investigations, so deeply buried in paper, so redundant. In America today, you can get a master's degree, build a house, bicycle across country, or make a baby in less time than it takes to put the average appointee on the job.

The thickening began in 1953. It was the Joseph P. McCarthy period, and in a bow to the security mania of the time President Dwight D. Eisenhower issued Executive Order 10450, which required that all candidates for Senate-confirmed presidential appointments be checked by the Federal Bureau of Investigation (FBI) as a kind of security clearance. The limited intentions of the order and its intended focus on national security concerns are clear from the language.

> The scope of the investigation shall be determined in the first instance according to the degree of adverse effect the occupant of the position sought to be filled could bring about, by virtue of the nature of the position, on the national security, but in no event shall the investigation include less than a national agency check (including a check of the fingerprint files of the Federal Bureau of Investigation), and written inquiries to appropriate local law enforcement agencies, former employers and supervisors, references, and schools attended by the person under investigation. . . . Should there develop at any stage of investigation information indicating that the employment of any such person may not be clearly consistent with the interests of the national security, there shall be conducted with respect to such person a full-field investigation, or such less investigation as shall be sufficient to enable the head of the department or agency concerned to determine whether retention of such person is clearly consistent with the interests of the national security. . . . The head of any department or agency shall designate, or cause to be designated, any position within his department or agency the occupant of which could bring about, by virtue of the nature of the position, a material adverse effect on the national security as a sensitive position.

Over the years, this national security review gradually evolved into today's lengthy, one-size-fits-all "full-field investigation," which often involves dozens of interviews, checking of academic and business records, and detailed inquiries into any matter that might raise questions not just about a nominee's fitness to hold public office but about any controversy his or her nomination might engender.

It is noteworthy that at no time after 1953 did any president communicate to the FBI a desire to enlarge the simple clearance that Eisenhower had ordered; the expansion resulted from decisions made within the FBI, often in response to the controversy or embarrassment of the day. No one in authority after 1953 seems ever to have asked for a reexamination of the nature and appropriateness of the evolving FBI full-field investigation. Like so much in the appointments process, it simply took on a life of its own.

Much the same is true of the brace of forms and questionnaires that appointees must now complete before their names go forward in formal nomination to the Senate. American presidents have occasionally weighed in with their personal views on whether so many and such diverse forms are actually essential, but they have done close to nothing to alter practices over which they have substantial control. President Clinton suggested, in typical frustration with the process, that "it's time to have a bipartisan look at the whole appointments process. It takes too long to get somebody confirmed. It's too bureaucratic. You have two and three levels of investigation. I think it's excessive."[35] At the end of his term, however, the appointments process was thicker and slower than ever.

One Clinton appointee's comment echoes the anthem of frustration sung by many others who have endured the modern process:

> Committees have very lengthy forms to be filled out, and of course you also have the FBI clearances and other things with very long forms that have to be filled out. None of it is coordinated, so they are all asking the same questions. . . . There are about 30 pages of information that you have to supply each one. But they're in different formats so that you have to go through this process [many times]. It's a very redundant thing. It is a very cumbersome, drawn-out process of just filling out paperwork, answering the same questions in different ways and in different order.[36]

Thickness in the appointments process is a product of defensiveness. Those charged with helping a president choose his appointees and those charged with helping Senate committees to confirm them dislike surprise, and they dislike embarrassment. To many of them the greatest sin may be a bad appointment, but the greatest fear is to have troublesome information appear after sign-off.

Full-field investigations by the FBI grew more comprehensive after information about John Tower that was not in his FBI file came out at his confirmation hearing in 1989. White House information forms began to include questions about taxes paid for domestic help after Zöe Baird's nomination ran aground on that shoal. After Donald Ginsburg's Supreme Court nomination was withdrawn in response to information about his adult marijuana use, questions on that subject crept into FBI inquiries and White House forms. It is a game Washington insiders like to play: match the question to the scandal.

Even when participants in the process make efforts to simplify it, they are often confounded by other participants who believe that simplification is somehow a lowering of standards. When the Office of Government Ethics (OGE) recommended to Congress that the SF 278, the financial disclosure form that all presidential appointees must complete, have fewer categories for reporting the value of assets, it was following a recommendation that had been made by several blue-ribbon commissions that had studied the appointments process.[37] The recommendation also followed a simple logic, that multiple reporting categories served no valuable purpose in enforcing the law. How did Congress respond? It increased, not reduced, the number of reporting categories, and thus further thickened the appointments process.

All these layers, all the forms and questionnaires, all the investigations often, ironically, accomplish the opposite of what they intend. Perhaps the thickening of the appointments process has made it harder for rogues to hide. That is difficult to measure. There are not many rogues in appointed positions in government these days. On the other hand, there were not many rogues before all this thickening occurred.

The thickening, however, has made the process much longer and slower, handicapping a president's ability to govern with his own team. The thickened process frustrates new appointees, dulling their own enthusiasm for public service and making pettiness and contention the characteristics of many of their initial interactions with the White House and the Senate. Moreover, the thickness of the process is sometimes a deterrent to people who would like to serve their country in government but choose not to do so because they cannot abide the uncertainty, the intrusive scrutiny, and the guilty-until-proven-innocent mentality that seem to them to be at the core of the contemporary appointments process.

A survey conducted by the Brookings Institution's Presidential Appointee Initiative in late 2000 explored the views of executives from Fortune 500 companies, presidents of leading colleges and universities, chief executive officers of major nonprofit organizations, think-tank scholars, and state and local officials—exactly the sorts of people who ought to be in the on-deck circle for presidential appointments. Their interest in public service was high, but their opinion of the presidential appointments process was low—low enough in a number of cases to be a powerful deterrent to accepting a presidential appointment. Fifty-nine percent of the sample described the appointments process as "confusing," and 51 percent called it "embarrassing." Forty-two percent said the White House is too demanding, making the appointments process an ordeal; 66 percent felt that way about the Senate.

Respondents who had been offered appointments turned them down for a variety of reasons, including a disinclination to enter the appointments process. "It became clear to me that this process was going to be very complex and very invasive of my privacy," said one. Another confessed, "I didn't want to go through the nomination and confirmation process, which I knew would be deadly and would probably fail. The threat of having [my] family vilified was too much for me."[38]

A Rational Appointments Process?

Here is a fantasy: The year is 2004, and a new administration has just been elected. Because it began its transition planning as soon as the president-elect had secured his party's nomination, after the March primaries, the week following the election adheres tightly to a carefully planned script.

Unlike his predecessors, the new president will have to fill only about 450 full-time positions in the departments and agencies. The number of appointees requiring Senate confirmation was reduced by nearly a third when the Congress passed the sweeping Appointments Process Renewal Act two years earlier. Career senior executives from the reformed and much more responsive senior executive corps, already on the job and fully knowledgeable about their responsibilities, now fill many of the positions that used to await the attention of a new president, often late in the first year of his term.

The transition personnel team, headed by an experienced hand who has agreed to seek no other position in the administration, has identified 125 high-priority positions for the new administration. The team has studied these jobs and consulted with previous incumbents. It has a clear idea of the kinds of people the president-elect should recruit to fill the slots. It has even begun to identify and to preclear some potential candidates for these jobs, though no one has yet been offered a position. Most of the preclearance has been done with the approval of the individuals under consideration but without any commitment to offer them an appointment.

The Appointments Process Renewal Act authorizes the relevant government agencies—the Office of Government Ethics, the FBI, and the designated agency ethics officials in the agencies and departments—to participate in these preclearances. It further specifies, following the recommendation of a bipartisan commission that examined the extensive array of clearances and investigations for presidential appointees, that simpler, less intrusive, less time-consuming reviews could be conducted for all nominees except those in critical national security positions. In the old days, these reviews were one-size-fits-all, but common sense now prevails, and most clearances can be completed in two to four weeks.

As soon as he returns from a postelection vacation, the president-elect begins to review the lists of candidates provided by his transition personnel team and to choose nominees for these high-priority positions. Recruitment will be easier than in previous transitions because changes have been made in the ethics laws to reduce the extensive array of postemployment restrictions on presidential appointees that had been steadily growing in law and executive order. Because they have already been cleared, the nominations can be formally sent to the Senate a few days later.

The Senate is well prepared for this transition, as well. Because the nominees have used the new interactive Nomination Forms Online website to submit all required information, each Senate committee can generate tailored and completed questionnaires electronically and distribute them to committee members. No time is lost explaining all the requirements to nominees, because they have been indicated on the Appointee Resource Center website and are well known by the transition personnel team. So Senate committee staffs can immediately begin their own reviews, hastening to prepare for confirmation hearings, which routinely begin before inauguration. A sense of urgency prevails in the Senate because, under the act, it now must complete the confirmation process within forty-five days of the formal receipt of a nomination.

The task of the Senate staffs is eased by the decision, also mandated in the act, to eliminate confirmation hearings for all noncontroversial nominees below the rank of executive-level 3 (EL-3). Instead of the dozens of confirmation hearings that used to be scheduled in the first year of a new administration, the busiest committees now have to cope with only ten to fifteen.

There may still be some senators who, for political reasons or because they have genuine doubts about a nominee, may want to place a hold on the nominations. Senate rules now limit holds on nominations to a total of two weeks, however, and no hold may postpone a vote beyond the forty-five-day period unless a majority of the full Senate agrees to a fourteen-day extension. So it is a certainty that a confirmation vote will occur within fifty-nine days of nomination even if holds are imposed for the full time permitted. The recent amendment to Senate Rule 22 prohibits the use of filibusters on nominations so that only a simple majority is necessary for confirmation, as the Constitution intended.

By inauguration day most of the original 125 nominations are moving through the confirmation process. The personnel team moves into the Executive Office Building on inauguration day and continues its work as the Office of Presidential Personnel. Because its systems were prepared and tested well before the election, it is already up to speed, preparing twenty-five to thirty nominations for the president to send to the Senate each week. At this pace, all the major nominations should be made by the end of March and confirmed by the middle of May at the latest. This will be the most rapid staffing of a new administration since 1968—as it should be.

How wonderful it would be if this were reality, not fantasy. Unfortunately, a rational presidential appointments process is a long way from reality. The evolution traced here has led us to a state of affairs that no one consciously chose—that no rational person could possibly choose—and that no one likes.

The contemporary presidential appointments process is a national disgrace. It encourages bullies and emboldens demagogues. It silences the voices of responsibility and nourishes the lowest forms of partisan combat. It uses innocent citizens as pawns in politicians' petty games and stains the reputations of good people. It routinely violates fundamental democratic principles, undermines the quality and consistency of public management, and breaches simple decency. Republicans and Democrats, legislators and chief executives, journalists and special interests all share responsibility for allowing one of the rare and genuine inventions of American political creativity to fall into a state of malignancy.

The presidential appointments process has changed in the past three decades, changed significantly, but none of those changes has improved it. The contemporary appointments process is slower, more cumbersome, more contentious, more repellent to talented Americans, and more distant from the purposes of good government than it has ever been. For too long, those who could stop the deterioration of the process have failed to do so, turning away from its excesses, accepting them as the inevitabilities of high-stakes, scorched-earth politics.

It is past time to begin rebuilding and reinvigorating the way we staff the executive and judicial branches of government. If we merely continue doing what we have been doing, then we will surely continue getting what we have been getting. That was not good enough for the late twentieth century, and it certainly will not be good enough for the twenty-first.

Notes

1. Arthur M. Schlesinger Jr., *A Thousand Days* (New York: Fawcett Crest, 1965), p. 625.

2. Martin P. Wattenberg, *The Decline of American Political Parties, 1952–1996* (Harvard University Press, 1998), p. ix.

3. Leo C. Rosten, *The Washington Correspondents* (Harcourt Brace, 1937), p. 3.

4. Stephen Hess, *News and Newsmaking* (Brookings, 1996), p. 20.

5. Rosten, *The Washington Correspondents*, p. 107.

6. F. B. Marbut, *News from the Capital: The Story of Washington Reporting* (Southern Illinois University Press, 1971), pp. 191–92.

7. Hess, *News and Newsmaking*, p. 12.

8. Ibid., p. 40.

9. Data from Stephen Ansolabehere and others, *The Media Game: American Politics in the Television Age* (New York: Macmillan, 1993), pp. 39–41; Hess, *News and Newsmaking*, p. 3; Times Mirror Center for the People and the Press, "Americans Going Online: Explosive Growth, Uncertain Destinations," press release, October 16, 1996.

10. John Quincy Adams, *Memoirs* (Philadelphia: J. B. Lippincott, 1874–77), vol. 7, pp. 424–25.

11. Quoted in James D. Richardson, *Messages and Papers of the President* (New York: Bureau of National Literature, 1897), vol. 2, pp. 448–49.

12. Arthur M. Schlesinger Jr., *The Age of Jackson* (Boston: Little, Brown, 1945), p. 47.

13. Dwight D. Eisenhower, *Mandate for Change* (New York: Signet, 1963), p. 137.

14. Sherman Adams, *First-Hand Report: The Story of the Eisenhower Administration* (Harper and Brothers, 1961), p. 57.

15. Quoted in Leslie H. Gelb, "Carter Finding Few Outsiders," *New York Times*, December 16, 1976.

16. Quoted in Richard L. Schott and Dagmar Hamilton, "The Politics of Presidential Appointments in the Johnson Administration: Notes on Work in

Progress," paper presented at the annual meeting of the Southern Political Science Association, November 4, 1977, p. 6.

17. Fred Malek, "Management and Non-Career Personnel: Recommendations for Improvement" (mimeograph, December 18, 1970), p. 1.

18. Remarks by Senator Warren G. Magnuson to the Consumer Federation of America, May 7, 1973. Washington.

19. Common Cause, "The Senate Rubberstamp Machine" (mimeograph, November 1977), pp. 34, 36.

20. Norman J. Ornstein and others, *Vital Statistics on Congress, 1997–1998* (Washington: CQ Press, 1998), p. 139.

21. For a catalogue of the requirements imposed on presidential appointees by the Ethics in Government Act of 1978, see G. Calvin Mackenzie and Robert Shogan, *Obstacle Course* (New York: Twentieth Century Fund Press, 1996), pp. 79–82.

22. "Staffing the Reagan Presidency," panel discussion at the annual meeting of the American Political Science Association, New York, N.Y., September 2, 1981.

23. G. Calvin Mackenzie, "If You Want to Play, You've Got to Pay: Ethics Regulation and the Presidential Appointments System, 1964–1984," in G. Calvin Mackenzie, ed., *The In-and-Outers: Presidential Appointees and Transient Government in Washington* (Johns Hopkins University Press, 1987), p. 86.

24. Quoted in "Legends in the Law: A Conversation with Robert H. Bork," *Bar Report* (December–January 1998), www.dcbar.org/about_bar/roberth.html (December 11, 2000).

25. Interview with Robert C. Byrd, *Booknotes,* C-SPAN transcript, June 18, 1989 (www.booknotes.org/transcripts/10031.htm [December 11, 2000]).

26. Quoted in Claudia Dreifus, "Jocelyn Elders," *New York Times Magazine*, January 30, 1994, p. 18.

27. G. Calvin Mackenzie, *The Politics of Presidential Appointments* (New York: Free Press, 1981), p. xix.

28. Joseph R. Harris, *The Advice and Consent of the Senate* (University of California Press, 1953), p. 377.

29. U.S. Senate, Committee on the Judiciary, *Hearings on the Nomination of Clement Haynsworth to Be Associate Justice, U.S. Supreme Court*, 91 Cong., 1 sess. (Government Printing Office, 1969), p. 327.

30. U.S. Senate, Committee on Agriculture and Forestry, *Hearings on the Nomination of Earl L. Butz to Be Secretary of Agriculture*, 92 Cong., 1 sess. (Government Printing Office, 1971), p. 144.

31. Mackenzie, *The Politics of Presidential Appointments*, p. 274.

32. Quoted in "Assault by Legislators Prompts Anthony Lake to Ask President Clinton to Withdraw Nomination," Reaganradio.com (www.reagan.com/HotTopics.main/HotMike/document-3.18.1997.6.html [December 11, 2000]).

33. Quoted in "Recruiting Presidential Appointees: A Conference of Former Presidential Personnel Assistants," occasional paper (Washington: National Academy of Public Administration, December 1984), p. 4.

34. Lauren Cohen Bell, *Warring Factions: Interest Groups, Money, and the New Politics of Senate Confirmation*, unpublished manuscript, p. 193.

35. Quoted in Twentieth Century Fund, *Obstacle Course*, p. 7.

36. Quoted in Paul C. Light and Virginia L. Thomas, *The Merit and Reputation of an Administration: Presidential Appointees on the Appointments Process* (Brookings and Heritage Foundation, 2000), p. 12.

37. See Presidential Appointee Project, *Leadership in Jeopardy: The Fraying of the Presidential Appointments System* (Washington: National Academy of Public Administration, 1985); Twentieth Century Fund, *Obstacle Course*.

38. Quoted in Paul C. Light and Virginia L. Thomas, *Posts of Honor: How America's Corporate and Civic Leaders View Presidential Appointments* (Brookings, 2001).

CHAPTER TWO

Presidential Appointments: Recruiting Executive Branch Leaders

JAMES P. PFIFFNER

THE UNITED STATES Constitution vests the "executive power" in the president and commands that "the laws be faithfully executed." To fulfill this constitutional responsibility, each president appoints the major officers of the government. The ability of the government to carry out its primary function—responding to the wishes of its citizens through execution of the laws—depends crucially on capable civil servants. The effectiveness of these civil servants in the executive branch, in turn, is intimately linked with the quality of the leadership of the executive branch—that is, presidential appointments.

Each new president comes to office with the opportunity to appoint thousands of men and women who will help lead the executive branch. No individual could possibly make these selections alone, and so the Office of Presidential Personnel (OPP) in the White House Office is the organizational entity that assists the president in recruiting leaders for the executive branch. Career civil servants are recruited on a continual basis by the Office of Personnel Management and individual agencies, but with each change of administration the Office of Presidential Personnel is formed anew to recruit leaders for the top levels of the executive branch.

The primary duty of the Office of Presidential Personnel is to help repopulate the leadership levels of the executive branch, a crucial task in serving the nation. The first section of this chapter examines the development of the recruitment function in American government and the institutionalization of the Office of Presidential Personnel over the past fifty years. The OPP did not exist in 1960; by 1981, more than a hundred people were working on political recruitment.

In addition to serving the presidency, the Office of Presidential Personnel also serves individual presidents. All presidents want to mold their administrations to fit their policy agendas and to reflect the values of the coalitions that put them in office. This task calls for close attention to the wishes of the individual president not merely to recruit the individuals the president personally knows and wants to appoint but also to seek out those individuals who share the president's values and have the skills, character, and experience to carry out his or her policy directives. The second section of this chapter explores the OPP's relationship with the president in recruiting presidential and other political appointees.

Third, the OPP has important obligations to the individual Americans it is trying to recruit. The presidential nomination and appointments process is complex, conflictual, and difficult. Evidence collected by the Brookings Institution's Presidential Appointee Initiative shows that many presidential nominees, despite their enthusiasm for coming to work in Washington, are less than enchanted by the way they have been treated in the process of presidential nomination and confirmation by the Senate. The final section of this chapter examines the appointments process from the perspective of the nominees and suggests ways that their experience might be improved in the future.

The Office of Presidential Personnel: Serving the Nation

Although presidents had made thousands of political appointments through the years, until the middle of the twentieth century they lacked the personal staff needed to exercise significant control over those choices. As presidents began to assert more personal control over appointments, they increased their own institutional capacity to recruit their own nominees for positions in the government. The creation of this institutional capacity began slowly and only gradually superceded the traditional reliance upon the political parties. As the institutional capacity necessary to support a growing presidency evolved, however, it also acquired some of the drawbacks of large organizations. The whole process began to slow, and the time necessary for bringing on board the president's team increased significantly.

The Institutionalization of the Office of Presidential Personnel

President Harry S Truman was the first president to place one person, Donald Dawson, in charge of advising him on appointment decisions; Dawson had one assistant. Dawson's main activities were clearing candidates for office, placing them in specific positions, and managing patronage by coordinating placements with the Democratic National Committee.[1] He did not have the capacity to operate independently of the Democratic Party, but his appointment was the first significant step toward the development of presidential independence.

President Dwight D. Eisenhower did not believe that party patronage should play a large role at the top levels of American government. He had been a professional military officer and was suspicious of turning over important government responsibilities to people whose main qualification was loyal service to the party. Instead of a Republican regular, Ike designated Charles Willis, who had founded a nonpartisan group to draft Eisenhower, as his aide for political appointments.

Despite his personal distrust of patronage, Eisenhower was subjected to heavy pressure from the Republican Party for jobs after twenty years of Democratic control of the government. The Republican National Committee complained that the new administration was not sensitive to the needs of the party faithful. These pressures were so great that the control of patronage was brought into the White House and placed in the hands of Eisenhower's chief of staff, Sherman Adams.

Shortly after his inauguration in March 1953, Eisenhower created, through executive order, a new class of political appointments, known as Schedule C positions. By design, these positions were at lower-than-executive levels and policy determining or confidential in nature. About two hundred positions were created by the order, though subsequent presidents would increase this number. By Eisenhower's second term the need for more White House control was indicated by the creation of a new position, special assistant for personnel management.

When John F. Kennedy was elected, he did not want to turn recruitment for political appointments over to the Democratic National Committee and assigned his aides in the White House the task of handling political personnel. His campaign manager, Larry O'Brien, and several other staffers took care of placing political loyalists who had supported Kennedy in the campaign as well as managing patronage more broadly. To fill the top levels of his administration, however, with "the best and the brightest," Kennedy created a "talent hunt" that was headed by a separate team under Sargent Shriver. This appointments team would not merely screen applications that came in but would also reach out to find talented people who were committed to Kennedy's New Frontier policies. As Kennedy aide Dan Fenn explained it, they wanted to avoid the syndrome of the usual approach to staffing an administration: BOGSAT—that is, "a bunch of guys sitting around a table" asking each other "whom do you know."[2]

Lyndon B. Johnson continued Kennedy's practice of putting his own aides in charge of political personnel. He asked John Macy to come to the White House to run his recruitment operation at the same time that Macy was chair of the Civil Service Commission. Macy spent mornings at the civil service building and afternoons and evenings at the White House, helping Johnson select presidential appointments. Macy expanded the political personnel staff from four to seven professionals and began to use computers to organize job files.[3]

The campaign run by Richard M. Nixon had not been dependent on the Republican National Committee, and he intended to run his White House with his handpicked supporters. After the inauguration, the personnel operation was taken over by Peter Flanigan, who initially had fifteen staffers working for him. The ability of the White House to control presidential appointments was undercut, however, by President Nixon's original intentions to have his cabinet secretaries pick the best people for their departments rather than tightly controlling appointments from the White House.

Nixon soon became disillusioned with his "cabinet government" approach to political appointments: he felt that his cabinet secretaries were not implementing his priorities and were choosing appointees who were loyal to them but not necessarily to Nixon himself. So in 1970 he brought Fred Malek from his position at the Department of Health, Education, and Welfare to run the political appointments process at the White House. Malek planned to create a "professional executive search capacity" in the White House. In his opinion, before his arrival the search was primarily reactive rather than actively seeking out the best executive talent. "What they were doing then was more dependent on what came in over the transom through the political system. They were not clearly delineating the nature of a job, the requirements of a job, and then going out and searching through society to find the best candidates for that kind of job, to meet the criteria. So we established a professional team of executive recruiters and endeavored to find the best people."[4] Malek eventually had thirty to forty staffers working in the White House personnel office.

Jimmy Carter's personnel operation began in the summer of 1976. Carter took his possible transition into office seriously, and because he did not have Washington experience, he decided to set up a transition team in Atlanta. One of the main tasks of the transition operation was to create a talent inventory program to prepare lists of possible appointees to political positions. The operation in Atlanta, headed by Jack Watson, collected thousands of resumés for cabinet and subcabinet positions, but much of the preparation work they did was ignored once Carter was elected because campaign officials, under the direction of Hamilton Jordan, felt that campaign workers had been excluded from serious consideration. In the battle following the election, Jordan won.

Even if all of the work of the talent inventory program operation had survived intact, however, it would probably not have made a major impact on presidential appointments because of President Carter's commitment to "cabinet government." Part of his approach to governance was to delegate to cabinet secretaries broad authority to select their subcabinet subordinates. Not all cabinet secretaries were as supportive of White House policy direction as Carter had expected, however, and many of the subcabinet appointees were more loyal to their immediate superiors than to Carter.

In 1978, having decided to abandon his cabinet government approach, President Carter brought in Tim Kraft, and then Arnie Miller, to tighten White House control over presidential appointments. According to Miller, the Carter White House "had given away the store and they wanted to take it back. . . . He gave away hiring. I was brought in to take it back."[5] Miller began to take control of the appointments process, but it was already halfway through the administration, and, as John Ehrlichman was fond of saying, once the toothpaste is out of the tube, it is very difficult to get it back in.

President Ronald Reagan decided to take a deliberate approach to political appointments, and in April 1980, Ed Meese asked Pendleton James, a professional headhunter, to begin planning personnel operations for a possible Reagan administration. Mindful of the frustrating experiences of Presidents Nixon and Carter, the Reagan administration decided to control all political appointments tightly in the White House. In contrast with previous administrations, this would include political appointments below the presidential level, such as noncareer Senior Executive

Service (SES) and Schedule C appointees. To emphasize the importance of political appointments, James was given the title of assistant to the president for presidential personnel and an office in the West Wing of the White House, two important precedents. To handle the large volume of appointments and tighter scrutiny, the Office of Presidential Personnel was expanded considerably, and James had about a hundred people to assist him. The Reagan personnel operation was the most thorough and sophisticated approach to date.

President George Bush continued to maintain control of political personnel in the White House through Chase Untermeyer and Constance Horner, directors of his Office of Presidential Personnel. The tight White House control was loosened a bit, and more leeway was given to cabinet secretaries over nonpresidential political appointments, but the principle that all political appointments were at the president's discretion was enforced.

President Bill Clinton's transition efforts were centered with the president-elect in Little Rock, Arkansas, but his political personnel operation was at the Washington end of the transition. Including volunteers and professionals, the total number of people working on personnel operations approached three hundred.[6] The operation handled a huge volume of applications and resumés, aided by new scanning and computer technology. The personnel efforts were hindered, however, by a disruptive turnover in leadership. Clinton appointed Richard Riley to head the personnel operation, and Riley conscientiously consulted his predecessors about how best to handle the duties of heading the personnel office. Soon after his appointment, however, Clinton designated Riley to be his secretary of education. Clinton then appointed his aide, Bruce Lindsey, to be head of political personnel, but Lindsey was also handling other important duties for Clinton, and the appointments process suffered. In January he turned to Veronica Biggins, an Atlanta bank executive, to head up presidential personnel. In March 1993 the Office of Presidential Personnel had about a hundred people working in it, though by the summer of 1993 that number had been cut in half and was down to thirty-five by the end of September.[7]

Thus the presidential recruitment function was transformed in the second half of the twentieth century. It developed the following characteristics:

—The political parties, which had dominated presidential appointments for the previous century, were gradually replaced by an increasingly professionalized executive recruitment capacity.

—The recruitment capacity, which began with one person in charge in the Truman administration, was gradually institutionalized in a potent and permanent place in the White House Office, headed by an aide with the title of assistant to the president.

—The reach of the OPP was extended not only to presidential appointments but also to what are technically agency head appointments (noncareer SES and Schedule C positions).

—The size of the office grew from six people in the Kennedy administration to more than a hundred staffers at the beginning of the Reagan and Clinton administrations.

The Slowing Pace of Appointments

Part of the cause of this institutionalization was the increasing number of appointments that are handled by the Office of Presidential Personnel. An important consequence of these increasing numbers is a significant slowing of the appointments process. Both of these developments have had negative consequences for the presidency and the national government.

Seeking out potential appointees for the highest-level appointed positions like cabinet secretaries, agency heads, the subcabinet, and regulatory commissioners is a challenge in its own right, but the task of the Office of Presidential Personnel is quite a bit broader. The OPP must also recruit many other presidential appointees, including full-time positions on commissions as well as ambassadors (185), U.S. district attorneys (94), and U.S. marshals (94). A total of 1,125 full-time presidential appointments require Senate confirmation.

In addition to presidential appointments, lower-level political appointments are available to each administration to help implement its priorities. These include noncareer appointments in the Senior Executive Service (created in 1978), which can amount to 10 percent of the total career SES of around 7,500. Noncareer SES appointments presently number about 720. Schedule C positions, a total of 200 when first created in 1953, now number 1,428. These latter two categories of political positions are technically appointed by cabinet secretaries and agency heads. Since the Reagan administration, however, they have been controlled by the Office of Presidential Personnel. Although noncareer SES and Schedule C appointments are not as important as presidential appointees, their screening and control by the OPP create a significant additional burden on the office.

These appointments are directly concerned with the leadership and control of the executive branch by the president, but the OPP also advises the president on several thousand part-time appointments, many to boards and commissions that may meet several times a year. A total of 490 part-time presidential appointments requiring Senate confirmation are made at the president's discretion, in addition to 1,859 that do not require Senate confirmation.

Regardless of how one counts or which categories are included, the number of political appointees has increased considerably over the past fifty years, and the OPP faces a daunting challenge in helping the president fill the positions. Although in the nineteenth and early twentieth centuries the number of appointees, including postmasters, customs inspectors, and other field positions, was considerably greater than at present, those positions were filled as patronage by political parties. Now the positions are used directly to provide leadership for the executive branch; they require significant skills, experience, and expertise and are controlled by the president through the OPP.

Given the increasing numbers of political positions and the increasing scope of coverage of the OPP, it is not surprising that the pace of appointments has slowed considerably in the past four decades. One indicator of the difficulty that recent presidents have had is the total number of nominations and appointments they have been able to make in the first year of their presidencies. This information is presented in table 2-1.

The slower pace of the Bush administration is explained by the fact that his was a "friendly takeover." That is, Bush took over following eight years of the Reagan administration, with political positions already filled with loyal Republicans, and he had no need to rush appointments. In contrast, during a party turnover transition, the top levels of the government are vacant, and there is an urgent need to fill the positions with the new president's appointees. Despite this need, recent administrations have been taking longer to get their people on board.

From the perspective of individual nominees and their experience, the process is often frustratingly slow. The Presidential Appointee Initiative asked presidential appointees from the Reagan, first Bush, and Clinton administrations how many months had passed from the time they were first contacted by the White House until they were confirmed by the Senate. Evidence for the slowing process can be seen in table 2-2, which illustrates a comparison of the experiences of those appointees from 1984 to 1999 with those of a sample from 1964 to 1984 who were surveyed

Table 2-1. *First-Year Nominations, by Administration, 1977–93*
Number

	Carter (1977)	*Reagan (1981)*	*Bush (1989)*	*Clinton (1993)*
Nominations requiring Senate confirmation	682	680	501	673
Total confirmed	637	662	432	499

Source: Data from James P. Pfiffner, *The Strategic Presidency: Hitting the Ground Running*, 2d ed. (University Press of Kansas, 1996), p. 168.

earlier by the National Academy of Public Administration. Table 2-3 demonstrates the increasing time necessary for a new administration to get its appointees on board in a different way, by comparing the past three administrations.

The increased numbers of positions and the increasing scope of the OPP are the primary, but by no means the only, factors involved in the slowing pace of presidential appointments. Since 1978 a number of ethics laws have tightened requirements for holding high positions in the government, including the disclosure of financial information. Nominees often have to hire consultants to help them, and filling out the forms takes a considerable amount of time. With scandals in recent administrations, those who vet nominees have become more cautious, taking extra time to make sure there are no skeletons in the closets of potential nominees. This caution has rubbed off on the Federal Bureau of Investigation (FBI): not wanting to miss something important, they take extra care and time to do their background investigations. The resources and personnel of

Table 2-2. *Duration of Appointments Process as Reported by Nominees, 1964–99*
Percent unless otherwise specified

Duration of process	*1964–84*	*1984–99*
1 or 2 months	48	15
3 or 4 months	34	26
5 or 6 months	11	26
More than 6 months	5	30
Number of appointments	532	435

Source: Data from Paul C. Light and Virginia L. Thomas, *The Merit and Reputation of an Administration: Presidential Appointees on the Appointments Process* (Brookings and Heritage Foundation, 2000), p. 8.

Table 2-3. *Duration of Appointments Process as Reported by Nominees, by Administration, 1984–99*

Percent unless otherwise specified

Duration	*All*	*Reagan*	*Bush*	*Clinton*
1 to 2 months	15	21	23	7
3 to 4 months	26	36	25	21
5 to 6 months	26	29	24	26
More than 6 months	30	11	25	44
Number of appointments	435	107	127	201

Source: Data from Light and Thomas, *The Merit and Reputation of an Administration*, p. 8.

the FBI are stretched thin at the beginning of each administration in performing hundreds of clearances simultaneously.

The above factors affect any administration coming into office, but the priorities of an individual president may also increase the time between inauguration and the completion of top-level appointments. The Reagan administration took extra time to find nominees who were ideologically compatible with the administration's goals. The Clinton administration took extra time to ensure gender and racial diversity among its appointees. If the president wants to be personally involved in a large number of lower-level nominations, as did President Clinton and Hillary Rodham Clinton in 1993, it will take longer. The size of the OPP staff is also a factor. Although the number of OPP staffers in recent administrations has been sufficient to the task, the Clinton OPP was sharply reduced in size by the summer of 1993, which contributed to a slower process.

The slowness of the process hurts an administration by keeping it from fully pursuing its policy agenda throughout the government. Presidential appointees need to be present not only at the very top but also several levels down (to the assistant secretary level) for policy change to be pursued effectively, either within the executive branch or through legislation. Even relatively routine administrative actions, such as procuring information technology or office space, require approval at various political levels. Career civil servants are quite capable of doing the analysis, but they hesitate to move very far before their new political superiors are on board.

For instance, when President Clinton proposed the controversial "gays in the military" policy early in his administration, only a few appointees were on board at the Pentagon. It would have helped if he had had the appointees at the assistant secretary level to explain and defend his policy to the career military officers whose support was crucial to implementation of the policy. By the end of June 1993, only ten of twenty-four Defense Department positions requiring Senate confirmation had been filled, and of the twenty-two positions in the armed services, only one had been confirmed.[8] By December 12, 1993, the Department of Defense had filled nineteen of the forty-six available jobs.[9] By April 28, 1993, the Clinton administration had more than three top officials in only two of the fourteen cabinet departments, and in seven of the departments only the secretary had been confirmed.[10]

The Office of Presidential Personnel: Serving the President

The first job of the OPP is to advise the president in matching the right nominee with the right position, but for several reasons this is not a simple task. The personnel office must be ready to act the day after the election, so advance planning is crucial but often neglected in the pressure of the campaign. The onslaught of office seekers will hit immediately, and the OPP must be ready to handle the volume with some political sophistication. A process must be set up that strikes the right balance between the president's personal attention and the need to delegate much of the recruitment task to the OPP. Intense pressure for appointments will buffet the process from the campaign, Capitol Hill, interest groups, and the newly designated cabinet secretaries. Perhaps most important, the newly elected president's policy agenda will not be fully implemented until most of the administration's appointees are confirmed and in office. Each of these factors presents a challenge to an incoming administration.

The Initial Onslaught and the Need to Plan

Whereas the number of positions that can be filled by each new president amounts to several thousand, the number of applicants for those positions is many multiples of the number of positions available. Presidential campaigns generate enthusiasm for the winner, and people are not reticent about offering their talents to the new administration. Most of these offers come in "over the transom"—that is, unsolicited by the administration. The deluge begins the day after the election (and sometimes even before), and the OPP must be ready to handle the flood of paper.

Thus preelection preparation is crucial, but it is also risky. The risk is that the press will get wind of personnel preparation and try to find out who is being considered for which posts. If word gets out, public attention shifts from the campaign, and campaigners get suspicious that the planners are dividing the spoils of victory before the victory is even won. If this preelection planning is not also coordinated with the campaign, rival power centers will emerge.

This was the case in 1976, when Jimmy Carter, running as an outsider, set up a transition planning operation in Atlanta. The planning was a wise move, but it was not sufficiently coordinated with the campaign. In April 1980, Edwin Meese asked Pendleton James to begin planning a transition, even before Reagan had been nominated. Meese was in charge of both the campaign and the transition operation, so the conflict that marked the Carter transition was absent, and because the planning was done entirely in secret, the attention of the press did not generate rivalries within the Reagan camp.

Former presidential recruiters attest to the need for the personnel operation to be ready to move immediately. Arnie Miller, President Carter's recruiter, characterized the pressure of applicants as "that avalanche, that onslaught at the beginning, that tidal wave of people coming from all over the country, who've been with a candidate for years, and who have been waiting for this chance to come in and help."[11] "Presidential personnel cannot wait for the election because presidential personnel has to be functional on the first day, the first minute of the first hour. . . . Personnel can't take ten days," Pendleton James observed. "The guys in the campaign were only worried about one thing: the election night. I was only worrying about one thing: election morning."[12]

By the inauguration in 1989, about 16,000 resumés had come into the Bush transition operation, including a ten-foot stack of 1,500 resumés from the Heritage Foundation. There was no letup after the inauguration, and by the end of May more than 45,000 applications and recommendations had been received, a staggering amount of paper. During the Clinton transition the personnel operation had received 3,000 resumés by the end of their first week, and by February 1993 they were receiving 2,000 a day.[13] According to Robert Nash, the OPP director for President Clinton, the office's computers contained 190,000 resumés in the last year of the administration.[14] Many of them were not solicited or from serious candidates, but the numbers are nonetheless daunting.

Part of the problem is that, although many of these applications for jobs are unsolicited and come from people who are clearly unqualified, some come from people with powerful sponsors, especially in Congress.

The staff reading these applications must have the political sensitivity to be able to judge when the recommendation from Capitol Hill is serious and when it is merely a courtesy sent to please a constituent. The appropriate letter must then be generated to reply to the member. There also has to be someone who will recognize an applicant who is an old friend of the president and thus needs to be taken seriously.

Presidential personnel staff can also expect that they will be personally pursued by eager office seekers. Jan Naylor Cope, the deputy director of the presidential personnel office in the Bush administration, has recalled that at a Washington social occasion at a hotel an eager office seeker pursued her into a stall in the women's room to present her with a resumé. She was also approached in restaurants and in church by office seekers.[15] Looking forward to a break from work, Veronica Biggins, the OPP director for President Clinton, went to a lunch with a friend. When she arrived at the restaurant, however, her friend had "a stack of resumés" to discuss. "There is no such thing as friendship when you are indeed director of Presidential Personnel," she concluded.[16] Edwin Meese recalls that during the Reagan transition three resumés were thrust upon him while he was attending the funeral of a relative.[17]

Personal Presidential Participation in the Recruitment Process

By the time of the inauguration, the president and the OPP will have had to establish procedures to have potential nominees vetted by the White House counsel's office for conflict of interest, cleared by FBI investigations, and checked for taxes paid through the IRS. The substantive vetting and judgment about candidates are the job of the OPP and the president, however. Some presidents have been closely involved in the process of selecting nominees, and some have largely delegated that task to the director of the OPP and the chief of staff.

President Johnson was closely involved with the selection process and took personal interest in individual selections. John Macy, also chair of the Civil Service Commission at the time, has remarked that Johnson "was deeply involved in a large number of appointments. He had a fantastic memory, and he could recall some detail on a summary that we would send him, months and months afterwards."[18] President Gerald R. Ford was also actively involved personally in recruiting appointees for his administration. His personnel recruiter, Douglas Bennett, had three regularly scheduled meetings with the president each week, sometimes alone and sometimes with the chief of staff.[19] William Walker, when he was head of recruitment, met with Ford for an hour every Tuesday and Friday afternoon.[20]

Presidents Nixon, Carter, and Bush preferred to work from paper memorandums and most often approved the recommendations made by their OPP directors in conjunction with the chief of staff. Fred Malek saw President Nixon personally only about once a month. He and Chief of Staff H. R. Haldeman would come to an agreement, and most often the president approved their recommendations.[21] President Carter also preferred to work from paper—that is, he would read memorandums and reports in detail and respond on paper rather than personally discussing potential appointees. According to Arnie Miller, "We had a similar problem with Carter really only reading memos—five or six on appointments every night."[22] Miller sometimes wanted the president to personally ask a prospective nominee to take the job, but "I couldn't get Carter to ask."[23]

Chase Untermeyer has observed that "presidents often hate personnel" recruitment; once he and Chief of Staff John Sununu had agreed on a nominee, President Bush would virtually always go along with their recommendation. "Under the arrangement we had with President Bush almost never were there meetings in the Oval Office talking about personnel. . . . It was all done by paper. President Bush would see a memo recommending somebody with initials from John Sununu and me. In 99.9 percent of the cases he then signed it."[24] Untermeyer would occasionally talk with the president on the phone about a nominee, but this did not happen on a regular basis.

One of the most organized personnel operations was set up by Pendleton James in the early Reagan administration. Those involved in deciding on presidential nominees agreed on an explicit set of criteria that each nominee would have to meet. These included a philosophical commitment to the Reagan agenda, unquestioned integrity, the toughness required to take political buffeting, the necessary competence to handle the position, and the ability to act as a "team player."[25] Once a name was being seriously considered for recommendation to the president, it had to go through a set of checkpoints to ensure that anyone who had serious reservations about a candidate could register them. The process included the OPP, the departmental secretary, the troika (Edwin Meese, James A. Baker, and Michael Deaver), the counsel's office, the legislative liaison, Lyn Nofziger's political shop, and the domestic or national security adviser.[26]

James met with the troika daily at five o'clock in the afternoon to consider the candidates. Finally, James—sometimes with others of the troika—met with President Reagan every Tuesday and Thursday at three in the afternoon for final decisions on nominees. Each candidate would have a four-page file: The first page described the position and the qualifications the official needed. The second page contained a summary of the candidate's qualifications; sometimes there were several candidates. The third page would have a summary of recommendations for the candidate from important politicians. The final page would list the people who had been considered but rejected by those making recommendations.[27]

President Clinton's personal involvement, along with the First Lady's influence in political personnel selection, slowed the Clinton personnel operation considerably at the beginning of his administration. Cabinet members complained about appointments languishing in the president's in-box.[28] Although it is clearly the prerogative of the president to be personally involved—after all, these are presidential appointments—the process tends to work more smoothly when the president delegates much of the winnowing process to his OPP, reserving the final choices to himself.

Later in his administration President Clinton scaled back his personal involvement in selecting nominees. When Robert Nash returned in 1995, to be director of the OPP, President Clinton told him, "I want you to find capable, competent people who believe in what I'm trying to do for this country, and I want it to look like America." Nash did not talk much with the president about nominees, but he coordinated with the chief of staff. "My decision memos go to the chief of staff's office . . . and then from the chief of staff's office to the president."[29]

Given the range of relationships between the president and the chief personnel recruiter, there is no one best way to structure the process. Presidents have different personal preferences, and the processes should be set up to serve the president. It is the view of many experienced presidential personnel recruiters, however, that several principles should guide those who manage the appointment process.

First, the role of the director of the OPP should be that of a neutral broker who is not trying to foster personal policy preferences. Pendleton James argues that he or she should be a person who "[has the] confidence of the president, [is] an honest broker, stays in the job, has no hidden agenda, understands the president and his philosophy—what he wants to accomplish, what his goals are. You really have to know your president because you want to bring in men and women who are there to carry out his agenda, his team, his approach, his philosophy."[30]

Next, the process has to impose a discipline on recruitment so that there is one central control point and that all nominees have gone through the same screening and coordination steps. According to James, "You've got to control the process. The appointment process is a nightmare because you have coming at you from all angles the President, his senior staff, senior colleagues, friends of the President—they're all coming forward. You've got to avoid being blind-sided."[31]

James illustrates the problem of end runs with a story: President Reagan, approached at a social occasion to make a certain appointment, agreed on the spur of the moment. As it turned out, the person making this request had not supported Reagan in the campaign, and the personnel operation had another person who was just as qualified and had supported Reagan strongly. "But what that taught the president is that he's going to be end-run all the time. He's going to be at parties, cocktails, dinner, and somebody is going to say, 'You haven't appointed the assistant secretary of wildlife. My brother-in-law would be good in that job.' So Reagan would say, 'Sounds good to me. Put it in the process.'"[32] Arnie Miller has complained that in the Carter administration the credibility of the personnel operation was undercut by other White House staffers attempting to place certain candidates outside the process but also notes that "we were able to finally put a lid on that."[33]

The point is that all recommendations for appointments (including those of the president) should be coordinated through the OPP so that they can all come under the same scrutiny and vetting. The president can then make a fully informed decision. If discipline is not enforced from the top down, the process will be subject to end runs, and the president will not be well served. Thus one of the major functions of the OPP is to buffer the president from personal pleading for positions. A personnel request made to the president should be directed to the OPP. The president who short-circuits the process and decides on an appointment without using the process will soon be overwhelmed by office seekers. Using the OPP as a buffer does not take away the president's personal right to decide, it merely puts personnel decisions into an orderly process.

Constance Horner has summarized the elements of a successful OPP operation:

> Advance planning. Delegated authority for decision making in the personnel realm as well as some others. Clear lines of authority. No ambiguity about who is making the decisions. Even though you can have multiple locuses of decisionmaking, [the decisionmakers] have to be clearly in power so everyone knows the rules. It sounds very banal to say it, but prioritizing. . . . The thing is it all has to be done simultaneously and immediately. That's the problem. There's no way you can sequence these things.[34]

The challenge for the OPP is to set up a system that allows the president to be as personally engaged in personnel selection as desired, but which lifts as much of the burden as possible. The wise president will set the tone and determine the criteria for selection but will delegate most of the footwork to the OPP.

Conflict over Subcabinet Appointments

Political patronage has a long and colorful history in the United States. The purposes of patronage appointments are to reward people for working on the campaign and for the political party and to ensure that the government is led by people who are committed to the political philosophy and policy agenda of the sitting president. As long as these purposes are consistent with putting qualified people in charge of government programs, there is no problem.

From the perspective of the OPP, however, pressures for patronage are frustrating. Pressures for appointments come from all sides: the campaign, the political party, job seekers, and Congress. Everybody, it seems, wants to ride the president's coattails into Washington jobs. According to Pendleton James, "The House and Senate Republicans just start cramming people down your throat."[35] After the election of President Nixon, Senator Robert Dole complained that the administration was not making enough appointments of candidates proposed by members of Congress. He sarcastically proposed that when congressional Republicans wrote letters to recommend appointments to the White House they include the line, "Even though Zilch is a Republican, he's highly qualified for the job."[36]

President Carter was criticized by the Democratic National Committee and by members of Congress for not appointing enough members of the party faithful to his administration. Carter's memoirs reflect his frustration over the pressures for political appointments: "The constant press of making lesser appointments was a real headache. Even more than for Cabinet posts, I would be inundated with recommendations from every conceivable source. Cabinet officers, members of Congress, governors and other officials, my key political supporters around the nation, my own staff, family and friends, would all rush forward with proposals and fight to the last minute for their candidates."[37] The problem was that Carter had not used his OPP as a buffer in his early months in office. Insofar as the president can channel pressures for jobs to his OPP, he is under less immediate pressure to make a decision. When the candidate and the position have been run through the OPP process, he can make a fully informed decision with confidence.

In every administration there will be tension between the White House and cabinet secretaries over the selection of subcabinet appointees. From the White House staff perspective, these are presidential appointments and should be controlled by the White House. From the cabinet secretary's perspective, these appointees will be part of his or her management team, and because the secretary will be held accountable for the performance of the department, substantial discretion should be delegated to department heads. Cabinet secretaries also suspect that the White House OPP is more concerned with repaying political debts than with the quality of subcabinet appointments.

According to Chase Untermeyer, a politically savvy cabinet secretary will come armed with a list of what he or she calls "my appointments." The OPP director has to counter this approach and assert the primacy of the OPP. One of the ways to do so is to have a list of potential nominees ready. As the old political saying goes, "You can't beat somebody with nobody." More important, however, the president should establish in the beginning that the OPP will control presidential appointments. Untermeyer would like the president to say to cabinet secretaries,

> I'd like to introduce you to my assistant for presidential personnel. This individual has my complete confidence. This individual has been with me many years and knows the people who helped me get elected here. P.S., while you were in your condo in Palm Beach during the New Hampshire primary, these people helped me get elected so you could become a cabinet secretary. Therefore, I will depend upon the assistant for presidential personnel to help me see that those people who helped us all get there are properly rewarded.[38]

The perspective of the cabinet secretary was expressed by Frank Carlucci, the secretary of defense in the Reagan administration: "Spend most of your time at the outset focusing on the personnel system. Get your appointees in place, have your own political personnel person, because the first clash you will have is with the White House personnel office. And I don't care whether it is a Republican or a Democrat. . . . If you don't get your own people in place, you are going to end up being a one-armed paperhanger."[39]

Managing the Appointments Process

Some lessons have been learned over the past several administrations about how to design the most effective recruitment operation for the president. First, if the OPP is to be an effective recruiter and screener for the president, its authority must be established from the very beginning. One of the messages is sent by the status of the OPP director and the location of his or her office. Pendleton James was given the title of assistant to the president, the highest rank on the White House staff, and his office was in the West Wing, the most prestigious location in the government. These status symbols send the message that the OPP director will have access to the president and will be a serious figure in the administration, and they are particularly important in the beginning of an administration.

Next, the ground rules for political appointments must be laid out for the administration: all recommendations for appointments must go to the president through the process set up by the OPP. The Carter and Nixon administrations had so much trouble with their appointees in part because these presidents began by delegating to cabinet secretaries the authority to recruit their own subcabinet appointees. Arnie Miller recalls, "I came [to the White House] in 1978. The president had given away the store for the first two years. He thought that appointments were appropriately the responsibility of Cabinet members. He then realized that this was a mistake and asked us to come in and try to take that power back."[40]

The Reagan administration decided that it had to control nominations from the beginning and insisted that all nominations be run through the OPP process. The Reagan process was to bring in the cabinet secretaries before they were nominated and get their understanding and agreement that nominations would all have to go through the OPP process and that they would not have carte blanche to pick their own subcabinet appointees, though their input would be sought and their wishes would be considered.[41]

Pen James advises that the OPP director has to control the appointments process.

> Being the head of presidential personnel is like being a traffic cop on a four-lane freeway. You have these Mack trucks bearing down on you at sixty miles an hour. They might be influential congressmen, senators, state committee chairmen, heads of special interest groups and lobbyists, friends of the president's, all saying, "I want Billy Smith to get that job." Here you are, knowing you can't give them all [that they want], and you have to make sure that the president receives your best advice. So presidential personnel is buffeted daily and sometimes savagely because they want to kill . . . me . . . because I'm standing in the way of letting [them have their appointment].[42]

The Office of Presidential Personnel: Serving Presidential Nominees

The first duty of the OPP is to help form the leadership of the government for the nation, and its second obligation is to the individual president who has been elected, but the OPP also has important obligations to the Americans who want to serve their country. The United States has a long legacy of individual citizens serving in both the executive and the legislative branches of government for several years and then returning to private life. This practice brings in energetic people with new ideas who want to participate in the governance of their country. The problem is that recently many of these idealistic Americans have had distressing experiences with their nominations to high office.

Although high-level political appointments have sometimes encountered opposition and occasional confirmation battles in the Senate, the process has in recent administrations been exacerbated by active interest group involvement and public controversy. The confirmation process can be harrowing when the political opponents of the president search for troublesome incidents from the lives of nominees that they can use to embarrass the president and defeat a nomination. In a suicide note, President Clinton's' deputy White House counsel, Vincent Foster, wrote, "I was not meant for the job or the spotlight of public life in Washington.

Here ruining people is considered sport."[43] Another Clinton nominee, Henry Foster, was dismayed to find that most of the political controversy surrounding his nomination as surgeon general concerned the small number of abortions he had performed rather than his career as a public leader and doctor, during which he had delivered thousands of babies.

The media avidly investigate the backgrounds of high-level nominees, searching for embarrassing peccadilloes that can be magnified to gain partisan leverage. "Opposition research" by the opposing political party or interest groups often finds its way into the newspapers. Stephen Carter, in his book *The Confirmation Mess*, writes that

> in America today are hundreds, perhaps thousands, of people in private life who might otherwise be brilliant public servants but will never have the chance, because for some reason they are not enamored at the thought of having the media and a variety of interest groups crawl all over their lives in an attempt to dig up whatever bits of dirt, or bits of things that could be called dirt . . . [turning] tiny ethical molehills into vast mountains of outrage, while consigning questions of policy and ability to minor roles.[44]

After the hearings on the nomination of Clarence Thomas to the Supreme Court, Senator John Danforth expressed his frustration with the process.

> If the president calls to say that he will nominate you for a job subject to confirmation by the Senate, just say no. . . . Why risk the reputation you have worked so hard to earn by subjecting yourself to what can become of presidential nominees. . . . The real issue is whether there are any limits to how far we can go in using a presidential nomination for the purpose of making a political point, or furthering a philosophical position, or establishing our own moral superiority, or embarrassing the president of the United States, whatever party may at the time occupy the White House. Today there are no such limits.[45]

Although these extreme examples are not typical, there is ample evidence that the experience of the average presidential nominee has been deteriorating in recent administrations. The Presidential Appointee Initiative, which has surveyed appointees since 1984 about their experiences as nominees, has found that they have a number of justified complaints.

Current and former presidential appointees were asked about their general impressions of the whole nomination and confirmation process. Although 71 percent thought of the process as "fair," many also gave negative reports of their experiences. Twenty-three percent thought their experience was "embarrassing," 40 percent thought it "confusing," and 47 percent had accepted it as a "necessary evil."[46] These are disappointing findings for a process that is intended to bring citizens into the government for what should be considered a high honor. Appointees were clearly put off by the intrusiveness of the process in delving into their personal finances, the investigations into their backgrounds to ensure that nothing in their past could lead to a political scandal, and the time it took for them to be confirmed. These factors all added up to an unhappy experience for many.

Having gone through it, many of the candidates clearly understood the process but still were critical of it. When asked whether "the White House as a whole acts reasonably and appropriately in the way it processes potential presidential nominees," fully 30 percent replied that "it has become too demanding and thus makes the nomination process an ordeal." This indictment is striking, given that it comes from those who have successfully survived the process and have served as presidential appointees in the government. As for the Senate confirmation process, 46 percent thought that it was too demanding and made the process an ordeal. The experience of becoming a presidential appointee also calls for the collection of lots of information necessary for filling out financial disclosure forms. Those appointees who served between 1984 and 1999 who found collecting this information difficult or very difficult amounted to 32 percent (compared to 17 percent of appointees from 1964 to 1984). Making the financial calculations to fill out the financial disclosure forms was complicated enough that 25 percent of appointees spent between one thousand and ten thousand dollars for outside expert advice, and 6 percent had to spend more than ten thousand dollars.[47]

One of the main problems with the nomination process is that having agreed to serve, nominees are often left in limbo for some time, with little information about the progress of their nomination. When asked to grade the White House personnel operation, many appointees were satisfied, but enough found problems that their views have to be seriously considered. When asked how well the OPP "stayed in touch" with them during the process, 51 percent graded the OPP's performance as average or below average. Significant numbers also gave average or lower grades to the OPP for competence (35 percent), responding quickly to questions (36 percent), and caring about the nominee's confirmation (38 percent). Thirty-nine percent of appointees said that they received either not enough information or "no information at all" from the White House about the process, and as a result 62 percent went to outside sources for help on the legal aspects of appointments and 48 percent for the financial aspects.[48]

The causes of much of this dissatisfaction are varied. Public scrutiny of nominations has increased; financial disclosure has become more complicated; and the process takes longer. Another factor to be considered is the huge volume of nominations that the OPP must handle and the limited resources that it has at its disposal. The OPP is under pressure, as are all units in the Office of the White House, to limit the number of personnel so that the White House staff does not look bloated and present a fat target for critics of the president. Extra pressure was added when the Clinton administration made good on its promise to cut the White House staff by 25 percent.[49] A number of steps could be taken, however, to improve the experience of presidential nominees.

Conclusion: Improving the Appointments Process

Although the capacity of the OPP and the appointments process might be improved, the institution itself and its location in the Office of the White House are appropriate. Proposals to move the recruitment function to political parties or elsewhere in the government are unrealistic. Some have suggested that the Office of Management and Budget (OMB) might be a better location and provide more institutional memory. More institutional memory is certainly desirable, but the priority of recruiting politically loyal appointees and its inherent political sensitivity makes the OMB the wrong home for the presidential personnel office. The OMB is the home of some of the best civil servants in the government, and their role of neutral competence is crucial. If political recruitment were lodged in the OMB, the danger of politicization would be real and too high a price to pay.[50] The OMB is not the place for the Office of Presidential Personnel.

Others have suggested that the national headquarters of the political parties would be a good location for the political recruitment function. Political sensitivity is the strong point of national party committees, and they could keep data banks over periods of time when the presidency was controlled by the other political party. Although on the surface this might seem like a good idea, there are profound historical reasons that the personnel recruitment function should not be located in party headquarters.

During the second half of the twentieth century, the personnel function shifted from the political parties, where it had resided in the nineteenth and early twentieth centuries, to the White House. The reason for this shift is that presidents felt they needed more personal control over their appointments. The proliferation of primaries after 1968 accelerated the shift in control over appointments. With the increase in the number of primary elections, political parties had to remain neutral among the various candidates of their party until the nomination had been made. As a result, individual candidates had to build their own campaign teams, and when they won, their teams followed them into the White House. Thus the winning presidential candidate and the entourage do not trust the political party with something as sensitive as political recruitment. As former Democratic Party chair Robert Strauss has noted,

> It is rare that a nominee acquires the nomination of his party without thinking he did it despite the party and despite the chairman. The chairman has been neutral if he's a decent chairman. . . . I would hate for the parties to be the repository of any great lists of skilled people and count on those lists being maintained the way they should be. . . . The Democratic Party, from my experience, is not equipped to keep lists and maintain them.[51]

The Executive Clerk's Office in the White House keeps track of each presidential appointment and law signed by the president. The clerk's office does not have the resources to recruit presidential personnel, and to give it the job would risk unduly politicizing a strictly nonpartisan office essential to the presidency.

One reform proposal that is worth considering is a reduction in the total number of political appointees. This proposal has been made by a number of prestigious groups and commissions, including the National Academy of Public Administration, the National Commission on the

Public Service (the Volcker Commission), and the National Research Council of the National Academy of Sciences.[52] The rationale for these proposals is that the need for the OPP to recruit and screen for thousands of positions reduces its effectiveness and unduly lengthens the appointments process. This in turn slows the staffing of new administrations.

Presidents believe that having their own people in place throughout the government will give them the extra leverage they need to have a responsive government. The reality is, however, that no president knows most of the people who are appointed in his or her name. Appointees are drawn from throughout the political system, and these people may or may not be personally or ideologically loyal to the president. They may also be responsive to their sponsors in Congress or elsewhere in the political system. In addition, the growing number of appointees multiplies the layers of hierarchy between the president and those who actually do the work of government and contributes to the "thickening" of the government.[53]

According to Bush's OPP director, Constance Horner,

> There are too many low-level political appointees. This really clogs up the process. And I say that as someone who believes that presidents should have a large apparatus for changing policy, and I believe that there should be a thousand presidential appointees, but the number of political appointees that require the attention of presidential personnel, that can cause trouble. . . . The number of lower-level political appointees requires too much overhead and maintenance for the value to the president, substantively or politically. . . . Those special assistants interject themselves into the decisionmaking process beyond their substantive capacity because of the weight of their political influence. What that means is that other layers are created between the presidential appointee and the senior career civil service, and that weakens the utility that a president can get out of the civil service.[54]

The point has been made that early planning is essential for an effective appointments process. A personnel operation has to be ready to go the day after the election. The effectiveness of the selection process will be undercut if the president changes the person who is in charge of recruitment, as President Clinton did during his transition. The director should ensure that people who work in the OPP are not there for the primary purpose of finding themselves a job in the administration. According to Chase Untermeyer's deputy, Jan Naylor Cope, Untermeyer "got a commitment from each of us that we would stay in the position a minimum of one year before we even thought about what we might want to do next with our lives. So people were really focused on the task at hand and not trying to cherry-pick their next job."[55]

The appointments process might serve the president better if the people who come into the government, particularly those who have not had experience working in the federal government before, were given an orientation to the political and administrative context of their new jobs. Chase Untermeyer has remarked that, even though he had previous government experience, the orientation program he went through in preparation to be assistant secretary of the navy "was extremely valuable."[56] A number of attempts at orientation programs for new appointees were made in the Ford, Reagan, and Bush administrations, but they have never been institutionalized. Arnie Miller agrees that "a good way to start is with an orientation program for all new key appointees."[57]

People coming into government from the business world may especially need to hear the advice of respected veterans of government service. According to Pendleton James, who has had a long career in the private sector as an executive recruiter, in addition to his government experience, "Businessmen make the worst appointees because they are used to command and control. . . . Government doesn't work that way. Some businessmen, we know, have made that transition. Some businessmen cannot. They just get terribly frustrated with the bureaucracy, and government is bureaucracy, and you have to persuade the bureaucracy to move or change or whatever."[58]

Fred Malek, with impressive private sector experience, also emphasizes the differences between government and business.

> In business you have to satisfy a CEO and through the CEO the board of directors. In government . . . you have a much more complex array of people whose needs have to be met. Business is complicated. You have customers and business partners and the like, but it's tough, more complicated in government. . . . You have to be able to subjugate your ego. . . . You have to be indefatigable. It's very hard work. The government works harder than the private sector, without question.[59]

Any new administration would benefit from a systematic orientation program for its new appointees, but such a program must be taken seriously. It needs to be held under the auspices of the White House itself, and it has to include influential members of the White House staff if new appointees are to take the time out of their hectic schedules. The issues that need to be covered include the legal dimensions of conflict-of-interest regulations, how to deal with the press, relations with Congress, the functions of the OMB, and the role of the White House staff in the new administration. The people who deliver these messages should include top officials in the new administration as well as high-level veterans of previous administrations.[60]

From the surveys of the former appointees cited earlier, it is clear that the nomination and appointment process has room for improvement, but the good news is that many of the problems cited by respondents are not difficult to alleviate. One theme that came through clearly is that once contacted by the OPP, many potential nominees felt that they had been abandoned and did not have sufficient information about how the process would proceed. Chase Untermeyer points out "the sad truth" that "often nominees feel abandoned in the confirmation process. . . . It's extremely important for that nominee of the President to have somebody holding his or her hand in getting through the process."[61]

According to Constance Horner, "The nominee becomes an orphan because the White House Legislative Office doesn't have anywhere near the staff needed to squire nominees. . . . I strongly recommend the creation of a permanent, very small White House career staff to serve as a checkpoint for nominees—someone who knows everything there is to know technically about this process."[62] Arnie Miller agrees:

> A separate confirmation unit should be established in the White House with members of the PPO [Presidential Personnel Office], the counsel's office, and the Office of Congressional Liaison to assist nominees with conflict-of-interest and disclosure questions and prepare them for confirmation hearings. From the moment they are selected, appointees should feel well-supported by the confirmation unit and already a part of an administration they will be proud to serve.[63]

In addition, nominees need to be given realistic expectations about the process. One told the Presidential Appointee Initiative that he or she would have appreciated "more realism about how much time it takes.

Everybody says, 'Oh, it's two months, maximum.' Turned out to be six months. And that's pretty off-putting because your whole private life is on hold . . . while this is going on. And it's also kind of nerve-wracking."[64] Veronica Biggins, the director of the OPP during the Clinton administration, says that potential nominees should be warned that they may be treated harshly in the press but that the political attacks are often not personal. "It is important that appointees know that this can happen and that these individuals know that the candidates understand it's not them, it's politics." Edwin Meese has added to the advice that should be given to those contacted by the OPP, "Don't give up your day job until you're sure."[65]

Other possible improvements to the process include giving nominees clearance forms immediately, even before their nominations are certain, so that they can get a head start on gathering the information. Veronica Biggins suggests that during the transition a new administration might give to the FBI the names of those it expects to nominate, even if it is not certain which positions they will be nominated for, just to give the bureau a head start on investigations.[66]

Despite all of these complaints and difficulties with the presidential personnel process, the overwhelming majority of nominees have had rewarding experiences serving the president and the nation. Fifty-four percent of the appointees would "strongly recommend" to friends that they take a presidential appointment if given the opportunity, and 29 percent would "somewhat encourage" that. Only 8 percent would discourage a friend from taking such an appointment.[67] The rewards of the job are many—the highest ranking are "accomplishing important public objectives" and "dealing actively with challenging and difficult problems."[68]

The presidential appointments process has much room for improvement, but the bottom line is that few people have such an opportunity to serve their country and work for a president whom they admire. It is a rich and rewarding experience, and few who have had the opportunity would take back their years at the highest levels of the government.

Notes

Unless otherwise noted, all quotations in the notes are taken from interviews conducted by Martha J. Kumar in 1999 or 2000 as part of the White House Interview Program.

1. See Thomas J. Weko, *The Politicizing Presidency* (University Press of Kansas, 1995), pp. 15–20.

2. G. Calvin Mackenzie, *The Politics of Presidential Appointments* (New York: Free Press, 1981), p. 27.

3. See Weko, *The Politicizing Presidency*, p. 32.

4. Fred Malek, interview by Martha Joynt Kumar, White House Interview Program, November 23, 1999, p. 2.

5. Arnie Miller, interview by Martha Joynt Kumar, White House Interview Program, December 16, 1999, pp. 13, 6.

6. Weko, The *Politicizing Presidency*, p. 100.

7. Ibid., pp. 100, 125, 126.

8. "The Pentagon's Missing Civilians," editorial, *Washington Post*, June 27, 1993, p. C6.

9. "Help Wanted, Call Clinton (EOE)," *Washington Post*, December 10, 1993, p. A29.

10. Jon Healey, "Administration Fills Its Slots, Congress Plays Waiting Game," *Congressional Quarterly Weekly Report*, vol. 51, no. 18 (May 1, 1993), p. 1060.

11. *Recruiting Presidential Appointees: A Conference of Former Presidential Personnel Assistants* (Washington: National Academy of Public Administration, 1984), p. 10.

12. Pendleton James, interview by Martha Joynt Kumar, White House Interview Program, November 8, 1999, pp. 21, 5.

13. See James P. Pfiffner, *The Strategic Presidency* (University Press of Kansas, 1996), p. 164.

14. Robert Nash, interview by Martha Joynt Kumar, White House Interview Program, September 1, 2000, p. 13.

15. Jan Naylor Cope, interview by Martha Joynt Kumar, White House Interview Program, June 8, 2000, pp. 28–29.

16. "Staffing a New Administration," panel discussion, May 16, 2000, in Alvin S. Felzenberg, ed., *The Keys to a Successful Presidency* (Washington: Heritage Foundation, 2000), p. 19.

17. Ibid., p. 20.

18. Quoted in Richard L. Schott and Dagmar S. Hamilton, *People, Positions, and Power: The Political Appointments of Lyndon Johnson* (University of Chicago Press, 1983), p. 5.

19. Douglas Bennett, interview by Martha Joynt Kumar, White House Interview Program, November 15, 1999, p. 2.

20. *Recruiting Presidential Appointees*, p. 11.

21. Ibid., p. 12.

22. Ibid.

23. "Staffing a New Administration," p. 20.

24. Chase Untermeyer, interview by Martha Joynt Kumar, White House Interview Program, July 6, 1999, p. 43.

25. "Staffing a New Administration," p. 10.

26. See Pfiffner, *The Strategic Presidency*, p. 61.

27. James, interview, p. 10; *Recruiting Presidential Appointees*, p. 14.

28. Miller, interview, p. 9.

29. Nash, interview, pp. 34–35.

30. James, interview, pp. 15, 16.
31. "Staffing a New Administration," p. 11.
32. James, interview, p. 8.
33. *Recruiting Presidential Appointees*, p. 10.
34. Constance Horner, interview by Martha Joynt Kumar, White House Interview Program, March 23, 1999, p. 31.
35. Quoted in Pfiffner, *The Strategic Presidency*, p. 70.
36. Quoted in Mackenzie, *The Politics of Presidential Appointments*, p. 46.
37. Jimmy Carter, *Keeping Faith* (Bantam Books, 1982), p. 61.
38. Untermeyer, interview, p. 10.
39. Frank Carlucci, secretary of defense in the Reagan administration, interview by the staff of the National Academy of Public Administration Presidential Appointee Project, Washington, 1985, quoted in Pfiffner, *The Strategic Presidency*, p. 66.
40. *Recruiting Presidential Appointees*, p. 13.
41. James, interview, p. 7.
42. Ibid., p. 7.
43. The note is printed in Elizabeth Drew, *On the Edge: The Clinton Presidency* (Simon and Schuster, 1994), p. 258.
44. Stephen L. Carter, *The Confirmation Mess* (New York: Basic Books, 1994), p. 5.
45. Quoted in "A Presidential Nomination? Forget It," *Washington Post*, June 25, 1993, p. A25.
46. The results of the survey are reported in Paul C. Light and Virginia L. Thomas, *The Merit and Reputation of an Administration: Presidential Appointees on the Appointments Process* (Brookings and Heritage Foundation, 2000), p. 25.
47. Ibid., pp. 29, 27.
48. Ibid., pp. 15, 7.
49. For an analysis of the cuts in White House staff during the Clinton administration, see James P. Pfiffner, "Cutting Staff No Easy Task for Clinton," *Maine Sunday Telegram*, December 12, 1993, pp. C1, C11.
50. For an analysis of the OMB, see James P. Pfiffner, "OMB: Professionalism, Politicization, and the Presidency," in Colin Campbell and Margaret J. Wyszomirski, eds., *Executive Leadership in Anglo-American Systems* (University of Pittsburgh Press, 1991), pp. 195–218.
51. *Recruiting Presidential Appointees*, p. 21.
52. See, for example, *Science and Technology Leadership in American Government: Ensuring the Best Presidential Appointments* (Washington: National Academy Press, 1992); National Commission on the Public Service, *Leadership for America: Rebuilding the Public Service* (Washington, 1989), p. 18; National Commission on the Public Service, "Politics and Performance: Strengthening the Executive Leadership System," in *Task Force Reports* (Washington, 1989), pp. 157–90; Presidential Appointee Project, *Leadership in Jeopardy: The Fraying of the Presidential Appointments System* (Washington: National Academy of Public Administration, 1985); Pfiffner, *The Strategic Presidency*, pp. 190–99.

53. Paul Light, *Thickening Government* (Brookings, 1995).

54. Horner, interview, p. 34.

55. Cope, interview, p. 7.

56. Untermeyer, interview, p. 28.

57. Arnie Miller, "Personnel Process for a Presidential Transition," in Mark Green, ed., *Changing America: Blueprints for the New Administration* (New York: Newmarket Press, 1992), pp. 739–50, 747.

58. "Staffing a New Administration," p. 47.

59. Malek, interview, pp. 8, 7.

60. For a more thorough analysis of orientation programs for new political appointees, see James P. Pfiffner, "Strangers in a Strange Land: Orienting New Presidential Appointees," in G. Calvin Mackenzie, ed., *The In-and-Outers: Presidential Appointees and Transient Government in Washington* (Johns Hopkins University Press, 1987), pp. 141–55.

61. "Staffing a New Administration," pp. 16–17.

62. Horner, interview, pp. 18, 5.

63. Miller, "Personnel Process for a Presidential Transition," p. 749.

64. Quoted in Light and Thomas, *The Merit and Reputation of an Administration*, p. 21.

65. "Staffing a New Administration," p. 18, 41.

66. Ibid., p. 18.

67. Light and Thomas, *The Merit and Reputation of an Administration*, p. 5.

68. Ibid.

CHAPTER THREE

Why Not the Best? The Loyalty-Competence Trade-off in Presidential Appointments

GEORGE C. EDWARDS III

EVERY NEW ADMINISTRATION promises to nominate highly talented, well-qualified people to fill appointed positions in the executive branch of the federal government.[1] Yet every president nominates to positions of responsibility more than a few persons who do not satisfy the National Academy of Public Administration's call for "able, creative, and experienced people" who will serve as "the most important ingredient in the recipe for good government."[2]

Although there may be disagreement on just who qualifies as a "quality" appointment, almost everyone agrees that, overall, the quality of appointees could—and should—be higher. A survey conducted for the Brookings Institution's Presidential Appointee Initiative queried 435 senior-level appointees who served in the second-term Reagan and the Bush and Clinton administrations. Table 3-1 illustrates their mixed reviews of their fellow appointees. Clearly, there is room for improvement.

Given the intentions of all administrations to nominate "good" people, why do they so often fail to do so? Equally important, what can a new administration do to avoid making the mistakes of past administrations? To answer these questions, this chapter focuses on the competing criteria by which the White House evaluates potential appointees, delineates the reasons that presidents feel they need to emphasize loyalty in making their appointments, and then challenges both the necessity and the utility of weighing loyalty over competence.

Table 3-1. *Appointees' Assessment of Fellow Appointees, 1984–99*

Statement	*Percent agreeing*
Fellow appointees represent the best and the brightest America has to offer	11
Fellow appointees are a mixed lot: some are highly talented, while others do not have the skills and experience their positions require	79
Fellow appointees are not the most talented Americans, but they are adequate to perform the tasks assigned to them	8
Overall, the talents of fellow appointees are not adequate to the demands of their positions	1

Source: Data from Paul C. Light and Virginia L. Thomas, *The Merit and Reputation of an Administration: Presidential Appointees on the Appointments Process* (Brookings, 2000), p. 33.

The Dimensions of Quality

Although there is widespread agreement that presidents should make high-quality appointments to positions that supervise the bureaucracy, this consensus may quickly dissolve when one begins to define terms. Just what is a "quality" appointment?

Quality, like beauty, is in the eye of the beholder. Evaluations of quality depend heavily on what the evaluator wants from the bureaucracy. At a minimum, everyone wishes to avoid corruption and scandal. Most of those who urge higher-quality appointments explicitly or implicitly refer to job-related characteristics of appointees, such as analytical intelligence, substantive expertise, and managerial skills. Their primary goal is that policies be implemented efficiently and effectively. Conversely, the White House places a premium on reliability and trust over such impersonal qualities, because the president's highest priority is the responsiveness of the executive branch to his policies. In addition, the president faces a need to reward individuals, constituencies, and contributors who helped him win office and to respond to the demands of high-level appointees to name some of their subordinates.

Integrity

Everyone agrees that integrity is the sine qua non of appointment criteria. Officials lacking in integrity are unlikely to provide good advice and competent administration. Equally important, lapses in integrity can cause the president serious harm. Integrity is essential, but it is a filter with a wide mesh that will screen out only a few potential nominees.

Thus, although it is a necessary dimension of a quality nominee, integrity is not a sufficient criterion for choosing among potential officeholders. If quality is related to performance, it must represent more than the absence of ethical problems.

Loyalty to the President

Presidential recruiters agree that one important criterion for a quality presidential appointment is loyalty to the president as a person. According to George Bush's White House personnel director, Chase Untermeyer, this is the kind of loyalty that holds up when the going gets tough—as it inevitably will.[3]

Although there are many exceptions, the loyalty credential is most typically established by working on the presidential campaign. The campaign is a trial by fire in which devoted followers choose among rivals for the nomination and sacrifice themselves for the candidate, battling adversaries within and outside the party during a protracted struggle. It is only natural that this process creates strong bonds between the candidate and his supporters and that this bond continues into the presidency.

The question, of course, is whether those who are skilled at helping the president obtain the White House are also those best suited to governing once the election is over. There are significant differences between campaigning and governing. Implementing government programs is largely an anonymous, long-term service-delivery activity in which success is measured in terms of productivity, operational efficiency, cost-effectiveness, and client benefit. A political campaign, on the other hand, is a relatively short-term enterprise that markets a particular person and whose object is to demonstrate why one choice is good and the other is bad. Campaigns lend themselves to superficial treatment of complicated issues through short commercials or news sound bites, and success is measured in terms of the number of votes cast.[4] Although the skills required for governing and campaigning overlap, effective governing, which is primarily the implementation of public policy, requires more than expertise in running political campaigns.

Commitment to the President's Program

Related to loyalty to the president is adherence to his political philosophy and commitment to his program. The Reagan administration placed an especially high priority on ideological screening. As the former White House personnel director, Pendleton James, has put it, "You have to keep thinking, What does the President want?" From this perspective, being a good manager or a policy expert is not enough. When the going gets tough, the issues that become politicized are usually value issues, not technical questions. Appointees committed to the president's program are more likely to display the toughness, courage, and stamina necessary to implement his policies in the face of resistance from many quarters of the political system.[5] People who disagree with the president's policies are unlikely to implement his directives with the same vigor as those who agree with the policies. In addition, those who are committed to the president's program are more likely to mobilize the resources of their agencies to think creatively about advice they offer the president to further the accomplishment of his goals.

For these reasons, Donald Devine and Jim Burnley argue, the most important criteria for selecting political appointees are their character, toughness, and reliability and their loyalty to the president and his program. Only when these qualities have been established, they say, should an evaluation of a potential appointee's skills come into play.[6] The danger in such a formulation is that loyalty trumps skill, and in that event the president will end up with committed appointees who are ineffective in achieving their collective goals.

Ability

What most people mean when they discuss the quality of an appointment is a person's ability. Ability has many dimensions, however, including intellectual, political, managerial, and personal.

INTELLECTUAL ABILITY. One important component of ability is a person's intellectual skills. These include both analytical skills and substantive expertise. Few would argue against naming intelligent and knowledgeable people to positions of responsibility, but opinions are mixed about the priority to assign brainpower in evaluating job candidates. Pendleton James argues, for example, that appointees do not have to be brilliant. Rather, they need only "a minimum of competence."[7] Others argue that people who have gained program knowledge by working in an area with which their agencies have a close relationship are often the least desirable appointees because they may find it difficult to be loyal to the administration rather than to the interest with which they have been associated.[8]

POLITICAL SKILLS. Both the White House and more-detached observers agree that an ideal appointee would have savvy in the ways of

Washington and possess significant political skills. These skills include prowess at the critical tasks of dealing with the press, Capitol Hill, the courts, state and local officials, and interest groups. Proficiency at negotiating and public speaking may also be important to an appointee's success.

There are many examples of failure to meet these standards. Bill Clinton's first surgeon general, Jocelyn Elders, had to resign because of her insensitivity to the political implications of her public remarks. In the Reagan administration, Secretary of the Interior James Watt and Environmental Protection Agency director Anne Gorsuch Burford displayed a similar insensitivity, as well as a heavy-handed approach in implementing policies. The resultant popular outcry and the mobilization of opposition groups led the Reagan administration to remove both from office and to retreat from its own policy goals in the area of environmental protection.

MANAGERIAL SKILLS. Most high-level appointees have responsibility for managing a part of the federal bureaucracy, and thus it makes sense that these appointees be skilled at working within a bureaucracy. Managerial skills are varied, ranging from planning, organizing, and motivating employees to creating open communication with subordinates and good working conditions for employees. Equally important, managers must develop administrative strategies for accomplishing the president's goals. A poor design can be detrimental to the goal of bringing about change.

PERSONAL CHARACTERISTICS. A final component of ability is the personality of the appointee. For our purposes, personality includes job-related characteristics such as interpersonal skills, personal stability, a sense of self-esteem, flexibility, tolerance for conflict, the ability to accept criticism, and a sense of duty.[9] Persons lacking in these characteristics are less likely to be effective leaders within their agencies.

Presidents also value appointees who are team players, able to work with both the White House and other administration officials. The president is not apt to nominate persons whom he views as likely to be uncooperative or to engage in visible self-promotion.

Why Does the White House Distrust the Bureaucracy?

Tension exists between the White House's need for loyal and committed appointees and the country's more abstract requirement for men and women of exceptional integrity and ability to run the executive branch.

Why do different observers and participants weigh dimensions of quality differently? The essence of the explanation is that the White House feels it needs to use appointees to lead career bureaucrats, whose responsiveness to the president it distrusts.

Agency Discretion

Laws often permit agency heads wide latitude in making public policy. They may influence the rules, procedures, design, and substance of agency action.[10] This latitude provides implementers with a certain margin of freedom in giving new meaning to policies, which sometimes inhibits intended change or brings about unintended consequences.

The leeway in policy implementation can be attributed to several factors. Perhaps the most important is the sheer complexity of policymaking. When they establish policy, presidents and members of Congress have neither the time nor the expertise to develop and define all the requisite details for how it will be carried out. They have to leave most (and sometimes all) of the details to subordinates (usually in the executive branch). Thus, although it is the president's responsibility to implement the policies of the national government no matter who initiates them, much of this responsibility must be delegated to others.

The difficulty in reaching consensus on policy goals also inhibits clarity in implementation directives. In the United States we share wide agreement on the goals of avoidance of war, equal opportunity, and efficiency in government, but this consensus often dissolves when specific policy alternatives are under consideration. As Lyndon Johnson once said, "If the full implications of any bill were known before its enactment, it would never get passed."[11]

Imprecise decisions make it easier for presidents to develop and maintain winning coalitions. Different people or groups can support the same policy for different reasons, as each may hold its own conception of the goal or goals the program is designed to achieve. Ambiguous goals also may make it less threatening for groups to be on the losing side of a policy conflict, which may reduce the intensity of their opposition.

The problems of starting up a new program may also produce confusion in the implementation instructions. Often, the passage of a new policy is followed by a period of administrative uncertainty in which a considerable time lag occurs before any information on the program is disseminated. This period is followed by a second phase in which rules are made but are then changed quickly as high-level officials attempt to deal with unforeseen problems of implementing the policy and of their own earlier directives.

A cynical yet realistic explanation for the lack of clarity in federal statutes is that the Congress does not want them to be detailed. Some members of the legislature would rather let the executive branch agencies (and sometimes the courts) provide the specifics, not because of the latter's expertise but because the agencies and judges can later be assigned the blame for the rules that turn out to be unworkable or unpopular. Such broad language allows Congress to sidestep many touchy questions and leave their resolution to the president and his appointees. Moreover, individual members of Congress can gain credit with their constituents by intervening on their behalf regarding the application of regulations. In addition, if the goals are not precise, Congress cannot be held accountable for the failure of its policies to achieve them.

Inconsistency as well as vagueness in guidance from the president and Congress may provide operating agencies with substantial discretion in the interpretation and implementation of policy. For example, the Immigration and Naturalization Service is often confronted with inconsistencies: The agency is supposed to keep out illegal immigrants but also to allow needed agricultural workers to enter the country. It must carefully screen foreigners seeking to enter the country but facilitate the entry of foreign tourists. It must find and expel illegal aliens yet not break up families, impose hardships, violate civil rights, or deprive employers of low-paid workers. As James Q. Wilson points out, "No organization can accomplish all of these goals well, especially when advocates of each have the power to mount newspaper and congressional investigations of the agency's failures."[12] Similarly, the Forest Service is supposed to help timber companies exploit the lumber potential in the national forests and also preserve the natural environment.

Many of the factors that produce unclear communications are also responsible for inconsistent directives. The complexity of public policies, the difficulties in starting up new programs, and the multiple objectives of many policies all contribute to inconsistency in policy communications. Another reason decisions are often inconsistent is that the president and top officials are constantly attempting to satisfy a diverse set of interests that may represent views on both sides of an issue. Consequently, policies that are not of high priority to the president may simply be left to founder in a sea of competing demands.

Agency Parochialism

Government agencies have a tendency toward inbreeding, as the selective recruitment of new staff serves to develop homogeneous attitudes. People who are attracted to the idea of working for government agencies are likely to support the policies carried out by those agencies, whether they are in the field of social welfare, agriculture, or national defense. Naturally, agencies prefer to hire like-minded persons. Within each agency, the distribution of rewards creates further pressure to view things from the perspective of the status quo: personnel who do not support established organizational goals and approaches to meeting them are unlikely to be promoted to important positions. Moreover, all but a few high-level members of the civil service spend their careers within a single agency or department. Even with the introduction of the Senior Executive Service in 1978, very few of its career officials have moved across agency lines.[13] Because people want to believe in what they do for a living, this long association strongly influences the attitudes of bureaucrats.

Related to longtime service in an agency is the relatively narrow range of each agency's responsibilities. Officials in the Department of Education, for example, do not deal with the budget for the entire national government but only with the part that pertains to their programs. It is up to others to recommend to the president what amount is best allocated to education and what portions should go to national defense, health, or housing. With each bureaucratic unit focusing on its own programs, few people are in a position to view these programs from a wider, national perspective.

Influences from outside an agency also encourage parochial views among bureaucrats. When interest groups and congressional committees support an agency, they expect continued bureaucratic support in return. Because they generally favor the policies the bureaucracy has been carrying out all along, which they probably helped initiate, what these outsiders really want is to perpetuate the status quo.

The combination of these factors results in a relatively uniform environment for policymaking. Communications within organizations pass mainly among persons who share similar frames of reference and reinforce bureaucratic parochialism by their continued association.

The influence of parochialism is strong enough that some presidential appointees, who are in office for only short periods of time, are "captured" and adopt the narrow views of their bureaucratic units. The dependence of such officials on their subordinates for information and advice, the need to maintain organizational morale by supporting established viewpoints, and pressures from their agencies' clienteles combine to discourage high-ranking officials from pursuing changes in policies.

President Richard M. Nixon has observed that "it is inevitable when an individual has been in a Cabinet position or, for that matter, holds any position in Government, [that] after a certain length of time he becomes an advocate of the status quo; rather than running the bureaucracy, the bureaucracy runs him."[14] Thus parochialism can lead officials to see different faces on the same issue.

President Ronald Reagan had the same concerns about bureaucratic parochialism. For this reason, his administration went to considerable lengths to insulate new cabinet appointees from the traditional agency arguments in defense of programs that the White House had slated for cuts. The appointees received their initial briefings from the president, the director of the Office of Management and Budget, and citizens groups rather than from the bureaucracy; they were often assigned deputies who had close personal and ideological ties to the White House; and they were given little time to react to the president's proposals before having to agree to support them as a condition of appointment.

White House Distrust

The fact that bureaucrats hold particular policy views and have discretion in the implementation of policy does not in itself pose problems for presidents. Implementers who are well disposed toward a particular policy are likely to carry it out as the president intended. Other policies, however, fall within a "zone of indifference." Bureaucrats lacking strong feelings about such policies should nevertheless implement them faithfully.

The core of the tension over standards of quality is the view, brought to Washington by recent administrations, that the bureaucracy is not a neutral instrument. As the author of one prominent study has put it, "It is a rare political appointee . . . who does not take up his or her office convinced that senior career officials are . . . recalcitrant adversaries, saboteurs-in-waiting, obstinately committed to existing programs, and resistant to new policy initiatives."[15]

The new president and his staff believe that officials and the agencies they represent have interests of their own to advance and protect and may not necessarily view issues from the president's perspective.[16] If policies are in direct conflict with their policy views or personal or organizational interests, implementers may exercise their discretion, sometimes in subtle ways, to hinder implementation. Moreover, bureaucrats "have resources of organization, time, and information that enable them to pursue those interests with vigor and persistence."[17]

The White House emphasizes political appointees because it distrusts the career bureaucracy.[18] A principal responsibility of political appointees is to elicit responsiveness of career officials to their directions. Many White House officials view this task as posing a challenge to even the most committed, adroit, and persistent appointees. As the size and scope of the federal government have grown since the 1960s, so has distrust toward it, especially among Republican presidents and the general public. Richard Nixon told his cabinet, "We can't depend on people who believe in another philosophy of government to give us their undivided loyalty or their best work."[19] Similarly, former president Gerald R. Ford has observed that "there are bureaucratic fiefdoms out in the states or in various regions, and the people who occupy those pockets of power want to do things in their own way. They are pros at it. They have been disregarding Presidents for years, both Democratic and Republican."[20]

As a result, presidents are more likely to focus on increasing their control of the bureaucracy than on improving the quality of the management of it.[21] According to Terry Moe, "Whatever his particular policy objectives, whatever his personality and style, the modern president is driven . . . to seek control over the structures and processes of government. . . . He is not interested in efficiency or effectiveness or coordination per se, and he does not give preeminence to the 'neutral competence' these properties may seem to require."[22]

The White House has acted to constrain the exercise of bureaucratic discretion by requiring clearance of regulations and congressional testimony, limiting agency budgets, and establishing process restrictions on procurement and other spending.[23] Perhaps most important, the White House has sought to control personnel decisions more centrally and has deepened the penetration of political appointees into departments and agencies. The number of political appointees at the top of the executive bureaucracy has increased substantially, as has the number of political appointees at lower ranks.[24] Employing a related technique, presidents have also made efforts to place political appointees in career positions just before leaving office. In addition, presidents and their appointees have used provisions of the Civil Service Reform Act of 1978, which allows them to reassign top-level civil servants.

In short, presidents and their advisers have taken to heart the findings of scholars of public administration who more than a half century ago discredited the notion of a dichotomy between administration and politics.[25] The White House, instead, sees administration pervaded by politics, and it fears that politics will not serve its interests.

What evidence is there to support the expectation that the bureaucracy will not be responsive to the president? The agendas of executive departments and independent agencies are set by laws that predate the president's arrival in office and serve as a force for continuity rather than change. In addition, it does not stretch the imagination to consider that the way officials exercise their discretion depends to some degree on their dispositions toward the policies and rules they administer.[26] There is plenty of evidence that at times the ideologies of the White House and senior members of the civil service have clashed, although this potential for resistance to presidential initiatives has varied across agencies.[27] Verifying that the policy predispositions of civil servants are critical to their compliance with their political principals is more difficult.

In his study of political appointees, Hugh Heclo concludes that bureaucratic sabotage of political appointees is common, but he does not provide systematic evidence in support of this conclusion.[28] He also maintains that most sabotage is not proactive but rather takes the form of passive acceptance of orders and failure to share with appointees information that would help them accomplish their goals. In a more rigorous study, B. Dan Wood and Richard Waterman have found that the Environmental Protection Agency (EPA) maintained and even increased its inspections and citations of violations of environmental regulations in the face of strong efforts by the Reagan administration to constrain the enforcement of environmental protection laws.[29] Marissa Golden has found some resistance to Reagan initiatives in the Civil Rights Division of the Justice Department.[30]

Are Careerists Responsive to the President?

Despite some evidence of bureaucratic resistance to presidential initiatives, there is good reason to expect the bureaucracy to cooperate with the president's wishes. The professional norms of career civil servants offer political appointees considerable flexibility in directing agencies.[31] Francis Rourke argues that cases of bureaucratic challenge to presidential authority have been "a rare occurrence" and that senior bureaucrats follow the election returns and defer to the president.[32] "What is surprising," agrees James Q. Wilson, "is not that bureaucrats sometimes can defy the president but that they support his programs as much as they do. The reason is simple: . . . bureaucrats want to do the right thing."[33]

Richard Waterman and Kenneth Meier conclude that "all political-bureaucratic relationships are not a caldron of conflict."[34] Steven Stehr finds that during the Reagan administration, high-level bureaucrats thought the president's political appointees were very influential in their agencies and wanted even more influence to be exercised by key political executives as opposed to other influences on policy implementation.[35] Patricia Ingraham, who interviewed officials in health, housing, and transportation, has found that on the whole key career participants have not opposed change.[36]

Other scholars, including Terry Moe, B. Dan Wood, James Anderson, Richard Waterman, and Evan Ringquist, have found substantial evidence of bureaucracies' changing their implementation of policy in line with the president's wishes, even in areas of political controversy.[37] These agencies include the Equal Opportunity Employment Commission, the Federal Trade Commission, the Food and Drug Administration, the Office of Surface Mining and Reclamation, the Securities and Exchange Commission, the Nuclear Regulatory Commission, the National Highway Traffic Safety Administration, the Environmental Protection Agency, the National Labor Relations Board, the Justice Department's Antitrust Division, and the Interstate Commerce Commission.

James Pfiffner argues that despite their initial suspicion and hostility, political appointees usually develop trust in the career executives who work for them. He and others have found the relationship between political appointees and career executives to be characterized by a "cycle of accommodation." This cycle has occurred among most presidential appointees in all recent presidential administrations. Table 3-2 shows the results of surveys of appointees in the Johnson through first-term Reagan administrations. *Regardless of party, ideology, or administration, the overwhelming majority of political appointees find that career executives are both competent and responsive*.[38] As Paul Light has noted, "In interview after interview, presidential appointees celebrate the dedication of their bureaucrats."[39]

Similarly, a survey of Bush political appointees has found that they relied heavily on careerists for all aspects of their jobs, from formulating policy to implementing it. The political appointees also report that they

Table 3-2. *Appointees' Assessment of Career Civil Servants, by Appointees' Political Characteristics, 1964–84*

Percent

Appointee characteristic	*Careerists are competent*	*Careerists are responsive*
Party		
Democratic	92	86
Independent	85	87
Republican	83	78
Ideology		
Liberal	78	84
Moderate	90	85
Conservative	82	80
Administration		
Johnson	92	89
Nixon	88	84
Ford	80	82
Carter	81	86
Reagan[a]	77	78

Source: Data from Presidential Appointee Project, *Leadership in Jeopardy: The Fraying of the Presidential Appointments System* (Washington: National Academy of Public Administration, 1985). This table is adapted from Paul C. Light, "When Worlds Collide: The Political-Career Nexus," in G. Calvin Mackenzie, ed., *The In-and-Outers: Presidential Appointees and Transient Government in Washington* (Johns Hopkins University Press, 1987), p. 158.

a. Data for Reagan appointees are for 1981 to 1984 only.

found career civil servants helpful in everything from mastering substantive policy details and anticipating policy implementation problems to liaison with the Congress and other components of the bureaucracy.[40]

Table 3-3 presents the results from another survey of Bush political appointees. Most report that civil servants brought valuable experience to the job and had good leadership qualities and management skills. Equally important, these political appointees see senior civil servants as working hard to carry out administration policies. Indeed, on average they perceive of themselves as less likely to have valuable experience and be good managers than the civil servants who have worked for them.

The most recent data on the views of political appointees regarding career officials come from the Presidential Appointee Initiative. The data in table 3-4 indicate, once again, that political appointees under the past three presidents find the career officials with whom they have worked to be both responsive and competent. In addition to the percentages given in the table, another 11 percent of the appointees found careerists to have medium responsiveness, and another 13 percent found them to display medium competence. It is especially interesting that Reagan administration officials,

Table 3-3. *Bush Administration Appointees' Assessment of Career Civil Servants and Political Appointees*

Statement	*Percent agreeing*
Career civil servants bring valuable experience to the job	98
Political appointees bring valuable experience to the job	82
Career civil servants have good leadership qualities	59
Political appointees have good leadership qualities	64
Career civil servants have good management skills	61
Political appointees have good management skills	55
Career civil servants work hard to carry out administration initiatives and priorities	71
Political appointees work hard to carry out administration initiatives and priorities	100

Source: Data from Joel D. Aberbach and Bert A. Rockman, *In the Web of Politics: Three Decades of the U.S. Federal Executive* (Brookings, 2000), p. 123.

ostensibly the most antibureaucracy appointees, were most likely to find career officials to be competent and responsive.

When asked to rate the difficulty of the various elements of their jobs, only 25 percent of appointees found it difficult to direct career employees (see table 3-5). To put this finding in perspective, political appointees were more likely to find every other task on the list to be difficult. A significantly higher proportion of appointees—36 percent—found dealing successfully with the White House to be difficult.

The clashing of beliefs between career managers and political appointees has receded over time as the political views of the permanent

Table 3-4. *Reagan, Bush, and Clinton Administration Appointees' Assessment of Career Civil Servants*

Percent

Administration	*Careerists are competent*	*Careerists are responsive*
All	83	81
Reagan	86	87
Bush	85	83
Clinton	82	78

Source: Data from Light and Thomas, *The Merit and Reputation of an Administration*, pp. 9, 31, 32.

Table 3-5. *Reagan, Bush, and Clinton Appointees' Assessment of the Difficulty of Job Tasks*

In your (current/most recent) job, how difficult (do/did) you find it to master . . . ?

Percent

Task	*Very difficult*	*Somewhat difficult*	*Not too difficult*	*Not at all difficult*	*Don't know/ refused*
Substantive details of the policies	5	26	39	28	2
Decisionmaking procedures of department or agency	9	31	35	24	7
Informal political networks affecting the work of agency or department	11	31	36	20	3
Federal budget process	19	32	24	20	3
Directing career employees	5	20	37	36	3
Dealing successfully with Congress	11	38	32	16	3
Dealing successfully with the White House	8	28	32	25	7
Managing a large government organization or program	9	34	32	23	3

Source: Data from Light and Thomas, *The Merit and Reputation of an Administration*, p. 31.

bureaucracy shifted to the right and the senior civil service became more centrist. An increasing number of Republicans and independents have moved into career managerial positions.[41] Moreover, the Civil Service Reform Act of 1978 has given the White House the opportunity to place senior civil servants of its choosing in key positions. There is little need to make a trade-off between ability and loyalty in order to "control" the civil service.

In sum, the bulk of the evidence supports a view that federal bureaucrats are "principled agents."[42] As Joel Aberbach and Bert Rockman point out, there is little evidence to support assertions of recalcitrant career civil servants in the presence of effective administrative leadership, including open channels of communication, willingness to listen to advice, clear articulation of goals, and mutual respect. Good management is not incompatible with good politics.[43]

Why do new administrations persist in the expectation of facing bureaucratic resistance in the face of strong evidence of bureaucratic responsiveness? The answer seems to be that most political appointees have viewed their experience with careerists as somehow unique, believing that the careerists with whom they served were different from others.[44] The recalcitrance of bureaucracy is such a strong element of the conventional wisdom about how government works that it perseveres even in the face of widespread contradictory experience.

One of the greatest obstacles to presidential direction of the bureaucracy is the fact that bureaucracies have multiple principals. Congress passes the laws that establish and fund the programs that bureaucrats administer, and with increasing frequency courts issue orders affecting the implementation of policies. In addition, agencies have extensive ties with external groups and congressional committees.[45] From one perspective, then, career civil servants have a strong political base from which to resist White House direction, including the ability to play other political actors off against one another to diminish presidential influence.[46]

Nevertheless, many would agree with James Pfiffner that the "frustration of presidential desires is more often due to opposition from interest groups, Congress, and the president's own appointees than from the career bureaucracy." As likely as not, the cleavages may run between agencies and programs with appointees and careerists on the same side. The primary instigators for resistance to presidential policies are likely to be members of the Congress, interest groups, and executive agencies rather than career officials.[47]

At other times, the president's efforts to change the course of policy mobilize opponents, as happened when Reagan's efforts to reduce enforcement activity in the EPA's Office of Water Quality encouraged citizen suits that had the effect of producing lower levels of political control in the long run.[48] More broadly, the Reagan efforts to reduce the rigor of EPA regulation reinvigorated a flagging environmental movement and infuriated the EPA's patrons in the Congress, who resented what they saw as a blatant attempt to circumvent legislative intent by administrative action.[49]

In sum, a trade-off between ability and loyalty may not be necessary. Unless the president is aiming at altering the core mission of an agency, the White House is unlikely to meet stiff resistance from the bureaucracy. A president who does wish to change the fundamental role of an agency would be wise to concentrate on obstacles to change that lie outside the executive branch. In either case, he will need able managers to successfully implement policy.

Are There Costs to Emphasizing Loyalty above Ability?

An emphasis on ideological and personal loyalty may not be necessary to achieve the president's administrative goals. Whether necessary or not, does such an emphasis contribute to improving policy implementation?

A president-elect's transition team will be inundated with studies regarding the nomination and confirmation processes, the retention of appointees, and the many ethics requirements for appointed officials. In addition, hundreds, indeed thousands, of studies address the impact of organizations, procedures, budgets, personnel resources, organizational cultures, decision rules, and related matters on the implementation of public policy. What is striking is that almost nothing is known about the impact of individual appointees on the quality of performance of the federal executive branch. Indeed, not a single study focuses systematically on this critical question. Thus much more is known about the process of placing appointees in their positions than about the difference they make once they are in place.

Despite the absence of systematic data on the performance of appointees, there is no shortage of commentary on it. For example, David Cohen, a former career senior executive, has forcefully argued that no matter what the selection criteria, appointees are often not responsive to the White House because they come with personal agendas, have multiple loyalties, and are layered upon one another.[50] Patricia Ingraham adds that the links between White House and political appointees are frequently unclear and tenuous, providing everyone more discretion.[51]

Even where they are responsive to presidential agendas, Cohen says, appointees tend to lack the managerial skills necessary to enact those agendas successfully. No matter how loyal to the president the appointees are, they need to know what to do and how to do it once they obtain their positions. Most appointees are lawyers, legislators, congressional staffers, academics, lobbyists, presidential campaign workers, and trusted aides to senior appointees. Some of these officials may have substantial policy expertise, but almost all of them are essentially individual entrepreneurs, not team players, and have little managerial experience. Many of them are quite young.[52]

In addition, Cohen argues, noncareer Senior Executive Service appointees are often ideologues, possessing only political credentials. Policy or technical expertise is rarely a criterion for Schedule C appointments. Instead, past working relationships and loyalty to relevant political executives may be key, or these appointees may have been outplaced by the White House or may be connected to members of the Congress or influential groups. Some have policy expertise, others do not; some are experienced, others are not. The point is that the White House and department or agency officials essentially ignore managerial experience or competence in filling these positions.[53]

Thus, Cohen maintains, when it comes to selecting the top leadership of the executive branch of government, the White House largely abandons professional standards. When professional standards are employed, they are limited to technical and program expertise. The abilities to manage, design, and effectively carry out new programs, implement key legislation, and deliver services are not prominent criteria for evaluating potential appointees. Would any large corporation, Cohen asks, place at the head of a major operating division a person with no experience in managing funds or supervising people? What enterprise would fill every senior management position with persons with little or no inside experience? Who would accept the "mindless notion that any bright and public-spirited dilettante can run a government agency"?[54]

Paul Light provides evidence to support Cohen. He has found that preparation for the job, whether defined in terms of management experience, negotiating skills, congressional relations, or personal style, makes a difference. Most important, appointees' preparation for office directly affects their ability to use the career service to an administration's advantage. Among those Light studied, the better prepared for office political appointees were, the more they saw the careerists with whom they worked as responsive and competent. Good preparation for their jobs helps political appointees to mobilize the resources of the career bureaucracy. Those appointees who knew what they wanted and how to get it were most inclined to view the career service as helpful in all areas, including management, substantive policy, technical analysis, and congressional relations. Good preparation also helps appointees evaluate the strengths and weaknesses of careerists and know which questions to ask. Thus "skills are the crucial link between appointees and careerists."[55]

Political appointees face many challenges. One of the greatest is simply learning their new jobs. The short tenure in the same job of typical political appointees diminishes their ability to implement policy effectively, undermining the president's administrative strategy.[56] As administrative positions become more and more complex, both politically and substantively, it takes appointees more time to learn their jobs and to forge the relationships that make effective implementation possible. Moreover, the more layers in a bureaucracy, the more complex the management job becomes. Carolyn Ban and Patricia Ingraham find that the greatest tension between appointees and careerists occurs where the tenures of political appointees are the shortest and where they are trying to implement sharp change from past policies.[57] It is reasonable to conclude that a well-qualified, and thus well-prepared, appointee has the greatest probability of mastering the demands of his or her position and effectively implementing policy before the inevitable turnover in personnel starts the process anew.

The administrative strategies of recent presidents, by which they have sought to take control of the bureaucracy, have been premised on the perceived need to influence the behavior of bureaucrats in agencies as they exercise discretion over the policies and programs for which they are responsible.[58] Success in many policy areas, however, often requires less bureaucratic rigidity, not more. Patrick Wolf's analysis of 170 case studies of administrative performance in 104 federal agencies finds that the best predictor of effective bureaucratic performance is autonomy from direct political control.[59]

In addition, hierarchical control designed to limit bureaucratic discretion seems inappropriate for new approaches to public administration. Rather than being direct service providers or regulators, large elements of the federal service are becoming arrangers and monitors of proxy or third-party government. Thus the success of policy implementation now frequently depends on how adroitly federal agencies operate in nonhierarchical, loosely coupled networks of organizations that cut across the public, private, and nonprofit sectors, in which discretion either is shared or shifts entirely to bureaucrats in the private and nonprofit sectors. In any case, control is beyond the range of any single federal agency.[60]

Even when implementation follows a more traditional mode, the design of a policy must be appropriate to the president's goals. Robert Durant challenges the assumption that presidents and their emissaries know what they are doing when they apply the tools of the administrative presidency. For example, the Reagan administration decreased staff in areas such as antitrust, civil rights, and environmental protection in an effort to reduce enforcement activities to which it was opposed.[61] Such a strategy may be useful for stopping an activity, such as regulatory behavior, but, as Durant points out, it also undermines efforts to take the positive actions that the administration may desire.[62]

Laurence Lynn is one of the few scholars to focus on the impact of the quality of appointees on policy implementation.[63] He observes that the Reagan administration embraced the view that faithful supporters in key executive positions could be a potent tool of administrative leadership, serving as agents provocateurs, enforcers, and proconsuls in the agencies. The primary qualification for appointment—overshadowing managerial competence and experience or familiarity with issues—appears to have been the extent to which the appointee shared the president's values and could be expected to be reliable and persistent both in transfusing these values into agency practices and in executing central directives that were unpopular in the agency.

Lynn examines five agencies for evidence of lasting changes in the character of their core activity that were consistent with Ronald Reagan's policy preferences. Rather than being dependent on an appointee's loyalty to the president and commitment to his policies, he finds, the effectiveness of appointees in changing the behavior of an agency was related to four factors: the opportunities in the environment to accomplish change, the appointee's managerial skills and experience, the appointee's personality, and the appointee's design for achieving his or her goals. Although the environment of an agency is not subject to the discretion of the president, appointing skilled and experienced managers with appropriate personalities and designs for achieving goals is an option for the president, and one he should choose to exploit.

Conclusion

Every president has been dependent on the bureaucracy to achieve many of his goals. With divided government the norm over the past three decades, presidents more than ever have turned to the bureaucracy to accomplish changes in policy.[64] The president's greatest leverage with the bureaucracy comes from the appointments he makes to positions within it. The challenge for all presidents is to discover how to use his appointments to make the bureaucracy most responsive to his policies.

The conventional wisdom urges the president-elect to stress personal loyalty and commitment to his program in evaluating candidates for positions in the bureaucracy. Accepting this view, recent administrations have rarely assessed a candidate's intellectual ability, political and managerial skills, personality, and related factors in relation to the demands of an appointee's job. Yet the best evidence is that bureaucratic resistance to change does not pose a substantial obstacle to the president in achieving his goals.

In addition, loyalty to the president and commitment to his program are not sufficient for effective policy implementation. Skills and personal characteristics play an important role. Moreover, the greater the administrative challenge, and thus the more sophisticated the design needed to exploit it, the greater the premium on analytical ability, managerial and political skills, and personality. Moreover, different skills are appropriate for different situations. Expansion makes different demands on appointees than does contraction; controversial policies require more emphasis on coalition building, negotiation, and bargaining than on more traditional management skills.

No president is going to appoint political opponents to positions in the executive branch. This is not an either-or issue but rather one of relative emphasis. Quality matters. A president-elect who can see beyond the conventional wisdom and focus on the ability of potential appointees as the first (but not the sole) criterion of selection will increase the likelihood that his administration will effectively administer public policy.

Notes

1. Political appointees fall into three categories. The Executive Schedule appointees include the secretaries of cabinet departments, the heads of independent agencies and their deputies, and the heads of major departmental or agency bureaus or divisions such as assistant secretaries. These appointees are nominated by the president and confirmed by the Senate. There are nearly six hundred appointees in the Executive Schedule.

A second category of political appointees is made up of noncareer senior executives. These officials include senior staff in the immediate offices of cabinet secretaries, deputy secretaries, agency heads, and deputy assistant secretaries. There are currently more than seven hundred noncareer senior executives, whose appointments are not subject to Senate confirmation.

The more than seventeen hundred Schedule C employees constitute the largest category of political appointees. Most hold titles such as "executive assistant" or "special assistant" and provide confidential support services to those in Executive Schedule positions or to noncareer senior executives. A few hold management positions in special staff offices or small field offices. Nominations of these officials are also not subject to Senate confirmation.

2. Quoted in John W. Macy, Bruce Adams, and J. Jackson Walter, *America's Unelected Government* (Cambridge, Mass.: Ballinger, 1983), p. 100.

3. Chase Untermeyer, interview by Martha Joynt Kumar, White House Interview Program, July 6, 1999, Houston, Texas.

4. On this point, see David Cohen, "Amateur Government," *Journal of Public Administration Research and Theory*, vol. 8, no. 4 (October 1998), pp. 488–89.

5. Pendleton James, interview by Martha Joynt Kumar, White House Interview Program, November 8, 1999, Washington.

6. Donald J. Devine and Jim Burnley, "The Role of the Agency Head," in Charles L. Heatherly and Burton Yale Pines, eds., *Mandate for Leadership III* (Washington: Heritage Foundation, 1989), p. 806.

7. James, interview.

8. Devine and Burnley, "The Role of the Agency Head," p. 806.

9. For the importance of interpersonal skills, see Paul C. Light, "When Worlds Collide: The Political-Career Nexus," in G. Calvin Mackenzie, ed., *The In-and-Outers: Presidential Appointees and Transient Government in Washington* (Johns Hopkins University Press, 1987), pp. 165, 171.

10. On administrative discretion, see Gary S. Bryner, *Bureaucratic Discretion* (New York: Pergamon Press, 1987).

11. Quoted in Doris Kearns, *Lyndon Johnson and the American Dream* (Harper and Row, 1976), p. 137.

12. James Q. Wilson, *Bureaucracy: What Government Agencies Do and Why They Do It* (New York: Basic Books, 1989), p. 158.

13. See Mark W. Huddleston and William W. Boyer, *The Higher Civil Service in the United States: Quest for Reform* (University of Pittsburgh Press, 1995).

14. Richard M. Nixon, *Public Papers of the Presidents: Richard Nixon, 1972* (Government Printing Office, 1974), p. 1150.

15. Mark W. Huddleston, *The Government's Managers* (New York: Priority Press, 1987), p. 61.

16. See, for example, Rosemary O'Leary, "The Bureaucratic Politics Paradox: The Case of Wetlands Legislation in Nevada," *Journal of Public Administration Research and Theory*, vol. 4, no. 4 (October 1994), pp. 443–67.

17. David Lowery, "The Presidency, the Bureaucracy, and Reinvention: A Gentle Plea for Chaos," *Presidential Studies Quarterly*, vol. 30, no. 1 (March 2000), p. 93.

18. See Lawrence R. Jacobs and Robert Y. Shapiro, *Politicians Don't Pander* (University of Chicago Press, 2000), pp. 88–89, on the Clinton administration's distrust of civil servants to develop its health care reform plan in 1993.

19. Quoted in Carl M. Brauer, *Presidential Transitions: Eisenhower through Reagan* (New York: Oxford University Press, 1986), p. 150.

20. Gerald R. Ford, "Imperiled, Not Imperial," *Time*, November 10, 1980, p. 30.

21. Richard P. Nathan, *The Administrative Presidency* (New York: John Wiley and Sons, 1983).

22. Terry M. Moe, "The Politicized Presidency," in James P. Pfiffner, ed., *The Managerial Presidency*, 2d ed. (Texas A&M University Press, 1999), p. 147.

23. William T. Gormley, *Taming the Bureaucracy: Muscles, Prayers, and Other Strategies* (Princeton University Press, 1989); Paul C. Light, *The Tides of Reform: Making Government Work, 1945–1995* (Yale University Press, 1997);

Peri Arnold, *Making the Managerial Presidency: Comprehensive Reorganization Planning, 1905–1996* (University Press of Kansas, 1998); William F. West, *Controlling the Bureaucracy* (Armonk, N.Y.: M. E. Sharpe, 1995).

24. See Paul C. Light, *Thickening Government* (Brookings, 1995).

25. Herbert A. Simon, *Administrative Behavior* (New York: Macmillan, 1947); Dwight Waldo, *The Administrative State* (New York: Ronald Press, 1949); Paul H. Appleby, *Policy and Administration* (University of Alabama Press, 1949).

26. John Brehm and Scott Gates, *Working, Shirking, and Sabotage: Bureaucratic Responses to a Democratic Republic* (University of Michigan Press, 1997), p. 73 and chapter 5.

27. See, for example, Joel D. Aberbach and Bert A. Rockman, "Clashing Beliefs within the Executive Branch: The Nixon Administration Bureaucracy," *American Political Science Review*, vol. 70, no. 2 (June 1976), pp. 456–68; Richard L. Cole and David A. Caputo, "Presidential Control of the Senior Civil Service: Assessing the Strategies of the Nixon Years," *American Political Science Review*, vol. 73, no. 2 (June 1979), pp. 399–413; Robert Maranto, "Still Clashing after All These Years: Ideological Conflict in the Reagan Executive," *American Journal of Political Science*, vol. 37, no. 3 (August 1993), pp. 681–98; Marissa Martino Golden, "Exit, Voice, Loyalty, and Neglect: Bureaucratic Responses to Presidential Control during the Reagan Administration," *Journal of Public Administration Research and Theory*, vol. 2, no. 1 (January 1992), pp. 29–62; Robert A. Maranto, *Politics and Bureaucracy in the Modern Presidency: Careerists and Appointees in the Reagan Administration* (Westport, Conn.: Greenwood Press, 1993); Judith E. Michaels, *The President's Call: Executive Leadership from FDR to George Bush* (University of Pittsburgh Press, 1997).

28. Hugh Heclo, *A Government of Strangers* (Brookings, 1977), pp. 171–72, 224–32.

29. B. Dan Wood, "Principals, Bureaucrats, and Responsiveness in Clean Air Enforcements," *American Political Science Review*, vol. 82, no. 1 (March 1988), pp. 213–34; B. Dan Wood and Richard W. Waterman, "The Dynamics of Political-Bureaucratic Adaptation," *American Journal of Political Science*, vol. 37, no. 2 (May 1993), pp. 497–528; B. Dan Wood and Richard W. Waterman, *Bureaucratic Dynamics* (Boulder: Westview Press, 1994).

30. Golden, "Exit, Voice, Loyalty, and Neglect."

31. Robert Maranto and B. Douglas Skelley, "Neutrality: An Enduring Principle of the Federal Service," *American Review of Public Administration*, vol. 22, no. 3 (September 1992), pp. 173–88.

32. Francis E. Rourke, "Bureaucracy in the American Constitutional Order," *Political Science Quarterly*, vol. 102, no. 2 (Summer 1987), p. 219; Francis E. Rourke, "Grappling with the Bureaucracy," in Arnold J. Meltsner, ed., *Politics and the Oval Office: Towards Presidential Governance* (San Francisco: Institute for Contemporary Studies, 1981), p. 137.

33. Wilson, *Bureaucracy: What Government Agencies Do and Why They Do It,* p. 275. See also Colin Campbell and Donald Naulls, "The Limits of the

Budget-Maximizing Theory: Some Evidence from Officials' Views of Their Roles and Careers," in Andre Blais and Stephane Dion, eds., *The Budget-Maximizing Bureaucrat: Appraisals and Evidence* (University of Pittsburgh Press, 1991), pp. 85–118.

34. Richard W. Waterman and Kenneth J. Meier, "Principal-Agent Models: An Expansion?" *Journal of Public Administration Research and Theory*, vol. 8, no. 2 (April 1998), pp. 173–202, 197.

35. Steven D. Stehr, "Top Bureaucrats and the Distribution of Influence in Reagan's Executive Branch," *Public Administration Review*, vol. 57, no. 1 (January–February 1997), pp. 75–82.

36. Patricia W. Ingraham, "Political Direction and Policy Change in Three Federal Departments," in Pfiffner, *The Managerial Presidency*, pp. 209–11.

37. Terry M. Moe, "Regulatory Performance and Presidential Administration," *American Journal of Political Science*, vol. 26, no. 2 (May 1982), pp. 197–24; Terry M. Moe, "Control and Feedback in Economic Regulation: The Case of the NLRB," *American Political Science Review*, vol. 79, no. 4 (December 1985), pp. 1094–116; Wood, "Principals, Bureaucrats, and Responsiveness in Clean Air Enforcements," pp. 213–34; B. Dan Wood and James E. Anderson, "The Politics of U.S. Antitrust Regulation," *American Journal of Political Science*, vol. 37, no. 1 (February 1993), pp. 1–39; B. Dan Wood and Richard W. Waterman, "The Dynamics of Political Control of the Bureaucracy," *American Political Science Review*, vol. 85, no. 3 (September 1991), pp. 801–28; Wood and Waterman, "The Dynamics of Political-Bureaucratic Adaptation," pp. 497–528; Wood and Waterman, *Bureaucratic Dynamics*; Evan J. Ringquist, "Political Control and Policy Impact in EPA's Office of Water Quality," *American Journal of Political Science*, vol. 39, no. 2 (May 1995), pp. 336–63.

38. James P. Pfiffner, *The Strategic Presidency*, 2d ed. (University Press of Kansas, 1996), pp. 78–81; James P. Pfiffner, "Political Appointees and Career Executives: The Democracy-Bureaucracy Nexus in the Third Century," *Public Administration Review*, vol. 47, no. 1 (January–February 1987), pp. 57–65. See also Light, "When Worlds Collide"; Robert Maranto, "Does Familiarity Breed Acceptance? Trends in Career-Noncareer Relations in the Reagan Administration," *Administration and Society*, vol. 23, no. 2 (August 1991), pp. 247–66.

39. Light, "When Worlds Collide," p. 166.

40. Michaels, *The President's Call*, pp. 234–35.

41. Joel D. Aberbach and Bert A. Rockman, with Robert M. Copeland, "From Nixon's Problem to Reagan's Achievement: The Federal Executive Reexamined," in Larry Berman, ed., *Looking Back on the Reagan Presidency* (Johns Hopkins University Press, 1990); Joel D. Aberbach and Bert A. Rockman, "The Political Views of U.S. Senior Federal Executives, 1970–1992," *Journal of Politics*, vol. 57, no. 3 (August 1995), pp. 838–52; Joel D. Aberbach, "The Federal Executive under Clinton," in Colin Campbell and Bert A. Rockman, eds., *The Clinton Presidency: First Appraisals* (Chatham, N.J.: Chatham House Publishers, 1996); Joel D. Aberbach, "The President and the Executive Branch," in Colin Campbell

and Bert A. Rockman, eds., *The Bush Presidency: First Appraisals* (Chatham, N.J.: Chatham House Publishers, 1991).

42. Brehm and Gates, *Working, Shirking, and Sabotage*, p. 202 and chapter 5. Brehm and Gates also find that federal employees do not shirk and are hard workers.

43. Joel D. Aberbach and Bert A. Rockman, "Mandates or Mandarins?" in Pfiffner, *The Managerial Presidency*, p. 168.

44. Light, "When Worlds Collide," p. 160.

45. Scott R. Furlong, "Political Influence on the Bureaucracy: The Bureaucracy Speaks," *Journal of Public Administration Research and Theory*, vol. 8, no. 1 (January 1998), pp. 39–65.

46. Moe, "Control and Feedback in Economic Regulation"; R. Shep Melnick, *Regulation and the Courts: The Case of the Clean Air Act* (Brookings, 1983); George A. Krause, "Federal Reserve Policy Decision Making: Political and Bureaucratic Influences," *American Journal of Political Science*, vol. 38, no. 1 (February 1994), pp. 124–44; Richard W. Waterman, Amelia Rouse, and Robert Wright, "The Venues of Influence: A New Theory of Political Control of the Bureaucracy," *Journal of Public Administration Research and Theory*, vol. 8, no. 1 (January 1998), pp. 13–38; Waterman and Meier, "Principal-Agent Models: An Expansion?"; Jeff Worsham, Marc Allen Eisner, and Evan J. Ringquist, "Assessing Assumptions: A Critical Analysis of Agency Theory," *Administration and Society*, vol. 28, no. 4 (February 1997), pp. 419–40.

47. Pfiffner, *The Strategic Presidency*, pp. 73, 84–85.

48. See, for example, Ringquist, "Political Control and Policy Impact in EPA's Office of Water Quality."

49. Richard A. Harris and Sidney M. Milkis, *The Politics of Regulatory Change: A Tale of Two Agencies* (New York: Oxford University Press, 1989), p. 276.

50. Cohen, "Amateur Government," pp. 450–97.

51. Ingraham, "Political Direction and Policy Change in Three Federal Departments," p. 211.

52. Cohen, "Amateur Government," pp. 450–97.

53. Ibid., p. 463.

54. Ibid., pp. 450–52, 463.

55. Light, "When Worlds Collide." See also Paul C. Light and Virginia L. Thomas, *The Merit and Reputation of an Administration: Presidential Appointees on the Appointments Process* (Brookings and Heritage Foundation, 2000), p. 19.

56. See, for example, Ingraham, "Political Direction and Policy Change in Three Federal Departments," pp. 212–13. On short tenure, see Heclo, *A Government of Strangers*; Carolyn Ban and Patricia Ingraham, "Short-Timers: Political Appointee Mobility and Its Impact on Political-Career Relations in the Reagan Administration," *Administration and Society*, vol. 22, no. 1 (May 1990), pp. 106–24; Maranto, *Politics and Bureaucracy in the Modern Presidency*; Michaels, *The President's Call.*

57. Ban and Ingraham, "Short-Timers," p. 114.

58. See Lowery, "The Presidency, the Bureaucracy, and Reinvention."

59. Patrick J. Wolf, "Why Must We Reinvent the Federal Government? Putting Historical Developmental Claims to the Test," *Journal of Public Administration Research and Theory*, vol. 7, no. 3 (July 1997), pp. 353–88.

60. See Donald F. Kettl, *Sharing Power: Public Governance and Private Markets* (Brookings, 1993); Thad E. Hall and Laurence J. O'Toole, "Structures for Policy Implementation: An Analysis of National Legislation, 1965–1966 and 1993–1994," *Administration and Society*, vol. 31, no. 6 (January 2000), pp. 667–86.

61. See, for example, Wood and Anderson, "The Politics of U.S. Antitrust Regulation"; Wood and Waterman, *Bureaucratic Dynamics*, chapter 4; and Ringquist, "Political Control and Policy Impact in EPA's Office of Water Quality."

62. Robert F. Durant, *The Administrative Presidency Revisited* (State University of New York Press, 1992).

63. Laurence E. Lynn Jr., "The Reagan Administration and the Renitent Bureaucracy," in Lester M. Salamon and Michael S. Lund, eds., *The Reagan Presidency and the Governing of America* (Washington: Urban Institute Press, 1985).

64. See, for example, Nathan, *The Administrative Presidency*; Moe, "The Politicized Presidency," pp. 144–61.

CHAPTER FOUR

First Impressions: Presidents, Appointments, and the Transition

STEPHEN HESS

A CURIOUS PRODUCT of our presidential system is that although the electorate casts its vote for only two individuals, it in effect chooses hundreds of individuals to govern. The president-elect must quickly build an administration of private citizens that reflects his or her vision. This act of administration building has been called "a uniquely American enterprise." In most democracies the pieces of the incoming government are already in place as members of a shadow cabinet take their places alongside the new leader. It is the very "formlessness" of the governmental transition in the United States, says the *New York Times*, that makes "a president-elect's task at once exciting and daunting."[1]

For those on the inside, notes Martin Anderson, who has been there twice, it is a time of "delicious chaos."[2] For those on the outside, bankable information is hard to come by. "Those who know aren't talking," said insider Edwin Meese during the 1980 transition, "and those who are talking don't know."[3] The selection of presidential appointees is a complicated business, largely conducted behind closed doors.

For the national press corps, the journalists who shape our collective judgment of what kind of president we are about to get, covering the transition mainly boils down to a simple story about people. Who is in? Who is out? Who are the ins, and why were they chosen? Whom do they represent? Are they competent? Controversial? Why does it take so long to assemble the president's White House team and cabinet?

Thus the initial success and lingering impression of each presidency will be largely determined by the selection of about thirty people picked in haste during the brief period between election and inauguration. These include the secretaries of the fourteen executive departments: State, Treasury, Defense, Justice, Interior, Agriculture, Commerce, Labor, Health and Human Services, Housing and Urban Development, Transportation, Energy, Education, and Veterans Affairs.

Congressional acts award cabinet rank to the U.S. trade representative and the "drug czar." The president fills out the rest of his cabinet as he sees fit. For instance, President Bill Clinton's second-term team included the administrator of the Environmental Protection Agency, the director of the Office of Management and Budget (OMB), the director of the Central Intelligence Agency, the U.S. representative to the United Nations, the administrator of the Small Business Administration, the director of the Federal Emergency Management Agency, the chairman of the Council of Economic Advisers, and the White House chief of staff. Notable also are other top members of the White House staff, such as the national security adviser, the White House counsel and press secretary, and the primary economic and domestic policy aides. In terms of a president's ability to get off to a fast and favorable start, these are the appointees who put a face on the administration.

Paradoxically these high-profile appointments are the easiest a president will ever make. Most of the men and women chosen are personally known to him. Some are among his closest friends. Some have just finished running his campaign. All have reputations that are easy to check out. Moreover, the historical record (as opposed to the anecdotal record) shows that the president is given considerable latitude by the public, the press, and even the Senate. Yet personnel mistakes, sometimes serious errors, have plagued chief executives even before they actually have taken office.

This chapter summarizes the experiences in this regard of the six most recent first-term transitions: those of Richard Nixon (1968–69), Jimmy Carter (1976–77), Ronald Reagan (1980–81), George Bush (1988–89), Bill Clinton (1992–93), and George W. Bush (2000–01). The mistakes and accomplishments of previous presidents give incoming administrations a roadmap by which to navigate successful transitions. Lessons can be drawn from prior events, and these lessons should be heeded early in the transition if presidents want to avoid the accusation of drifting and maintain control over their own messages.

In analyzing past transition periods, I find eight essential lessons for future presidents.

—Be prepared: preelection transition planning is essential.

—Act quickly: have your key White House staff in place by Thanksgiving and your cabinet secretaries announced by Christmas.

—Put the White House first: choose your White House team before selecting your cabinet.

—Think clusters: choose appointees as a team.

—Send a message: the appointments you make send a message about the administration's priorities.

—Choose your demographic goals: think about what you want your administration to look like.

—"Feed the beast": give the press corps something to cover.

—Smile and grovel: handle senators with care—it is they who must confirm your picks.

Richard Nixon, Elected November 5, 1968

Richard Nixon's transition exemplifies the importance of appointing the White House staff before choosing the cabinet. Sequencing of appointments is a matter of considerable relevance in transitions; the order in which presidents-elect choose their advisers has both symbolic and practical significance. The sequence that Nixon followed reflected the attention he gave to organizing his White House staff and the importance of finding ways to reach out to the opposition party.[4]

Of the twenty-five presidential elections of the twentieth century, only four have been close, and Nixon was involved in half of those, losing to John F. Kennedy in 1960 and defeating Vice President Hubert Humphrey eight years later. Facing President-elect Nixon in 1968 were the challenges of finding a way to conclude a divisive war in Vietnam and of building bridges to an opposition Congress. Indeed, Nixon was the first president in 120 years to enter office without his party's controlling at least one chamber of the Congress.

Every first-term transition is conducted in two cities, Washington and the home city of the winning candidate. Nixon's home was in New York; he had moved there after losing the California gubernatorial election in 1962. New York was the ideal city for transition purposes, close enough to the capital for the convenience of commuting politicians and big enough (unlike Plains, Georgia, or Little Rock, Arkansas) to divert an underemployed press corps. Nixon set up headquarters in the elegant Hotel Pierre, a block south of his Fifth Avenue apartment.

The president-elect's first substantive appointment (after the gracious gesture of appointing his longtime personal secretary, Rose Mary Woods) was Bryce Harlow to be chief White House assistant for congressional affairs, the job he had held in the Eisenhower administration. The Harlow appointment indicated Nixon's willingness to reach out to Democrats. A *New York Times* article, headlined "Harlow Is Liked by Both Parties," concludes that "[Harlow] brings to his job a quality few men have achieved even after years of effort—he has the confidence of both Democrats and Republicans in Congress."[5] This initial turn to Harlow also demonstrated Nixon's willingness to give the White House preeminence over the cabinet, despite his previous belief that the White House staff should be subservient to the cabinet.

Some of Nixon's earliest efforts were directed at finding "name" Democrats who might serve in his administration. He asked Humphrey to be the U.S. representative to the United Nations and was turned down. He asked Senator Henry Jackson of Washington to be secretary of defense and was turned down. Finally he considered offering the United Nations post to Sargent Shriver, President Kennedy's brother-in-law, who was at the time ambassador to France. As Nixon tells the story in his memoirs,

> Shriver expressed great interest and sent me a message stating the conditions for his acceptance. Among other things he required a pledge that the federal poverty programs would not be cut. It was intolerable to have a prospective ambassadorial appointee making demands relating to domestic policy, so I told Bill Rogers [Nixon's choice for secretary of state] to inform Shriver that I had decided against him and to let him know why. Rogers reported that Shriver realized that he had overstepped himself and had tried to backpedal, claiming that he had not meant his message to set forth conditions but to make suggestions. I told Rogers to say that my decision remained unchanged.[6]

The day after the Harlow announcement, Nixon announced that H. R. (Bob) Haldeman would be in charge of "the general administrative area" at the White House, a job description that shortly evolved into chief of staff. The next day he announced that John Ehrlichman would be his White House counsel. Haldeman and Ehrlichman had been top aides during the campaign. Robert B. Semple Jr., reporting the Ehrlichman appointment in the *New York Times*, wrote that "it can now be said with some authority . . . that much of Mr. Nixon's campaign staff will simply be transferred to Washington, where they will take up residence as members of the White House staff."[7] There followed a blizzard of announcements of young campaign workers joining the new White House staff. It was a logical plan, in that many campaign duties—press relations, scheduling, advance work, the personal care of the boss—need to be replicated in the White House.

Unlike the cabinet departments, where the structure is largely determined by law, there is some room for rearranging the boxes on the White House organizational chart to serve the individual needs of each president. One problem Nixon faced was what to do with his good friend Herbert Klein, a California newspaper editor who had served him loyally in four campaigns. Klein expected to be press secretary, but Nixon thought he was too independent. He decided to downgrade the press job and give it to twenty-nine-year-old Ronald Ziegler, a Haldeman protégé. But where did this leave Klein? Klein decided that "I could best bring the indecision on my role to a head either way by making my own power play on television." Appearing on CBS's *Face the Nation*, Klein said he would like to "have a role with [Nixon] if it were structured right. Otherwise, I would have to go back into private enterprise." The "structure" then agreed upon was a new entity called the White House Office of Communications, directed by Klein, which would be given government-wide responsibility for coordinating media relations.[8] Any revised government scheme for press relations gives journalists much to chew on. After Klein appeared on *Meet the Press* on December 8, the *New York Times* reported that "for perhaps the dozenth time since his appointment was announced, Mr. Klein also defended himself against assertions that he had been chosen to insure that nothing damaging to Mr. Nixon was allowed to leak out."[9]

Nixon announced that he would not reveal cabinet appointments until at least December 5. He mollified the restless press, however, with the appointment of Lee DuBridge, president of the California Institute of Technology, as his science adviser; the appointment of a well-respected economist, Paul McCracken of the University of Michigan, to chair the president's Council of Economic Advisers; and two surprising selections of distinguished Harvard professors to his White House staff. Henry Kissinger, foreign policy consultant to Nixon's archrival Nelson Rockefeller, would be the national security adviser, and Daniel Patrick Moynihan, who had served in the Kennedy and Johnson administrations, would be the president's assistant for urban affairs and director of a new Urban Affairs Council, which Nixon envisioned as the domestic equivalent of the National Security Council. "The academic community heaved a great sigh of relief," noted a *New York Times* story reported from Cambridge, Massachusetts.[10]

News from transition headquarters announced high-level study groups—such as one charged with outlining priorities in education, to be headed by Alan Pifer, president of the Carnegie Corporation, a major educational foundation. Such enterprises, which spring up during most transitions, cadge ideas on the cheap, spot talent for subcabinet jobs, and reward the deserving who do not wish to join the new administration. They also often generate misinformation and rumor that find their way into the political bloodstream.

The press was full of speculation in 1968 as November flipped into December, but it was more apt to be wrong than right. The predictions made by the *New York Times* three days before Nixon unveiled his cabinet proved to be a near-even split—five correct and six incorrect. Douglas Dillon, who had served as secretary of the treasury under President Kennedy, was to be Nixon's secretary of state, according to R. W. Apple Jr.[11] The *Chicago Daily News*'s predictions, published with pictures and biographies, were wrong in every case.[12]

The television extravaganza that Nixon produced on December 11 to introduce his cabinet has never been duplicated. The selections for all twelve departmental secretaries were announced at the same time—broadcast live, during prime time, on all networks. The president-elect, on a raised platform, commented on the "extra-dimension" qualifications of each selectee facing him in the front row. The cameras in turn focused on the chosen, smiling or immobile. The purpose of the presentation was to make a splash, to grab attention. In hindsight, however, the real value was that each nominee got less nitpicking attention; the story was greater than the sum of the parts. As columnist Tom Wicker put it, "A prime-time television spectacular tended to emphasize the collegiality of the whole thing; let's have a big hand for the new Government, [Nixon] seemed almost to be saying."[13]

Nixon's cabinet was composed of white male Republicans. As he had failed in his quest for a Democrat, so too had he failed to get an African American or a Hispanic American to accept an appointment. He was turned down by Senator Edward Brooke of Massachusetts and Whitney Young of the Urban League. (He did, however, use the cabinet presentation to announce that he was going to reappoint Walter Washington as mayor of Washington, D.C., the only major city at the time with a black chief executive.) There is no evidence that Nixon sought a woman, and no Jews were among the chosen. What is remarkable is how little outcry was caused by this absence of diversity. A front-page *New York Times* article on December 14 noted the regret of Bayard Rustin, the civil rights leader; but that was about it, although the article reported that Leonard Garment, a law partner of the president-elect, was heading "a small group" seeking minority candidates for subcabinet jobs.[14] The accent on diversity would become so pronounced over time that 1968 now looks like ancient history. Moreover, diversity simply became a more dominant theme in putting together a Democratic administration, given that party's greater support from minority groups.

Of the chosen dozen, three were governors: Walter Hickel of Alaska (Interior), George Romney of Michigan (Housing and Urban Development), and John Volpe of Massachusetts (Transportation). Three were close friends of the president-elect: William Rogers (State), John Mitchell (Justice), and Robert Finch (Health, Education, and Welfare). Nixon had never met two of his proposed cabinet members: George Shultz (Labor) and Clifford Hardin (Agriculture).[15] Nixon's notes for the cabinet announcement indicate that he did not know Shultz's first name or how to spell his last name at the time.[16]

The number of turndowns may have been above average; no one keeps such records or has complete knowledge of them. Nixon admits in his memoirs to having been rejected by Humphrey, Jackson, Brooke, and Young. Kissinger gives additional information on Nixon's choices. He writes in his memoirs, "Nixon told me that [Robert] Murphy had turned down the position [of secretary of state]."[17] Former Pennsylvania governor William Scranton, another likely secretary of state or UN ambassador candidate, made it clear that he did not want full-time employment in the government. The point, of course, is that a president's ultimate choices cannot be judged against the ideal because circumstances over which he has no control often intervene.

The president-elect had an additional decision to make before filling the subcabinet posts. Would he keep any of the government's key administrators? This activity is always watched closely by Washington insiders. The young John Kennedy had been particularly skillful in this regard, providing instant reassurance by quickly reappointing J. Edgar Hoover as director of the Federal Bureau of Investigation and Allen Dulles as director of the Central Intelligence Agency. Nixon took a page from Kennedy's playbook by again retaining Hoover and reappointing Richard Helms, who had been director of the CIA under President Lyndon Johnson. He also asked Ellsworth Bunker, the U.S. ambassador to South Vietnam, to remain in his post "for a period of time."

Second-echelon appointees generally do not get much press notice unless they come with celebrity status, as did the former University of Oklahoma football coach, Charles "Bud" Wilkinson, whom Nixon added to his White House staff, and America's best-known yachtsman, Emil "Bus" Mosbacher Jr., whom he appointed as the State Department's chief of protocol. There was one second-echelon controversy, however, when Nixon picked David Packard to be deputy secretary of defense. The problem was Packard's wealth, not his ability. As cofounder of Hewlett-Packard, the electronic instruments company and a huge defense contractor, Packard was faced with what he called "an impossible conflict-of-interest problem."[18] Previous Pentagon nominees, notably Charles E. Wilson of General Motors and Robert McNamara of Ford, had sold their stock in the companies they ran. Packard could not sell his 29 percent interest in Hewlett-Packard, however, without depressing the market price and thereby penalizing the other shareholders. Packard proposed putting his stock in a trust, with all income and increase in value going to educational and charitable institutions. "But is it logical to apply a looser conflict-of-interest standard to an appointee who happens to be wealthier?" asked the *New York Times*.[19] The Senate apparently thought so at the time, approving Packard (and his proposal) 82 to 1. The lone dissenter was Senator Albert Gore Sr.

Following a practice started in 1953, Senate committees now hold informal hearings on the president-elect's cabinet choices even before he takes office so that the appointees can be quickly considered once a new president is inaugurated and can formally make the nominations. Thus on January 20, 1969, Richard Nixon was sworn in and sent his cabinet nominations to the Senate, where they were approved during a twenty-minute session. The next day the new cabinet took the oath of office at the White House, with one exception—Walter Hickel, the president's nominee to be secretary of the interior, who had not yet been approved by the Senate.

Whereas Packard had been challenged for a potential conflict of interest, and another Nixon nominee had been questioned about a record of drunk driving, the concern over Hickel's appointment was less about his personal behavior than his policy beliefs. This was a rare departure for the Senate when considering a job that serves at the discretion of the president. The standard rule of thumb had always been, as expressed by Senator Henry Jackson, chairman of the Interior Committee, that if a candidate "[meets] the minimum standards, . . . the president is entitled to his choice."[20] The accusation against Hickel was that he was a business-oriented governor who was insensitive to conservation. The *New York Times* editorialized, "As chief steward of the nation's resources his inclination seems to be to put private profit ahead of the public interest."[21] Conservation groups deluged the Senate with mail urging that Hickel not be confirmed. As one senator put it, "Hell hath no fury like a conservationist aroused."[22] During five days of fierce committee hearings, however, Hickel expressed a devotion to conservation that had not been previously evident, and the Senate voted 73 to 16 in his favor. On January 23 the president conducted a full-dress swearing-in ceremony at the White House for his secretary of the interior, symbolically completing the work of his transition.

Right after the election, Herblock, the *Washington Post*'s liberal cartoonist, who was famous for depicting Nixon with dark jowls, drew a barbershop with the sign, "This shop gives every new president of the United States a free shave."[23] In general, it was that sort of transition.

Jimmy Carter, Elected November 2, 1976

James Earle Carter was the first president since Woodrow Wilson to lack Washington political experience. Carter had been a one-term governor of Georgia whose candidacy for the Democratic presidential nomination, according to 1975 bookmakers, was rated at only eight to one in a field of fourteen. The genius of his long-shot victory was that in a nation doubly shocked by the back-to-back events of Vietnam and Watergate, he offered absolution to the American people. All of this is not your fault, he seemed to say, it is the fault of politicians. "I want the government to be as good as you are."[24]

Carter's personal history had personnel consequences: it meant that he did not have wide knowledge of the sorts of people who usually populate presidents' cabinets. Unlike President Nixon, Carter chose to select his cabinet before appointing his White House staff. Importantly, the Carter transition shows the significance of thinking of the cabinet in terms of clusters. Furthermore, questions about using the transition selection process to fulfill demographic goals were first raised by Carter.

Better preelection planning might have helped close Carter's knowledge gap about potential appointees. During the summer before the election Carter created a small transition office in Atlanta, headed by Jack Watson, that compiled a working list of about seventy-five prospective candidates for high-level positions. After the election, however, campaign manager Hamilton Jordan had other notions of who should control personnel selection. The "bloodless duel" between Jordan and Watson ended with Jordan in charge of the transition's talent inventory program, as the people-picking process was formally known.[25]

When choosing the vice presidential candidate, Carter had first drawn up a list of about twenty members of Congress and then narrowed it down to seven. Because he did not know any of them well, he invited the finalists to come by for interviews. The exercise was highly publicized and demeaning for the losers, but Carter had been pleased with his choice of Walter Mondale and was determined he would now use the same procedure for selecting his cabinet.[26]

Conducting the cabinet search from Plains, Georgia, involved some logistical problems. As recounted by Robert Shogan of the *Los Angeles Times*, "Carter's hometown was served by no airline, railroad, or bus company. It was without any motel, hotel, or even a restaurant, except for a sandwich shop, which, as a sign posted behind the counter informs its patrons, lacks a rest room."[27] Carter eventually moved some of these discussions to Atlanta, using borrowed space at the governor's mansion.

Although his first appointment was press secretary Jody Powell, who had held the same position during Carter's term as governor, the president-elect made it clear that he would appoint the cabinet before the White House staff. According to "the principle of contrariness," every president responds to what he feels are the mistakes of his predecessor.[28] Carter's contrary act was to tear down the so-called Berlin Wall that had characterized Nixon's White House under Chief of Staff Bob Haldeman. The staff at the Carter White House would know its place, subservient to his cabinet, and there would be no chief of staff.

Outsider Carter had pledged to bring "fresh faces" to Washington. At one point Hamilton Jordan even declaimed that "if, after the inauguration, you find a Cy Vance as secretary of State and Zbigniew Brzezinski as head of National Security, then I would say we failed. And I'd quit."[29] Now that Carter had become the ultimate insider, however, he was finding that past Washington experience might be a valued asset for future Washington service. The concern for balancing old and new was symbolized by Carter's first cabinet appointments. On December 3, a month after the election, he announced that Cyrus Vance, a prominent establishment figure whose past government positions included deputy secretary of defense, would head the State Department and that Bert Lance, a self-styled "country banker" from Georgia who had no federal experience, would be director of the Office of Management and Budget. Carter praised each man as "a good manager," a quality he held high in making his initial selections.[30]

Carter promptly outlined broad guidelines intended to prevent conflicts of interest, including appointees' full disclosure of net worth, a pledge not to lobby before their agencies for at least a year after leaving government, and divestiture of holdings that were likely to be affected by their official acts.[31] Lance announced plans to sell his bank stock. The Nixon experiences had made "conflict of interest" yesterday's transition issue.

Key appointments were visualized in terms of clusters. Vance was part of the national security cluster; Lance was part of the economic cluster. The Vance cluster was largely completed with the selection of Harold Brown as secretary of defense and Brzezinski for the National Security Council slot. The economic cluster was completed with the appointments of Michael Blumenthal as treasury secretary and Charles Schultz as chairman of the Council of Economic Advisers. Five of the six nominees were experienced Washington hands. All were white males.

By December 15, Carter had not yet appointed a black or a woman. Wrote Paul Delaney, "The overwhelming support blacks gave to Mr. Carter—in his primary campaign as well as in the general election—marks the first time a president has been so indebted to a minority community, and blacks fully expect appropriate payoffs, perhaps too much so."[32] On December 16, Carter announced that Representative Andrew Young ("one of the best personal friends that I have in the world") was his choice to be U.S. representative to the United Nations. The appointment was far from being a "payoff": the president-elect was in Young's debt for taking the job.[33] A *New York Times* editorial noted that "the symbolism of a black American speaking for this country to all the nations of the world will not be lost either inside our boundaries or across the globe."[34]

Carter's response to criticism about the lack of diversity in his appointments was that prominent blacks were turning him down. He mentioned Mayor Coleman Young of Detroit, Mayor Thomas Bradley of Los Angeles, and Vernon Jordan of the National Urban League. According to a *New York Times* report, however, "Sources who had talked with the two Mayors said in interviews this week that they had not decided to take themselves out of consideration until it became apparent that the Housing and Urban Development job was the only one open to them."[35] As Carter filled the "inner cabinet" with white males, advocates for women and minorities complained that their constituents were being relegated to the "outer cabinet."

The public manner in which Carter floated names of potential appointees generated fierce lobbying. Would the president-elect choose John Dunlop to be his secretary of labor? George Meany and Lane Kirkland of the AFL-CIO came out swinging on his behalf, but the Congressional Black Caucus and women's groups were bitterly opposed.[36] Would the president-elect name Harold Brown or James Schlesinger to be his secretary of defense? The intrigue was captured by the Pentagon correspondent John Finney, who wrote that

> as soon as Mr. Schlesinger began figuring in speculation . . . some Congressional liberals mounted a campaign against his appointment. . . . They started a counter-campaign by floating the name of Paul C. Warnke. . . . Mr. Warnke is a liberal on defense matters, Mr. Schlesinger a conservative. The liberals probably never believed that Mr. Warnke would be appointed, but their tactic was to make Dr. Harold Brown . . . seem like a moderate and an acceptable compromise.[37]

In keeping with Carter's promise that the process would be finished by Christmas, cabinet selections were completed on December 23. A member of the *New York Times* editorial board had forecast on December 7 that "since several previous Presidents have had one woman appointee in the cabinet, Mr. Carter will have to appoint at least two if he is to make any impact. . . . One of them may be black."[38] Carter chose Juanita Kreps

(Commerce) and Patricia Harris (Housing and Urban Development); Mrs. Harris was black.[39] The secretary of the interior was a western governor, Cecil Andrus of Idaho. A Minnesota member of Congress, Representative Bob Bergland, was named secretary of agriculture. There was one Catholic, Joseph Califano (Health, Education, and Welfare), and one Jew, Michael Blumenthal (Treasury), both of whom had held high positions in previous Democratic administrations. There was even a Republican, James Schlesinger, the former secretary of defense, who would be on the White House staff until Congress could create a new department of energy. Carter's was a traditional cabinet within the Democratic Party's frame of reference. Ironically, he had chosen fewer newcomers to Washington than had either Nixon or Kennedy.

Two controversies would still arise before the Senate gave its blessing to the incoming administration, one predictable, one not. The controversy over the appointment of Griffin Bell to be attorney general could have been anticipated. A Georgian and a former federal appellate court judge, Bell was the only real friend among Carter's department heads. Despite candidates' talk about choosing the best qualified without regard for political consideration, most presidents-elect quickly realize that they need to have absolute confidence in the legal officer who will make decisions of immense political consequence. Kennedy chose his brother. Nixon chose his law partner. Reagan would choose his personal attorney. Carter must have known this, because he did not subject the attorney general nomination to the same kind of let-it-all-hang-out procedure that characterized the selections at Defense and Labor. The Senate would test Bell's commitment to civil rights. The case against him was that he belonged to private clubs that excluded blacks, that he had supported the unsuccessful nomination of G. Harrold Carswell to the Supreme Court, that he had not sufficiently promoted school desegregation when he was counsel to Governor Ernest Vandiver from 1959 to 1961, and that he had ruled against seating Julian Bond in the state legislature in 1966. The Judiciary Committee held six days of hearings, during which, not coincidentally, Bell announced his intention to appoint a black judge to be the solicitor general. The final Senate vote in Bell's favor was 75 to 21.

No controversy was predicted, however, over the nomination of Theodore Sorensen to be director of the Central Intelligence Agency. Unlike outsider Bell, Sorensen had been deeply enmeshed in the Washington scene since his days as President Kennedy's famous ghostwriter. Two days after the *New York Times* called his confirmation "virtually certain," the paper's front page headlined, "Sorensen Approval by Senate as Head of CIA Is in Doubt."[40] The sudden squall was set off by the Intelligence Committee's having been alerted that Sorensen had taken classified material with him when he left the White House staff in 1964 to write a book. The initial allegation, as is often the case in contentious nominations, produced a pileup of others: Republicans, elements of the Democratic Party not friendly to the Kennedys, and intelligence community professionals objected to Sorensen, protesting that he had been a conscientious objector in World War II, he lacked experience in the field, and his law firm represented certain foreign governments. At his confirmation hearing on January 17, Sorensen announced that he had asked Carter to withdraw the nomination. It was a defeat for the president-elect. If Carter had more carefully cultivated the committee before making the appointment, perhaps the outcome would have been different. Sorensen's prompt decision, however, minimized the damage. In early February the president nominated Admiral Stansfield Turner, an Annapolis classmate, who was unanimously confirmed.

The other cabinet nominations survived in the usual manner. Brock Adams, the representative from Washington state and Carter's choice for secretary of transportation, appeared before the Commerce Committee; in response to questioning by Senator Moynihan of New York, Adams promised to discuss with northeastern governors the possibility of using a large portion of their highway money for mass transportation, promised to review federal support for the Westway highway project in lower Manhattan, and said he understood the senator's point that a greater share of mass transit funds should be allocated to cities like New York.[41] "It's an educational process" for the appointees, noted a Senate committee staff director. "They often come up here feeling that the President and Cabinet run the country, and that the Congress stands by waiting for orders."[42]

A week before the inauguration the last piece of the mosaic, the White House staff, was put in place. Hamilton Jordan, even without the chief of staff title, would be the primus inter pares, the first among equals. Of the eleven persons with greatest responsibility, seven were from Georgia. In addition to the previously announced—Lance (OMB director) and Powell (press secretary)—Jordan would be joined by Robert Lipshutz (White House counsel), Jack Watson (cabinet secretary), Frank Moore (congressional relations), and Stuart Eizenstat (domestic affairs adviser). Of these, only Eizenstat had Washington experience. Two women, one of whom was black, and a Hispanic American were given exalted titles, but they were not in the inner circle. Press Secretary Powell, announcing the new appointments, used the "wheel" image, with the president as the hub, to describe the organization of the White House. The words he reiterated were "informal," "open-door," and "free access." Cabinet Secretary Watson stressed that the White House staff was not going to exercise any "command role."[43] If it was not obvious what the Carter administration was to be, there was no doubt that it would not be the Nixon administration.

Ronald Reagan, Elected November 4, 1980

Ronald Reagan's entrance into the Executive Office demonstrated the merits of being prepared. The Reagan campaign began the process early, and though it was not a transition entirely clear of bumps, it marked one the strongest beginnings for an administration.

The results of the election doubly advantaged Ronald Reagan's transition. He had won an overwhelming victory. Unlike Nixon and Carter, Reagan had no need to talk of bipartisanship in making appointments. Ultimately he chose one Democrat to serve in the cabinet, Georgetown University professor Jeane Kirkpatrick, to be U.S. representative to the United Nations, but her party affiliation was not an issue. Moreover, the election created a Republican majority in the Senate, for the first time in twenty-six years. The president-elect had the votes to confirm his nominees, some of whom, such as James Watt to be secretary of the interior, might have been turned down if the Democrats had remained in control.

Another notable difference between 1968 and 1976 was that a large reservoir of experienced Washington hands was available to join the new administration. Reagan's party was back in power after only four years. Observing the incoming transition team, an admiring Carter White House aide commented that "they're very competent. They're no strangers to Washington. They know their way around and they know what they want. They're more relaxed than we were four years ago."[44] Although this was especially helpful at the secondary level, the talent pool also produced the secretaries of state and defense, Alexander Haig and Caspar Weinberger.

Reagan tapped another talent pool from his two terms as governor of California. Every president's state contributes a body of supporters eager to move with him to the capital. In measuring governing skills, however, not all of the fifty states can be thought of as Washington writ small. A state's size and complexity make a difference, and lessons learned in a state like California are more transferable to the federal government than those learned in a state like Arkansas.

During eight years as his state's chief executive, Reagan had developed a personal style of leadership. His objectives were few and clear, he inspired great loyalty in those around him, and he delegated immense authority. Subordinates polished lists of potential appointees while this president-elect, wearing a bright orange ski parka and gloves, went to his meat locker for veal and beef slabs. Emerging, he waved at the reporters and photographers and asked, "You mean a farmer doing his work is of this much interest?"[45] He did not even announce the cabinet choices; he left this chore to his press secretary. It was not a problem for Reagan to remain in Los Angeles during most of the transition.

The president-elect turned over direction of the transition to Edwin Meese, who had been his chief of staff in Sacramento. It was Meese who shuttled back and forth between Washington and Los Angeles. Pendleton James, a corporate headhunter with experience in the Nixon White House, headed the transition division charged with personnel recruitment. By September he had assembled a staff and was preparing a short list of candidates for each top job, using a set of five criteria: "first, commitment to the Reagan philosophy and program; second, the highest integrity and personal qualifications; third, experience and skills that fit the task; fourth, no personal agenda that would conflict with being a member of the Reagan team; and, fifth, the toughness needed to withstand the pressures and inducements of the Washington establishment, and to accomplish the changes sought by the President."[46] The potential nominees were filtered through a "kitchen cabinet" of Reagan's California friends, led by his personal lawyer, William French Smith.[47]

Final decisions were made in Reagan's home on a hillside overlooking the Pacific. Lou Cannon, the most careful outside observer of the process, argues that Reagan was deeply involved in making the appointments that mattered most to him. These appointees included Haig (State), Weinberger (Defense), William Casey (CIA), Smith (Justice), Richard Schweiker (Health and Human Services), Raymond Donovan (Labor), Drew Lewis (Transportation), David Stockman (OMB), and Kirkpatrick (UN). Casey, Donovan, and Lewis had played important roles in the campaign, and Senator Schweiker had been a Reagan loyalist since 1976. "Reagan was uninterested in many of the other cabinet positions,"

Cannon writes, "and he was content in some cases to follow the lead of others who were more interested." Cannon cites Vice President–elect George Bush as the key player in picking Malcolm Baldrige (Commerce), Senator Robert Dole in picking John Block (Agriculture), and Reagan's friend Alfred Bloomingdale in recommending Samuel Pierce (Housing and Urban Development). Senator Paul Laxalt of Nevada would choose the secretary of the interior. Reagan cared least about the jobs at Energy and Education, two departments he promised to abolish.[48] The ultimate results were shaped less by Reagan's old California friends (despite the media's attention to these wealthy entrepreneurs) than by political realities of regionalism and clout.

All cabinets, from the presidents' perspective, are a collection of friends and strangers. The strangers' quotient in Reagan's cabinet, however, even exceeded that in Carter's. "When, on December 11, 1980, President-elect Ronald Reagan asked me to be his Secretary of State," Alexander Haig begins his memoirs, "I had spent no more than three hours alone with him," and an hour of that time had been in a helicopter in 1973. Donald Regan asks in his memoirs, "Why would President-elect Reagan appoint a man he had met only twice [at fund-raisers] to a post as important as Treasury?" Possibly as many as five other cabinet officers could have written, as did Secretary of Education Terrel Bell, "I had never met him."[49]

Conflict-of-interest and financial-disclosure requirements, the curse of Republican transitions, were exacerbated by new laws passed during the Carter administration. As described by William Safire,

> The Ethics in Government Act of 1978 . . . requires prospective appointees to fill out the "Executive Personnel Financial Disclosure Report," a form printed in cool green, the color of cash. Worse, moments after a person is told by the President-elect that he is to be a cabinet member, the new member of the team hears from "The Conflict-of-Interest Counsel." This friendly ferret drops by with a packet of forms including permission for the FBI to launch a full-field investigation and releases requesting former employers, schools, and credit bureaus to disgorge everything about the nominee.[50]

As a result, at least three of Reagan's choices elected not to join his cabinet: Walter Wriston of Citicorp would otherwise have been appointed secretary of the treasury; rancher Clifford Hansen, a former senator from

Wyoming, declined to be secretary of the interior; and Houston oilman Michael Halbouty turned down the Energy post. Others declined for the usual reasons. Theodore Cooper, asked to be secretary of education, had just taken a new job as executive vice president of the Upjohn Corporation. Anne Armstrong, one of the few women in Reagan's political inner circle, told Reagan that "I had been in government and politics for ten years and that I needed to go back to Texas and spend more time with my family."[51]

The orderly and leisurely appearance of the transition veiled a great deal of jockeying for position. George Shultz, a high-ranked candidate for secretary of state, was shot down by his former boss, Richard Nixon, who strongly endorsed Haig.[52] Campaign manager William Casey wanted to be secretary of state but had to settle for the CIA directorship. Stockman, a young representative from Michigan, lobbied for the OMB job with the aid of columnist Robert Novak.[53] Reagan passed over Meese for chief of staff but eased the hurt by giving him cabinet status as a chief policy adviser. The right wing of the conservative movement bitterly complained that Reagan's appointees were too moderate, "Nixon-Ford retreads."

Although the final cabinet announcement—Bell to head the unwanted department of education—was made on January 7, the transition team considered the heavy lifting to be over on December 22, in time for Christmas. On that date Reagan added the lone black (Pierce, as secretary of housing and urban development) and the lone woman (Kirkpatrick, as UN representative). The other unwanted department, Energy, was given to Senator Strom Thurmond's candidate, James Edwards, a successful oral surgeon and former governor of South Carolina. Only four of the nominees—Kirkpatrick, Bell, Watt, and Stockman—listed their net worth as less than five hundred thousand dollars.[54]

Several nominees had contentious Senate hearings, although they were eventually approved with ease. By choosing Haig, who had been Nixon's last chief of staff, Reagan presented the Senate Democrats and the press with a tempting target. The *New York Times* front-page headline on January 14 reported, "Haig and Democrats in Repeated Clashes on Watergate Views." Demands to produce Nixon tapes and papers went unheeded, with executive privilege supported by the Carter White House. The Foreign Relations Committee voted 15 to 2 and the Senate 93 to 6 to support the nomination.

Attorney General–designate William French Smith, when challenged for being a member of all-male clubs, responded, "I do not think that we have reached the point where belonging to the Boy Scouts or Girl Scouts, going to a woman's college or a men's college, or even playing on a female or male Davis Cup team should be viewed as evidence of discriminatory attitudes."[55] Judiciary Committee approval was unanimous; a single dissenting vote was cast in the Senate, by William Proxmire of Wisconsin.

James Edwards admitted that he was not up to speed on many energy matters. According to Edwards, the Three Mile Island nuclear accident showed that "the system worked; nobody was harmed, nobody was killed." The Energy Committee's favorable vote was 17 to 0; there were three nay votes in the Senate.

Reagan's choice for interior secretary, James Watt of the Denver-based Mountain States Legal Foundation, evoked strong opposition from conservationists who argued that he had a long record of favoring exploitation of the land at the cost of the environment. This did not impress the Energy Committee, whose members voted 16 to 0 to confirm, with Paul Tsongas of Massachusetts abstaining; Watt carried the Senate with an 83-12 majority.

Most serious was the case against Raymond Donovan, Reagan's nominee for secretary of labor. As an executive in a New Jersey construction company, Donovan had been accused by an underworld informer of delivering money to a union courier in an effort to buy labor peace from the teamsters. Donovan vehemently denied the allegations. After delaying the hearings to conduct an investigation, the FBI concluded that it could not corroborate the charges. On January 29 nine Republicans and two Democrats on the Labor and Human Resources Committee voted in Donovan's favor, and five Democrats, including ranking minority-party member Edward M. Kennedy of Massachusetts, voted "present." On February 3, the Senate approved the nomination 80 to 17.

Comparing Reagan's cabinet to Reagan's White House staff, Steven Weisman, who covered Reagan for the *New York Times*, observed that the White House aides "have one common attribute that most of Mr. Reagan's cabinet members don't have: a long-standing commitment to Mr. Reagan's political fortunes, which is the one commodity that Presidents usually end up valuing the most when they weigh conflicting advice."[56] Weisman was certainly describing Meese and Michael Deaver, who would be in charge of the president's message and image, respectively. Meese had been right, however, when he predicted early that "the senior White House staff is not going to be nine guys from California."[57] For besides loyalty, which is found on all White House staffs, what distinguished Reagan's aides was that they had more past experience in the executive branch than any previous incoming White House staff. Whereas the Kennedy and Johnson assistants came from Capitol Hill, a special part of Washington, the Reagan people came from secondary positions in the federal departments and the White House.

The most important of these was James Baker, Reagan's chief of staff. Baker and Meese were the president-elect's first appointments, announced jointly on November 14. Baker had come to Washington as under secretary of commerce in President Gerald R. Ford's administration. Others in the Reagan White House who had also served Washington apprenticeships during the Nixon or Ford presidencies included Fred Fielding (White House counsel), Martin Anderson (domestic policy adviser), Richard Allen (national security adviser), David Gergen (communications director), Edwin Harper (budget director), Pendleton James (personnel director), Lyn Nofziger (adviser for political affairs), and Richard Darman (staff secretary). Elizabeth Dole, who became assistant to the president for public liaison, had worked in the consumer affairs office in the White House under Presidents Johnson and Nixon and was a member of the Federal Trade Commission for six years. Max Friedersdorf, who was appointed as assistant to the president for legislative affairs, had been on the staff of an Indiana representative, a lobbyist for Nixon and Ford, and chairman of the Federal Election Commission. The new press secretary, James Brady, had handled press relations for the Office of Management and Budget in the Ford administration, had worked as chief spokesperson for a secretary of defense, and had been press secretary to a senator. Even the next tier down included people coming back to government after the Carter interlude. In the White House—if not in some of the departments—this was a presidency prepared to "hit the ground running."

George Bush, Elected November 8, 1988

It had not happened since Herbert Hoover succeeded Calvin Coolidge in 1929—an election resulting in the transfer of presidential power between administrations of the same party. A "friendly takeover" creates another dynamic, with different advantages and different liabilities. Crosscurrents exist that are not present in the us-versus-them transitions between parties, where all the players know which team they are on. There is no shortage of experienced hands to help the new president, but who gets the pink slips?

Thus the friendly transition from President Ronald Reagan to President George Bush was both an unusual political moment and a surprisingly rocky period. The Bush administration's experience illustrates the importance of taking the Senate very seriously, given its role in the advice-and-consent process.

On the morning following his victory, Bush announced the importance that international relations would have in his presidency. James Baker, his Houston friend of thirty years, would be secretary of state. The former Reagan chief of staff had been secretary of the treasury in Reagan's second term before resigning to run Bush's campaign.[58] For Baker, whose appointment had also been the initial announcement of the Reagan transition, this must have been something like being picked first in both the NBA draft and the NFL draft.

A few days later, Bush retained Secretary of the Treasury Nicholas Brady, Attorney General Richard Thornburgh, and Secretary of Education Lauro Cavazos. The three had joined the Reagan cabinet earlier in the year, following Bush's endorsement. Brady was a New Jersey industrialist and had briefly been a U.S. senator; Thornburgh was a former governor of Pennsylvania; Cavazos was the president of Texas Tech.

Others closely identified with Bush's career would serve on his White House staff: C. Boyden Gray (White House counsel), Chase Untermeyer (director of personnel), David Bates (cabinet secretary), James Cicconi (staff secretary), Andrew Card (deputy chief of staff), and Marlin Fitzwater, who had been Bush's press secretary before becoming Reagan's press secretary. Bush reached beyond his inner circle, however, to make his most important appointment: John Sununu, the New Hampshire governor with a reputation for abrasiveness, was to be chief of staff.

George Bush, the man with the golden resumé—member of the U.S. House of Representatives, ambassador to the United Nations and to China, national party chairman, CIA director, two-term vice president—would not assemble a government of strangers. Bush's career had been long on friends and short on ideology. He even went back to his prep school days to pick the director of the United States Information Agency. Said one old friend, "Loyalty is his ideology."[59]

Beyond the traditional competition of any transition, friendly or otherwise, there was in 1988 and 1989 an underlying bitterness among the so-called Reaganauts in Washington, who felt that they were more than losing jobs, they were being purged.[60] Yet right after the inauguration the *New York Times* published a list of Bush appointees: of fifty-three White House staffers, for instance, twenty-seven came from the Reagan government. In the cold light of history the Reagan loyalists were wrong: the Bush transition had struck a balance between the need to find places for campaign supporters and the retention of experienced executives. The reality of impressions, however, was that everyone knew somebody who had been fired.

Bush's government also reflected the revolving door of political Washington, as former officials returned to serve again. Brent Scowcroft, President Ford's national security adviser, returned to the same position after working as vice chairman of Kissinger Associates; Roger Porter, a Harvard professor, returned to the White House to direct domestic policy; and Richard Darman, a veteran of three Republican administrations, came back from Wall Street to head the Office of Management and Budget.[61]

The cabinet choices, besides Baker and the three holdovers, consisted of former Texas senator John Tower (Defense), Representative Jack Kemp of New York (Housing and Urban Development), Representative Manuel Lujan of New Mexico (Interior), former chief of naval operations James Watkins (Energy), U.S. Trade Representative Clayton Yeutter (Agriculture), and former secretary of education William Bennett (drug policy czar). Former Illinois representative Edward Derwinski was to be the first secretary of the new department of veterans affairs. Two women who had served in previous Republican cabinets were back: Elizabeth Dole as secretary of labor and Carla Hills as trade representative. Only three of the sixteen to whom cabinet status was given were new to Washington: Dr. Louis Sullivan, a hematologist at Morehouse Medical College, where Barbara Bush was a trustee, was to be secretary of health and human services; Samuel Skinner, secretary-designate of transportation, was a prominent lawyer from Illinois, where he had been Bush's campaign director; and Houston oil executive Robert Mosbacher, another Bush friend and chief campaign fund-raiser, was rewarded with the Commerce portfolio. The diversity total was two Hispanic Americans, one African American, and two women—a considerable advance over previous Republican cabinets.

One member of the inner circle who helped Bush on personnel matters noted of the process that "the purpose of the first meetings was not to make or come to conclusions on individuals, but rather to talk more generally about the sort of individuals needed."[62] Bush ultimately decided that what he most needed in the Energy Department was an expert on nuclear matters, an issue mired in controversy, and chose a retired admiral trained by Hyman Rickover.[63] On the other hand, former transportation secretary Dole had the sort of governing skills that could usefully fit into any outer cabinet slot. If the watchword of Carter's selection process had been "good manager," the watchword of Bush's was "team player."

Bush had strong feelings about what he wanted at the CIA and the United Nations, two jobs he had once held. The intelligence post had never changed hands during a transition until President Carter fired CIA director Bush in 1977. Now Bush endorsed the concept of continuity and retained CIA director William Webster. The CIA position had been elevated to cabinet status when Reagan gave the job to his campaign manager, William Casey. Bush believed the director of central intelligence "should not be in the policy business," however, and he removed his appointee from the cabinet. For the UN ambassadorship Bush picked a distinguished diplomat, Thomas Pickering, who also was not given cabinet rank. "There is no point in the United Nations Ambassador sitting around, as I did for a while, talking about ag policy."[64]

When all the pieces were in place, where were the "new faces" Bush had promised? In response to the question, Bush replied, "I didn't mean I was going to reach out and find everybody with no experience in government."[65] Yet after the initial burst of energy, the appointment pace slowed to a crawl. Some explanations are reasonable: There is a cumulative buildup of red tape over the history of transitions as each new type of controversy produces new procedures to protect the executive branch appointers and the legislative branch confirmers (and presumably the citizenry). Thus each new transition requires more time to staff the government than the previous transition. Moreover, the more serious the effort to seek diversity, the longer the process takes. Nevertheless, the conundrum of the Bush transition was why a team so knowledgeable in the culture of the capital and the workings of government had such severe startup problems. The matter of Louis Sullivan was an embarrassment. The matter of John Tower was a disaster.

For Dr. Sullivan, the hematologist, getting confirmed as secretary of health and human services proved to be, in the words of Steven Roberts, "a painful lesson in the perils and pitfalls awaiting an innocent traveler in the Washington wilderness."[66] Although Sullivan's wounds were self-inflicted, the Bush staff had not prepared him for his journey. One senior White House assistant called their performance "amateur hour." The problematic issue was abortion, and Sullivan was forced to reverse course twice to get in line with his president's position. In one case he found himself in the crossfire between two Republican senators, abortion foe Gordon Humphrey of New Hampshire and abortion supporter Bob Packwood of Oregon, to whom Sullivan had said privately that he supported *Roe* v. *Wade*. A "very upset and confused" Humphrey told reporters, "Let's put it plainly. Dr. Sullivan is the only black nominee to the cabinet. It would be embarrassing to the President, embarrassing to the Republican Party, if that nomination encountered any trouble."[67] Belatedly the White House put Sullivan through a cram course for troubled nominees. In Washington parlance this is called the "murder board," a simulation of a confirmation hearing, with former Senate aides and lobbyists playing legislators. The actors fire questions at the nominee and then pick apart his answers. After a week of getting murdered regularly, Sullivan told a friend, "I find that I need to learn the language, the culture, and the etiquette of Washington so I'm not misunderstood."[68] Finally on February 23, after Sullivan apologized to Packwood for "having misspoken," the Finance Committee unanimously approved the nomination. The Senate confirmed the nomination on March 1, 98 to 1, with Jesse Helms the only senator to vote against Sullivan.

John Tower, however, was no innocent traveler in the Washington wilderness. He had retired from the Senate in 1985 after twenty-four years of service. As the virtual founder of the modern Republican Party in Texas, Tower had long supported Bush's political aspirations and had stuck with him through some difficult times. Tower's knowledge of the Pentagon was profound. He badly wanted to be secretary of defense, and there is no indication that Bush seriously considered any other candidate.

When the Armed Services Committee opened hearings on the nomination, the *New York Times*'s Andrew Rosenthal noted that "Mr. Tower is unlikely to face opposition from the committee, of which he was chair from 1981 to 1985. But aides said senators wanted to avoid any suggestion that they did not question a former colleague carefully enough."[69] The Senate is a clubby place, and its rejection of a president's cabinet nomination is rare; it has happened only eight times in two hundred years, the last in 1959. It seemed highly unlikely that John Tower would be the ninth.

When Bush announced Tower's selection on December 16, he said he was "totally satisfied" with the findings of an extensive FBI check into the candidate's personal and professional background.[70] Once the committee hearings began in January, however, Tower was subjected to an almost daily barrage of allegations about drinking and womanizing, with other charges leveled against his defense industry connections. "As might be expected," wrote William Safire, "each week with the nominee twisting in the wind invites some old political enemy or ex-wife or disgruntled former staffer to make a new charge, setting the FBI off on another investigation, providing time for more new charges."[71]

On February 23 the committee split along party lines and voted down the nomination, 11 to 9. On March 9 the Senate rejected Tower, 53 to 47, with three Democrats voting for him and one Republican, Nancy Kassebaum of Kansas, voting against him, although she said she would have voted for him despite her misgivings if the president had needed her vote.[72] It was the first time that an incoming president had been denied a cabinet member of his choice.

The Bush people had put too much stock in the Senate's habit of looking out for its own. (Only one former senator had ever been denied a cabinet seat, and that was in 1868.) Many of the charges against Tower were easily disproved; nevertheless, he was a hard fellow to defend. "I can understand how over the years Tower might have left a lot of people unhappy with him," said Les Aspin, chairman of the House Armed Services Committee. "Everything was a struggle with him, everything was a fight."[73]

Furthermore, in its efforts to save the nomination the administration was all thumbs. Sam Nunn, the chairman of the Senate Armed Services Committee, was infuriated when White House officials excluded Democrats from a Senate briefing about Tower's FBI report. The president's counsel asked Nunn to postpone the vote, while other administration officials were pressuring for a quick vote. The committee vote came while Bush and his top aides were in Japan for Emperor Hirohito's funeral, leaving the trolling for stray Democrats in less competent hands.[74] Nunn was a methodical southerner, slow to reach judgment, who had built his Senate career on expertise in matters military. When he decided that doubts about Tower's sobriety made him unfit to stand in the chain of command of the nuclear arsenal, there may not have been anything Bush's people could have done to get their nominee through the Democratic

Senate.[75] Some in Washington questioned Bush's decision to go down fighting; still, Stuart Eizenstat of the Carter White House concluded that "the Bush people have mishandled this nomination, but they were smart to have stood and fought, rather than to have played their cards and walked away as we did with the Sorensen nomination."[76]

Bush quickly patched up relations with Congress by appointing Richard Cheney, the popular Wyoming representative who also had been President Ford's chief of staff, to the defense position. Yet he paid a heavy price for the Tower humiliation. Other cabinet nominations—those of Watkins, Bennett, and Derwinski—were not confirmed until March. Gerald Boyd reported in the *New York Times* of "a growing perception in Washington that [Bush's] Administration is adrift." The president acknowledged that "too much time has been wasted."[77]

Bill Clinton, Elected November 3, 1992

Except for sending a strong message about his economic priorities, Clinton's transition into the presidency, widely considered one of the most chaotic in modern times, could be judged a case study in what not to do. The Clinton team was not in place early and did not inspire confidence in either the Senate or the media, and the whole process moved extremely slowly. Its self-imposed task to create a diverse cabinet and White House staff had an impact on the pace of appointments. How does a president-elect, given a mere eleven weeks, construct an administration that "looks like America"? That had been Bill Clinton's campaign promise, and it was now his challenge.

Richard Nixon had made halfhearted attempts to find a Democrat and an African American to include in his cabinet but settled for a dozen white male Republicans, and he announced them all at the same time on December 11. Jimmy Carter had completed his selections on December 23, with two women and two blacks in the cabinet. One of the women was black, and the other black was the UN representative, a position that had been absent from the Nixon cabinet. Ronald Reagan's cabinet was all male and all white, except for an African American at Housing and Urban Development and a woman at the United Nations. George Bush worked harder at creating diversity, choosing two Hispanic Americans, one African American, and two women, but he did not complete the cabinet until the tenth week of the transition. In addition, of course, other pieces had to be fitted into the puzzle—ideological, geographical, political, personal, and substantive.

But never had a president-elect attempted so elaborate a construction as did Clinton in 1992 and 1993. Cabinet building seems to cry out for gaming metaphors: it is juggling, musical chairs, tug-of-war, a puzzle, jigsaw or crossword. All of these descriptions are useful in recalling the Clinton transition.

Clinton's selection process was contained in what has been described as "a very closed loop" consisting of his wife Hillary, Vice President–elect Al Gore, Warren Christopher, who had been deputy secretary of state in the Carter administration, and Arkansas friends Bruce Lindsey and Thomas (Mack) McLarty. "Most job seekers appeared to go through the same ritual in their treks to Little Rock," explained Richard Berke. "It starts with a phone call from Warren Christopher, the transition director, telling the person that he or she is under consideration for an appointment. The candidate is met at the airport by relatively low-level aides, and then may be escorted to meet transition officials before going to the [Governor's] Mansion for interviews that usually last at least an hour."[78] A premium was placed on secrecy and protecting the candidates' privacy, not easy to do in a city the size of Little Rock and within a cable culture whose stock-in-trade is political gossip. A widely read newsletter, *Hotline*, ran a daily "Transition Box Score," assigning handicaps to the candidates.[79]

"It's the economy, stupid!" had been the campaign's theme, and so it was important that the economic team should be the first order of the transition's business. This Clinton accomplished on December 10, with the appointments of Lloyd Bentsen, chairman of the Senate Finance Committee, as secretary of the treasury; Roger Altman, an investment banker and friend of Clinton's since college days, as deputy treasury secretary; Leon Panetta, chairman of the House Budget Committee, as director of the Office of Management and Budget; Alice Rivlin, former director of the Congressional Budget Office, as deputy director of the OMB; and Robert Rubin, the cochairman of Goldman Sachs, as the head of the National Economic Council, a new White House unit that had been promised in the campaign.

"My first appointment, intentionally, is the Secretary of the Treasury," announced Clinton. "In filling this post, I wanted someone who had the unique capacity to command the respect of Wall Street."[80] Following Kennedy's example, Clinton believed that calming the business community must be of paramount importance to a young Democratic president. The *New York Times* commented of the economic team appointments that "all five are cut from the same fiscally conservative cloth."[81] No need to muddy the message by also announcing the appointments of such liberals as Robert Reich and Ira Magaziner.

Women's groups had made clear that their highest priority was the appointment of a woman in one of the "big four" cabinet posts—State, Defense, the Treasury, and Justice. "A person with knowledge of the appointment process" let it be known that Clinton was seeking a woman for attorney general.[82] Clinton's next batch of appointments consisted of four social activists, three of whom were women. In addition to his old friend from Oxford, Robert Reich, to be secretary of labor, Clinton picked Donna Shalala, chancellor of the University of Wisconsin, as secretary of health and human services; Laura D'Andrea Tyson, a professor at Berkeley, to head the Council of Economic Advisers; and Carol Browner, a Gore protégé, to run the Environmental Protection Agency. Reported Gwen Ifill, "Mr. Clinton let slip some of this awareness of the symbolic intent of today's announcements when he asserted incorrectly that Ms. Browner would be the first woman to head the environmental agency and was quickly corrected by Mr. Gore." (Anne M. Gorsuch had held the post from 1981 to 1983.) Tyson was the first woman to chair the Council of Economic Advisers.[83]

No members of minority groups had yet been selected, but the *New York Times* revealed that Ronald Brown, chairman of the Democratic National Committee, after rejecting the UN ambassadorship, had accepted appointment as the first black secretary of commerce.[84] Clinton then announced that Henry Cisneros, the former mayor of San Antonio, was his choice for secretary of housing and urban development and Jesse Brown, director of the Disabled Veterans of America, would be his secretary of veterans affairs. Another African American, Representative Mike Espy of Mississippi, was the leading candidate for secretary of agriculture. As Clinton juggled the names and the jobs, he knew at least six white males that he wanted in his cabinet: Warren Christopher as secretary of state; Les Aspin, chairman of the House Foreign Affairs Committee, as secretary of defense; Richard Riley, a former governor of South Carolina, as secretary of education; Bruce Babbitt, a former governor of Arizona, as secretary of the interior; retiring senator Timothy Wirth of Colorado, who felt he had a cabinet claim at the Department of Energy, and either of two top-rated claimants for secretary of transportation,

William Daley, of the Chicago Daleys, and former Michigan governor James Blanchard.

With only Energy, Transportation, and Justice undecided, the box score was ten men and one woman, seven whites, three African Americans, and one Hispanic American. No serious effort was made to find a Republican, which caused Thomas Friedman to write that "Republicans seem to be of two minds about Mr. Clinton's cabinet. On the one hand they note that his promise to appoint a Republican to give his team a bipartisan air was ignored. On the other hand, Republicans almost seem relieved."[85]

Women's groups were now irate at their nonrepresentation. Eleanor Smeal, president of the Fund for the Feminist Majority, wrote to him, noting that "if the trend you have established continues, it is probable that you will appoint fewer women to the cabinet than Presidents Carter, Reagan, or Bush." Hurt by the criticism, Clinton lashed out at the women, calling them "bean counters."[86] Patricia Ireland, president of the National Organization of Women, replied that "[Clinton] has made a whole series of campaign promises, and he is going to be pushed and pulled in a lot of directions. Right now, he's just starting to squirm a little."[87]

Bean counters perhaps, but powerful bean counters, Clinton concluded. An anonymous "top adviser" to the president-elect told Adam Clymer, "[Clinton is] casting aside people he knows very well and had planned to choose in favor of people he knows much less well who will help him reach his diversity goals."[88] Wirth was out as energy secretary, and Hazel O'Leary, a black woman and little-known executive with a Minnesota utility, was in. Clinton also played the UN game. The position was again raised to cabinet status. When the national security team was announced on December 22, it consisted of six white men, one black man, and Madeleine Albright at the United Nations. The penultimate slot, secretary of transportation, went to neither Daley nor Blanchard but to Federico Peña, the former mayor of Denver, who had not been on any journalist's radar screen, thus giving Clinton's cabinet a second Hispanic name.

And then there was one. "The transition team was scrambling to find the best female attorney general rather than the best attorney general period," according to George Stephanopoulos.[89] Clinton had been turned down by his first choice, Judge Patricia Wald of the U.S. Court of Appeals for the District of Columbia Circuit. Finally on Christmas Eve, the mythic date by which presidents-elect aim to have completed their cabinets,

Clinton announced that his attorney general would be Zöe Baird, the general counsel of Aetna Life and Casualty Company, who had originally been penciled in to be the White House counsel, a position that does not require Senate confirmation.

Although the Clinton transition vetters had not seen it as a problem, their attorney general–designate had broken the law. She and her law professor husband had hired undocumented aliens to care for their child and additionally had failed to pay Social Security taxes on their wages. "Radio talk-show hosts across the nation had a field day, and the public responded with outrage. Why does a person who earns $500,000 a year need to hire help on the cheap? And how could the nation's chief law enforcer be a scofflaw herself?"[90] The confirmation hearing was brutal.

SENATOR THURMOND: You admit you did wrong?

BAIRD: Yes.

THURMOND: You're sorry you did wrong?

BAIRD: Absolutely.

THURMOND: You're repentant for doing wrong?

BAIRD: Yes, sir.[91]

The nomination was withdrawn. But the next person Clinton proposed for attorney general, U.S. district court judge Kimba Wood, also had a "nanny problem." There was an explanation, but the White House, correctly concluding that it was too complicated to untangle in thirty-second sound bites, withdrew her name. The situation reminded R. W. Apple Jr. of Casey Stengel's assessment of the 1962 New York Mets: "Can't anybody here play this game?"[92] On the third try the president chose Janet Reno, state attorney for Dade County, Florida, whose nomination sped through the Senate. Reno was confirmed on March 11.

"I did micromanage the Cabinet appointments," Clinton admitted. "I spent more time on the Cabinet appointments than anybody in history had, and I plead guilty to that."[93] One consequence was that Clinton failed to get around to naming his White House staff, with one exception, until six days before becoming president. The exception was the chief of staff, announced on December 12. Clinton made clear that he did not want a sharp-edged operator like John Sununu or an insider extraordinaire like James Baker. He turned instead to Mack McLarty, his friend since kindergarten and now the head of a natural gas company. About to enter the shark-infested waters of Washington, perhaps Clinton felt that what he most needed at his right hand was a chum. McLarty told reporters he would not be serving as a terribly aggressive gatekeeper.[94]

At the last news conference in Little Rock before leaving for the capital, Clinton announced the rest of his White House operation. There were very few surprises. Mostly the team consisted of the young men and women who had been closely associated with his campaign and transition, people like Dee Dee Myers, Bruce Reed, Gene Sperling, and Marcia Hale. The *New York Times* reported that "many staff members, relieved to have finally been given a job, cheered as their colleagues' names were announced."[95]

Clinton's transition effort to construct an administration that "looks like America" produced eight black, female, or Hispanic nominations to cabinet-level positions that had never before been held by members of their groups. Yet the fallout from the attorney general fiasco helped to create the impression that the new presidency would "hit the ground stumbling."[96]

George W. Bush, Election Concluded December 13, 2000

The contested election of 2000 provides an almost test-tube experiment of what can be gained or lost by cutting the traditional ten- to eleven-week transition period in half. Although George W. Bush quickly attempted to assume the mantel of the president-elect, he soon realized this was a public relations blunder. As long as the race's outcome was still in doubt the media regarded his transition planning as arrogant. In other words, until the U.S. Supreme Court announced its decision on December 12 and Al Gore made his concession speech, Bush could not outwardly assemble his administration.

Bush's only transition-related announcements between election day, November 7, and his victory speech on December 13 were those appointing Andrew Card his chief of staff and putting the vice president–elect, Dick Cheney, in charge of the transition, with Clay Johnson as the transition's executive director. Card had had considerable Washington experience, including a stint as secretary of transportation; Johnson had been the governor's chief of staff in Austin. Cheney was assuming a role that no incoming president had ever turned over to his running mate, dramatically foreshadowing the influence that he would have in the administration. On matters of personnel, Bush, Cheney, Card, and Johnson were the transition's inner circle.

On December 16, Bush announced his first cabinet appointment, the long-expected selection of Colin Powell to be secretary of state. The next day Condoleezza Rice, his chief foreign policy aide, was named national security adviser. To complete the national security cluster, Bush appeared to be leaning toward giving the defense portfolio to Dan Coats, a former senator from Indiana. The appropriate question was whether Coats would be strong enough to represent the institutional needs of the Pentagon, given the wattage of Powell at state and the closeness of Rice at the White House. Bush concluded that the answer was no and turned instead to Cheney's old mentor, Donald Rumsfeld, who had been secretary of defense under President Ford. When reporters asked Bush about this equation, he replied, "General Powell's a strong figure, and Dick Cheney's no shrinking violet *[laughter from the reporters]* . . . but neither is Don Rumsfeld, nor Condi Rice. I view the four as being able to complement each other."[97]

The White House staff was chosen promptly and with no surprises—no James Baker, no John Sununu. Chief of Staff Andy Card had been a Bush family loyalist since 1980. Personnel director Johnson had been the president-elect's friend since they were students at Phillips Academy, Andover. White House counsel Al Gonzales, a Texas Supreme Court judge, had served as counsel to Governor Bush for three years. Of the triad that ran the campaign, Karen Hughes would oversee the offices of communications, press secretary, and speechwriting; Karl Rove's responsibilities would include political affairs, intergovernmental affairs, and public liaison; and Joe Allbaugh was to head the Federal Emergency Management Agency. Ari Fleisher, an experienced Capitol Hill hand, had proved his worth during the campaign and was elevated to the role of presidential press secretary. Perhaps the staff's most interesting characteristic, according to Dana Milbank, was that there were "more women with more power than in any previous administration." Of Bush's top twenty aides, eight were women.[98]

The closeness of the election made it essential that Bush seek at least one Democrat for his cabinet. John Breaux, whom he would have liked for energy secretary, chose to remain in the Senate. In a December 28 press conference, Bush was asked if he was "having trouble getting a Democrat to join your administration?"

BUSH: That's an interesting question. *[Laughter]* I'm not having trouble getting Democrats to return my phone calls.

REPORTER: That's a different question, sir.

BUSH: Yes, it was, but the same answer.[99]

The president-elect finally found his Democrat, on January 2, in President Clinton's cabinet: Secretary of Commerce Norman Mineta would serve as the next secretary of transportation.

The matter of which federal jobs, in addition to the leadership of the fourteen executive departments, deserve cabinet status has become increasingly negotiable in recent years. Clinton created eight honorific cabinet offices. Bush limited himself to four: budget director and White House chief of staff (two positions that clearly rate inclusion), director of the Environmental Protection Agency, and U.S. trade representative. Making the EPA director a member of his cabinet was necessary to lure a sitting governor to Washington. The trade representative's status was the subject of lively discussion within the transition. "The position needs to remain a Cabinet-level position," Bush concluded, "because of the importance of trade in the global economy. It should reconfirm our nation's commitment to free trade."[100]

When Bush finished his cabinet selections, on the first working day of the new year, it was clear that his three staunchest conservatives—John Ashcroft (Justice), Gale Norton (Interior), and Linda Chavez (Labor)—would not be looked upon with favor by many in the Democratic Party, which now held half the seats in the Senate. Although confirmation hearings are conducted by different committees, filled with different interests and egos, there seems to be something holistic about the way the Senate considers an administration's initial slate of appointments. Perhaps the energy expended in fighting one nominee cannot be recycled. Perhaps there is a point past which opposition is perceived as obstructionism and becomes politically counterproductive. Bush understood this when he answered a reporter's question about the Ashcroft nomination: "Well, I expected at least one member of my Cabinet to get a pretty tough hearing. You know, it could've been John, it could've been somebody else."[101]

The syndicated columnist Linda Chavez, a foe of affirmative action and bilingual education, could expect a pretty tough hearing, presided over by Senator Edward Kennedy. Nevertheless in the history of confirmations, ideological opposition is generally not sufficient to defeat a person who serves at the will of the president; it takes a skeleton in the closet. Chavez's skeleton was that she had taken a battered woman into her home, an illegal immigrant from Guatemala, who in the course of two years had done occasional chores for the family and had been given at least fifteen hundred dollars in spending money. Did the work make her an employee? Was this Zöe Baird redux, although the facts are vastly different? Chavez, admitting to "bad judgment" in not telling the Bush vetters or the FBI, withdrew her name from consideration.[102] Senate Democrats were delighted. Yet it was at little cost to Bush. Unlike the senior Bush president's unsuccessful fight to confirm John Tower as his secretary of defense, the Labor portfolio is not significant in a Republican cabinet, and Chavez was not a member of the inner circle. Two days later Bush announced a replacement and was given credit for acting expeditiously.

Senators would find no skeleton in the closet of straight-arrow John Ashcroft, their recently defeated colleague from Missouri, whose views on abortion, gun control, and the death penalty were deeply controversial, as were his actions in blocking the nomination of a black state judge to the federal bench. What two weeks of anguished debate in the Judiciary Committee did produce, however, was a set of Ashcroft commitments to policies he had opposed as senator, including a statement that *Roe* v. *Wade* is "the settled law of the law" and "as attorney general I don't think it could be my agenda" to overturn it.[103] The nomination was approved 10 to 8, with all Republicans plus Democrat Russell Feingold voting for Ashcroft. The full Senate favored him 58 to 42. No Republican deserted, and Bush won a big victory. So too did the Democrats, who showed that they had the votes to sustain a filibuster if Bush ever proposed a Supreme Court nominee they felt was beyond their tolerance level. Senator Charles Schumer pointedly reminded the president that "what has happened with the Ashcroft nomination in terms of divisiveness would look small compared to the divisiveness that would occur if someone of Senator Ashcroft's beliefs were nominated to the United States Supreme Court."[104]

During the Ashcroft debate almost all Democratic opponents made statements like Senator Dianne Feinstein's: "I truly believe that a president is entitled to his or her cabinet. However, the background record of this nominee is not mainstream on the key issues."[105] Is the attorney general, as the chief law enforcement officer, a position that justifies a special vote of conscience? Are there key issues that demand special consideration? If so, is there agreement on what they are? Do any of them fall under other jurisdictions, such as the Departments of Agriculture, Labor, Commerce, Housing, or Veterans Affairs? Conservationists contend that they exist in the Department of the Interior.

Yet the undoing of Chavez and the intense attack on Ashcroft seemed to shield the Norton nomination. Environmentalists waged an expensive campaign, said to cost nearly $1 million, that portrayed her in the pro-business image of her mentor, James Watt. But she was easily approved by the Senate Energy and Resources Committee, 18 to 2, partly because of her silken performance as a witness and partly because of skilled lobbying by her Denver law firm and a bipartisan group of states' attorneys general.[106] The Senate vote was 75 to 24.

The Bush cabinet ultimately included two African Americans, a Japanese American, a Cuban American, a Chinese American (who was the replacement for a Hispanic American), and an Arab American. There were four women in the cabinet, and the national security adviser (who was not given cabinet rank) was a black woman. The press made favorable comparisons with Clinton's tortured 1992 efforts to create a cabinet that "looks like America."

In announcing his nominees, Bush kept remarking on their "wonderful stories." Mel Martinez, his choice for Housing and Urban Development, left Cuba at the age of fifteen, speaking no English, and lived with foster families until he was reunited with his parents. Colin Powell is the son of immigrants from Jamaica. Elaine Chao, labor secretary–designate, came from China when she was eight years old. Norman Mineta was forced into an internment camp during World War II. The hallmark of Clinton's cabinet was representativeness: it was imperative to have a woman attorney general, just as it was necessary to have more than one Hispanic American. Strangely, given the similar end result, this was not the primary thrust of Bush's labors. In mid-December, Bush was asked, "Mr. President-elect, in the last two days you have appointed two women, two African Americans, a Hispanic American. Aside from the fact that these are incredibly competent, qualified people, is there another message that you are sending to America with these first choices?" He replied, "You bet: that people that work hard and make the right decisions in life can achieve anything they want in America."[107]

Rather than representativeness, Bush's message was true grit. Clinton's outstanding numerical record of opening high-level government positions to minorities could not be matched by a conservative administration. What Bush did was free his minority appointments from tokenism. He had received only 9 percent of the black vote, yet Powell and Rice would be his premier advisers on foreign relations, and Rod Paige was made secretary of education, Bush's number-one domestic priority.

When Bush finished his cabinet selection, a reporter asked, "What does your Cabinet say, do you think, about your management style, about how you intend to make decisions as president?" The President-elect replied, "First, it says I'm not afraid to surround myself with strong and competent people. . . . I hope the American people realize that a good executive is one that understands how to recruit people and how to delegate, how to line authority and responsibility, how to hold people accountable for results, and how to build a team of people."[108]

Indeed, Bush had picked some very competent people in a very short time. Ann Veneman was more than a "first," the first woman to be secretary of agriculture. She had previously served as the department's deputy secretary and headed the agriculture department of California. Secretary of Transportation Mineta was intimately involved in his subject from his days as chairman of the Public Works and Transportation Committee in the U.S. House of Representatives. Anthony Principi had the best resumé of any secretary in the brief history of Veterans Affairs as a cabinet department. Christie Todd Whitman, the two-term governor of New Jersey, brought more political clout to the EPA than any past administrator. Don Rumsfeld at Defense and Paul O'Neill at Treasury, as well as Vice President Dick Cheney, had unique backgrounds, combining vast government experience with experience as chief executive officers of Fortune 500 corporations.

Perhaps Ed Meese, the director of Reagan's successful 1980 transition, was right: the 2000 transition was proving that the corollary to "Work expands to fill the available time" is "Work can be compressed to fill the available time." Yet is there not a downside to a presidential transition cut in half? Linda Chavez thought her downfall was partly the result of the Bush staff's not being able to follow the "normal procedure" of a lengthy background check.[109] Previous transitions that went full term, however, notably those of George Bush and Bill Clinton, had made more serious vetting mistakes. The real problem is that there had not been enough time to carry the selection process deeper into the administration's second ranks. So the inauguration came and went without deputy secretaries, under secretaries, and assistant secretaries in place. Where were those who would work hand in glove with the executive branch officers, filling in the details and running programs? When might they arrive? How high is the price for not having them on board when a president wants to "hit the ground running?"

Lessons from Past Transitions

Transitions have both long-term and short-term consequences. The immediate objective is to prepare the president-elect to be as ready as possible to start running the government on January 20, the day his contract begins. First impressions are important. If the transition goes well, there will be a bonus, the so-called honeymoon, during which the new leader gets kinder and gentler attention from Congress, press, and general public. This section offers suggestions on how better transitions make better honeymoons.

First, however, let me note a long-term consequence. How well the president picks his people might be measured by how long they stay with him, rather than by how long it took to get them there in the first place. Presidents are not usually adept at firing people. If mistakes are made, they should be corrected, but doing so can be messy and is inevitably time consuming. Because presidents make four-year commitments, the expectation is that their cabinet members should, too. Yet what is the record of the five former presidents whose transitions we have just reviewed? After four years, 79 percent of Clinton's and Bush's department secretaries were still in place. For Reagan and Carter, the retention rate was 46 percent, and for Nixon, 64 percent (after making appropriate adjustments).[110]

One reason these figures are so fascinating is that in the mythology of transitions President Reagan is considered to have had the best and President Clinton to have had the worst. These conclusions, which I share, are based on more than personnel selection. Clinton badly stumbled on several issues, notably gays in the military, but his remarkable retention record deserves attention. At the end of two terms he left office with four cabinet members from his original team still in place: Janet Reno, Bruce Babbitt, Donna Shalala, and Richard Riley. Two-term president Dwight D. Eisenhower retained only Agriculture Secretary Ezra Taft Bensen and Postmaster General Arthur Summerfield, and two-term president Reagan retained only Samuel Pierce at Housing and Urban Development.

Government officials are sometimes enticed by lucrative jobs outside government. Three of Reagan's losses fit in this category, and perhaps this happens most often in Republican administrations. More significant, however, is that in the period under study five cabinet officials were fired by their president, and at least six others were forced out, including one secretary of state, one secretary of defense, and two secretaries of the treasury. Another secretary of state resigned in a policy dispute.

What makes the history of failed cabinet officers so mystifying is that presidents have sometimes felt let down by their closest friends, such as Nixon by his secretary of health, education, and welfare, Robert Finch, and by those with pluperfect credentials, such as Clinton by his defense secretary, Les Aspin. Total strangers have worked well, and then again they have not. Every type of background—business, law, academe—has produced successes and failures.

Presidents are almost always happier with their cabinet changes: John Connally replacing David Kennedy as Nixon's treasury secretary; Patricia Harris replacing Joseph Califano as Carter's secretary of health, education, and welfare; George Shultz replacing Alexander Haig as Reagan's secretary of state; Lamar Alexander replacing Lauro Cavazos as Bush's secretary of education; Robert Rubin replacing Lloyd Bentsen as Clinton's treasury secretary. The sad conclusion is that presidents (even presidents who have been vice presidents) do not know what they most need until they have been in office awhile. This suggests the impossibility of telling them otherwise. They will make their own mistakes.

If, however, the presidents whose transitions have just been explored could be gathered in one room and asked what they now think they did right and wrong and what advice would be most helpful to the next president, I think they would agree on eight points of advice about top-level personnel selection.[111]

Be Prepared

Once upon a time no candidate would be so presumptuous as to plan for his presidency before the people had elected him. Surely the voters would punish the candidate who took them for granted. Carter took this risk, setting up a small group to prepare for his transition before election day, and still got elected. He discovered, however, that his sensible innovation caused friction within his organization. Reagan finessed this problem by putting an intimate aide in charge of the preelection planning. Yet when preelection planning involves personnel decisions as to who gets the spoils of victory, the possibilities of unauthorized leaks can make it a politically risky enterprise. Nevertheless, the value of presenting the victorious candidate with carefully vetted lists of those who should be considered for top jobs (much in the Reagan manner of 1980) is of inestimable value. "Start people through the FBI process the day after the election," advises former White House counsel Boyden Gray, "even if you don't know what jobs they're going to have."[112]

Act Quickly

Some well-meaning folks will surely tell a president-elect, "Look at the trouble your predecessors got into by rushing into decisions they later regretted. Take your time and get it right." This is good friendly advice and bad political advice. First of all, previous bad decisions were usually those that took the longest, those made as the transition clock was running down. The longer a president-elect delays, the greater the pressure he or she will be subjected to by job supplicants, interest group advocates, and the media. Every prompt decision means the president-elect will have to say no a lot fewer times. Quick decisions mean that the transition news will be momentum, not indecisiveness. The sooner appointments are made, the more time the appointees will have to prepare themselves for their jobs. A handy rule of thumb is to have key White House staff in place by Thanksgiving and cabinet secretaries announced by Christmas.

Put the White House First

Both Carter and Clinton, the two presidents who selected their cabinet secretaries before choosing their White House assistants, eventually concluded they had made a mistake. By election day, candidates probably do not know who they want as their secretaries of agriculture, commerce, or labor, but they probably do know who they want as their top White House aides. So why delay the announcements? Especially if a surprise is planned, a John Sununu or a James Baker, fast is best. White House aides are a president's processors. They need to be in place to facilitate the rest of a president's appointments: the chief of staff to give direction, the White House counsel to sort out ethics questions, the personnel director for initial screening, the press secretary for public announcements, and the congressional liaison to deal with the Senate confirmation process. Personal aides make life run smoother. But how does a president-elect mix White House and departmental policy advisers?[113]

Think Clusters

Thinking in clusters is one way a president-elect can use appointment powers to counter the centrifugal forces that pull the pieces of government into different orbits. For one shining moment at the administration's creation, the new chief executive has the opportunity to relate the parts to one another. If the secretaries of state and defense and the national security adviser chosen are in sync, if their egos and ambitions are properly aligned, the president-elect will have a better shot at achieving his or her objectives. Yet examples of past dysfunctionality are stunning. Did Carter imagine a harmonious national security cluster with Brzezinski as his White House anchor? What could Reagan have been thinking when he joined together Haig, Weinberger, and Allen? How fortunate for Bush that John Tower was rejected by the Senate. His connection with Baker and Scowcroft would have been a disaster, whereas Cheney, his replacement, was a perfect fit. The problems are more often caused by personality than by ideology. One wonders whether presidential transition teams should hire a resident psychologist.

Send a Message

Appointments, so microscopically examined and interpreted by the media, can be usefully employed by presidents-elect to send a message or make a statement. The ideological Reagan used his first appointment to choose the pragmatist Baker as his chief of staff. Outsider Carter chose insider Vance as his first cabinet appointment. Clinton first picked an economic team, signaling that this was to be his top priority. The message can come from the sequence or from the bundling. Nixon sent the most dramatic message when he announced his entire cabinet at the same time, although the expanded size and expected diversity of today's cabinets may take this option beyond the reach of twenty-first-century presidents. Unfortunately most presidents-in-transition simply announce their intentions as they make up their minds and thus fail to take advantage of these early opportunities.

Choose Your Demographic Goals

Deep in the archive of the candidates' minds should be a rough sketch of what they want or need their administrations to look like. This is personal property. Candidates who announce that they want the attorney general to be a woman paint themselves into a corner. So they must be prepared. Preelection planning should include the resumés of qualified individuals from the groups that are on their demographic wish lists. If the election is close, they may even need to reach across party lines. They should also remember, however, that this is a game that can be won by changing the dimensions of the playing field. The executive branch of the government has fourteen departments, with each department head an automatic member of the president's cabinet. Yet there are some units of government called agencies or even offices that are more important than the mighty departments. Is the secretary of veterans affairs really more important than the administrator of the Environmental Protection Agency? The answer is no, if a president-elect announces which positions are in his or her cabinet before making the appointments rather than after the fact, when the same appointments are denigrated as pandering to special interests.

Feed the Beast

"The beast" is what Washington insiders call the media. Give reporters "a constant supply of doggie biscuits," claimed Lloyd Bentsen's press secretary, and they will "gleefully lick the hand that fed them." Run out of treats and they will "devour your arm."[114] The problem can be particularly severe for a transition press secretary, who has little to report while the boss juggles the makeup of his cabinet. Clinton was the extreme case. He did not announce any appointments until the sixth week of his transition. In the meantime reporters waited in Little Rock, staring at the walls of their rooms in the Capitol Hotel, and wrote stories about how long it was taking him to get organized. "Thanks to snippets of video and a few remarks on the run, it is known that President-elect Clinton likes a morning jog and weekend golf," reported Susan Bennett in the *Philadelphia Inquirer.* "What is not known after more than thirty days of the transition is anything of substance."[115]

The transition press corps is a curious hybrid of reporters who have been covering the winning candidate's campaign, some of whom now will be assigned to the White House beat, and White House regulars. The campaign reporters know the president-elect but not the presidency; White House regulars know the presidency but may not know the president-elect.

The reporters covering the Clinton transition arrived in Little Rock with a healthy curiosity and a good deal of good will, which was soon undermined by Clinton's incompetent press operation, according to scholar Charles O. Jones's interviews with reporters.[116] The moral for future transitions is not simply that idle reporters are dangerous reporters. Having a press corps on hand and no hard news is an opportunity for the incoming administration to educate the journalists through daily briefings by visiting experts on all matters—economic, diplomatic, military, scientific, social—that a new president (and a new press corps) will confront in the next four years.

Smile and Grovel

Finally the nominations have been made and sent to the Senate, where the new president confronts a lot of brushfires and one truly horrendous confirmation fight. Senators seem to demand that there always will be one. Perhaps the president should designate one of his nominees as the sacrificial lamb so that the others can survive unscathed. Given that this will not happen, what do the nominees have to look forward to?

Nominees will need to be prepared to explain themselves: "What's this about your child's nanny, Ms. Baird?" They will learn what most worries the senators, especially senators on their oversight and appropriating committees: "We will be watching, Mr. Watt." They may be required to make promises: "As for pursuing arms reduction with the Soviet Union, we will hold you to your commitments, Mr. Haig." They will too often have to endure being confronted by growl and swagger. This is no easy task for people who also think they are important. The best advice of the political sherpas who are most experienced at leading nominees through the confirmation process is to accept the short-term pain, then smile and grovel. In the end, senators give the president pretty much what he asks for, once they get the respect they think they deserve.

At last the team is in place: president, cabinet, White House staff. The final act of the transition is for someone to quote the favorite line of all political junkies: at the end of the 1972 movie, *The Candidate*, a dazed Robert Redford, the winning candidate, suddenly realizes that he must actually govern. "What," he asks, "do we do now?"

Notes

1. "Building an Administration," *New York Times*, December 14, 1976, p. 36.
2. Martin Anderson, *Revolution: The Reagan Legacy* (Stanford, Calif.: Hoover Institution Press, 1990), p. 196.
3. Edwin Meese III, *With Reagan: The Inside Story* (Washington: Regnery Gateway, 1992), p. 63.
4. For the sequence of presidential appointments made between election day and inauguration day, see appendix 4A; for the sequence of cabinet appointments, see appendix 4B.

5. Felix Belair Jr., "Harlow Is Liked by Both Parties," *New York Times*, November 14, 1968, p. 34.

6. Richard Nixon, *RN: The Memoirs of Richard Nixon* (New York: Grosset and Dunlap, 1978), p. 338. A very different version of why Shriver did not get the job appears in R. W. Apple Jr., "Nixon Picks Yost as UN Delegate in Surprise Move," *New York Times*, December 21, 1968, pp. 1, 18.

7. Robert B. Semple Jr. "Nixon Appoints Ehrlichman Counsel," *New York Times*, November 15, 1968, p. 32.

8. Herbert G. Klein, *Making It Perfectly Clear* (Doubleday, 1980), p. 41. Also see John Anthony Maltese, *Spin Control: The White House Office of Communications and the Management of Presidential News* (University of North Carolina Press, 1992), pp. 22–27.

9. R. W. Apple Jr., "Laird Choice of Nixon to Head Defense," *New York Times*, December 9, 1968, pp. 1, 43.

10. Robert Reinhold, "Scholars Praise Two Nixon Choices," *New York Times*, December 4, 1968, p. 32.

11. R. W. Apple Jr., "Nixon's Cabinet Due in Few Days," *New York Times*, December 8, 1968, p. 84.

12. Jonathan Friendly, "Articles about Possible Cabinet Nominees Raise Questions on Journalistic Standards," *New York Times*, December 9, 1980, p. B18.

13. Tom Wicker, "In The Nation: The More Things Change, Etc.," *New York Times*, December 12, 1968, p. 46.

14. R. W. Apple Jr., "Rustin Regrets Lack of Negro in Nixon Cabinet," *New York Times*, December 14, 1968, pp. 1, 26.

15. John Ehrlichman, *Witness to Power: The Nixon Years* (Simon and Schuster, 1982), p. 88.

16. William Safire, *Before the Fall: An Inside View of the Pre-Watergate White House* (Doubleday, 1975), p. 108.

17. Henry Kissinger, *White House Years* (Boston: Little, Brown, 1979), p. 26.

18. Quoted in William Beecher, "Business Leader Is Named by Laird as Pentagon No. 2," *New York Times,* December 31, 1968, pp. 1, 12.

19. "Conflict-of-Interest Standards," *New York Times*, January 19, 1969, p. E22.

20. "Cabinet Approved Except for Hickel," *New York Times*, January 21, 1969, pp. 1, 30.

21. "Conservation Front: Cloudy," *New York Times*, December 20, 1968, p. 46.

22. Quoted in E. W. Kenworthy, "Nixon Is Reported Considering Conservationist for Key Post," *New York Times*, January 12, 1969, p. 69.

23. See Stephen Hess and Sandy Northrop, *Drawn and Quartered: The History of American Political Cartoons* (Montgomery, Ala.: Elliot and Clark, 1996), p. 121.

24. See Stephen Hess, "The President: Is He the People's Choice?" *Information Please Almanac, 1977* (Simon and Schuster, 1976), p. 10.

25. James T. Wooten, "Carter Aide Chosen to Guide Transition," *New York Times*, November 11, 1976, p. 13.

26. Transcript of Carter news conference, *New York Times*, November 16, 1976, p. 32.

27. Robert Shogan, *Promises to Keep: Carter's First Hundred Days* (New York: Thomas Y. Crowell, 1977), p. 82.

28. Stephen Hess, "Making It Happen," in Barry P. Bosworth and others, *Critical Choices* (Brookings, 1989), pp. 98–101.

29. Quoted in Cyrus Vance, *Hard Choices* (Simon and Schuster, 1983), p. 30.

30. Transcript of Carter news conference, *New York Times*, December 4, 1976, p. 12.

31. "Text of Carter Statement on Conflicts of Interest and Ethics: Appointees Guidelines," *New York Times*, January 5, 1977, p. 17.

32. Paul Delaney, "Blacks Expect Gains for Help to Carter," *New York Times*, November 7, 1976, p. 39.

33. Transcript of Carter news conference, *New York Times*, December 17, 1976, p. B4.

34. "Ambassador to UN," *New York Times*, December 17, 1976, p. 26.

35. David E. Rosenbaum, "Carter Says Many Have Declined Posts; Mentions Three Blacks," *New York Times*, December 17, 1976, pp. 1, B5. Previously two white business leaders, A. W. Clausen of the Bank of America and Irving Shapiro of Du Pont, had withdrawn from consideration for the treasury post. Jane Cahill Pfeiffer of IBM declined to be secretary of commerce.

36. Tom Wicker, "The Dunlop Signal," *New York Times*, December 14, 1976, p. 37.

37. John W. Finney, "Finding a Job for Schlesinger," *New York Times*, December 14, 1976, p. 28. Also see David E. Rosenbaum, "Public Controversy Helps Carter in Selecting Cabinet, Aide Says," *New York Times*, December 18, 1976, p. 28.

38. William V. Shannon, "Guessing Game," *New York Times*, December 7, 1976, p. 41.

39. The number of federal departments dropped from twelve to eleven when the Post Office Department became an independent entity. Subsequently the Energy Department was created in 1977 and the Education Department in 1979, at which time the Department of Health, Education, and Welfare became the Department of Health and Human Services; the Veterans Administration became a department in 1989.

40. John B. Oakes, "A Conversation with Mr. Sorensen," *New York Times*, January 14, 1977, p. 23; Wendell Rawls Jr., "Sorensen Approval by Senate as Head of CIA in Doubt," *New York Times,* January 16, 1977, pp. 1, 24.

41. David E. Rosenbaum, "Senators Cordial to Adams at Confirmation Hearing," *New York Times*, January 8, 1977, p. 6.

42. Steven V. Roberts, "Cabinet Hearings Cast a Long Shadow," *New York Times*, January 6, 1981, p. B10.

43. Powell quoted in James T. Wooten, "Free Access by Staff to Carter Is Planned," *New York Times*, January 15, 1977, p. 1. Watson quoted in Charles Mohr, "No Command Role Expected," *New York Times*, January 15, 1977, p. 11.

44. Quoted in Hedrick Smith, "Transition Shaping Up as a Very Fast Pit Stop," *New York Times*, November 16, 1980, p. E1.

45. Quoted in Judith Miller, "Reagan's Day: A Fitting, a $16.50 Clip, and Work," *New York Times*, December 18, 1980, p. B17.

46. Meese, *With Reagan: The Inside Story*, p. 63.

47. Steven R. Weisman, "Reagan's 'Kitchen Cabinet' Strengthening Its Influence," *New York Times*, November 30, 1980, p. 36.

48. Lou Cannon, *President Reagan: The Role of a Lifetime* (Simon and Schuster, 1991), pp. 84–87.

49. Alexander M. Haig Jr., *Caveat* (New York: Macmillan, 1984), p. 1; Donald T. Regan, *For the Record* (San Diego: Harcourt Brace Jovanovich, 1988), p. 139; Terrel H. Bell, *The Thirteenth Man: A Reagan Cabinet Memoir* (New York: Free Press, 1988), p. 2.

50. William Safire, "Reagan's Mr. Clean," *New York Times*, December 8, 1980, p. 27.

51. Associated Press, "Mrs. Armstrong Decides to Bar a Post in Cabinet," *New York Times*, November 27, 1980, p. 24.

52. Cannon, *President Reagan: The Role of a Lifetime*, pp. 78–79.

53. David A. Stockman, *The Triumph of Politics* (Harper and Row, 1986), p. 70.

54. Associated Press, "Financial Reports Show That Ten Members of Cabinet Are Worth $1 Million or More," *New York Times*, January 26, 1981, p. 24.

55. Quoted in "Unsolicited Advice for Mr. Smith," *New York Times,* January 20, 1981, p. 30.

56. Steven R. Weisman, "Reagan's Inside Team Will Hold Much of Real Power," *New York Times*, January 4, 1981, p. E2.

57. Quoted in Adam Clymer, "Manager of Only Show in Town," *New York Times*, November 7, 1980, p. 14.

58. See James A. Baker III, *The Politics of Diplomacy* (Putnam's Sons, 1995), pp. 17–19.

59. Quoted in Maureen Dowd, "Bush's Fierce Loyalty Raises Debate on Whether It Hinders His Judgement," *New York Times*, March 10, 1989, p. B6.

60. See Herbert S. Parmet, *George Bush: The Life of a Lone-Star Yankee* (Scribner, 1997), pp. 360–61.

61. "Bush's Team: The First Choices," *New York Times*, January 23, 1989, p. 20.

62. Gerald Boyd, "Circle of Senior Aides Helps Bush Fill Top Posts," *New York Times*, December 8, 1988, p. B22.

63. Transcript of Bush news conference, *New York Times*, December 20, 1988, p. B8.

64. Transcript of Bush news conference, *New York Times*, December 7, 1988, p. B12.

65. Quoted from *USA Today* in R. W. Apple Jr., "Bush's Beltway Team," *New York Times*, January 13, 1989, pp. 1, D18.

66. Steven V. Roberts, "Sullivan's Rough Trip from Halls of Academe," *New York Times*, February 2, 1989, p. B5.

67. Quoted in Steven V. Roberts, "Bush Will Stand by Nominee to Health Post, Officials Say," *New York Times*, January 25, 1989, pp. 1, 16.

68. Quoted in Steven V. Roberts, "Cabinet Choice Fielding Hard Questions in Drills," *New York Times*, February 5, 1989, p. 26.

69. Andrew Rosenthal, "Tower Begins Confirmation Hearings Today," *New York Times*, January 25, 1989, p. 17.

70. Gerald M. Boyd, "Bush Names Tower to Pentagon Post, Ending Long Delay," *New York Times*, December 17, 1988, pp. 1, 11.

71. William Safire, "Towering Inferno," *New York Times*, February 13, 1989, p. 21.

72. Michael Oreskes, "Senate Rejects Tower, 53-47," *New York Times*, March 10, 1989, pp. 1, B6.

73. Quoted in Susan F. Rasky, "Panel, Beginning an End to Ordeal, Sets Vote on Tower Nomination," *New York Times*, February 22, 1989, p. 17.

74. Andrew Rosenthal, "On the Road to the Vote on Tower: A Series of White House Missteps," *New York Times*, February 26, 1989, pp. 1, 26.

75. Tower blamed his downfall on the animus and ambition of Sam Nunn; see John Tower, *Consequences: A Personal and Political Memoir* (Boston: Little, Brown, 1991), pp. 203, 217.

76. Quoted in Andrew Rosenthal, "On Capitol Hill, a Struggle for the Record," *New York Times*, March 5, 1989, p. E1.

77. Gerald M. Boyd, "Bush Tries to Dispel 'Drift' Image, Says Administration Is 'on Track,'" *New York Times*, March 8, 1989, p. B7; George Bush quoted in R. W. Apple Jr., "An Attempt to Recover," *New York Times*, March 11, 1989, p. 10.

78. Richard L. Berke, "Job Interviews with Clinton: Mostly a Friendly Little Chat," *New York Times*, December 6, 1992, pp. 1, 30. Also see Elizabeth Drew, *On the Edge: The Clinton Presidency* (Simon and Schuster, 1994), pp. 21–35.

79. Gwen Ifill, "People in Line for Jobs: The 'Short List' Grows," *New York Times*, November 23, 1992, p. 14.

80. "Excerpts from Clinton's Announcement of Appointments to Economic Posts," *New York Times*, December 11, 1992, p. 36.

81. "The Clinton Anti-Gridlock Team," *New York Times*, December 11, 1992, p. 38.

82. Neil A. Lewis, "Clinton Expected to Name Woman Attorney General," *New York Times*, December 9, 1992, pp. 1, B12.

83. Gwen Ifill, "Clinton Widens His Circle, Naming Four Social Activists," *New York Times*, December 12, 1992, pp. 1, 10.

84. Ibid., p. 10.

85. Thomas L. Friedman, "Clinton's Cabinet Choices Put Him at Center, Balancing Competing Factions," *New York Times*, December 27, 1992, p. 22.

86. Smeal quoted in Gwen Ifill, "Clinton Wants Wife at Cabinet Table," *New York Times*, December 19, 1992, p. 8; Clinton quoted in Gwen Ifill, "Clinton Chooses Two and Deplores Idea of Cabinet Quotas," *New York Times*, December 22, 1992, pp. 1, B9. In response, E. J. Dionne Jr. wrote that "presidential Cabinets have always been the product of a similar kind of bean-counting.

What's changed is the nature of the beans we count" (*Washington Post*, January 12, 1993, p. 17).

87. Quoted in Catherine S. Manegold, "Clinton Ire on Appointments Startles Women," *New York Times*, December 23, 1992, p. 15.

88. Adam Clymer, "Push for Diversity May Cause Reversal on Interior Secretary," *New York Times*, December 23, 1992, pp. 1, 15.

89. George Stephanopoulos, *All Too Human: A Political Education* (Boston: Little, Brown, 1999), p. 118.

90. Jeffrey H. Birnbaum, *Madhouse: The Private Turmoil of Working for the President* (Times Books, 1996), p. 21.

91. Quoted in Michael Kelly, "Clinton Cancels Baird Nomination for Justice Dept.," *New York Times*, January 22, 1993, pp. 1, 14.

92. R. W. Apple Jr., "Case of Double Jeopardy," *New York Times*, February 6, 1993, pp. 1, 8.

93. Quoted in Gwen Ifill, "The Baird Appointment: In Trouble from the Start, Then a Firestorm," *New York Times*, January 23, 1993, p. 8.

94. Michael Kelly, "Clinton's Chief of Staff Ponders Undefined Post," *New York Times*, December 14, 1992, p. B6.

95. Richard L. Berke, "Clinton Selects a Mostly Youthful Group of White House Aides," *New York Times*, January 15, 1993, p. 14.

96. Russell Baker, "Must Be Democrats," *New York Times*, January 16, 1993, p. 21. The "hit the ground stumbling" impression was further exacerbated when Clinton was forced to withdraw his nomination of Lani Guinier to be assistant attorney general in charge of the Civil Rights Division after saying he could not defend many of the views expressed in her writings; see Neil A. Lewis, "Clinton Abandons His Nominee for Rights Post amid Opposition," *New York Times*, June 4, 1993, pp. 1, 18.

97. "Transcript of President-elect Bush's News Conference," December 28, 2000. Transcribed by eMediaMillWorks for www.washingtonpost.com/onpolitics (January 30, 2001).

98. Dana Milbank, "White House Distaff Staff Make Family a Priority," *Washington Post*, February 15, 2001, pp. C1, C4. Milbank notes that in 1998 six of the twenty-nine top Clinton staffers were women.

99. "Transcript of President-elect Bush's News Conference," December 28, 2000.

100. "Bush Introduction of Elaine Chao for Labor, Robert Zoellick as U.S. Trade Rep.," January 11, 2001. Transcribed by eMediaMillWorks for www.washingtonpost.com/onpolitics (January 30, 2001).

101. Ibid.

102. Dana Milbank and Thomas D. Edsall, "Chavez Pulls Out as Labor Nominee; Bush Pick Acknowledges She 'Wasn't Forthcoming' on Illegal Immigrant Issue," *Washington Post*, January 10, 2001, p. 1.

103. David S. Broder, "Who Is Ashcroft?" *Washington Post*, January 23, 2001, p. 17.

104. "Excerpts from Remarks in the Senate Debate on the Ashcroft Nomination," *New York Times*, February 2, 2001, p. 14.

105. Quoted in Neil A. Lewis, "Democratic Leader Assures Bush on Ashcroft Nomination," *New York Times,* January 25, 2001, p. 20.

106. Rebecca Adams, "Norton Outmaneuvers Critics," *Congressional Quarterly Weekly,* January 27, 2001, p. 230.

107. "President-elect Bush Names Staff Members," December 17, 2000. Transcribed by eMediaMillWorks for www.washingtonpost.com/onpolitics (January 30, 2001).

108. "Bush Announces Three Cabinet Nominees," January 2, 2001. Transcribed by eMediaMillWorks for www.washingtonpost.com/onpolitics (January 30, 2001).

109. Milbank and Edsall, "Chavez Pulls Out as Labor Nominee."

110. The figures exclude cabinet secretaries who died in office or were given more important positions in government or in their presidents' campaigns.

111. These suggestions are deeply influenced by three scholars and friends who have led the way in studying presidential transitions: Richard E. Neustadt, Charles O. Jones, and James P. Pfiffner.

112. Remarks spoken at Heritage Foundation conference, "Achieving Successful Transition," Washington, May 31, 2000.

113. Transition organizers should read Bradley H. Patterson Jr., *The White House Staff* (Brookings, 2000).

114. Quoted in Kenneth T. Walsh, *Feeding the Beast: The White House versus the Press* (Random House, 1996), p. 9.

115. Quoted in Stephen Hess, "President Clinton and the White House Press Corps: Year One," *Media Studies Journal* (Spring 1994), p. 2.

116. Charles O. Jones, *Passages to the Presidency* (Brookings, 1998), pp. 134–72.

Appendix 4A: Sequence of Presidential Appointments

Sequence based on dates when the president announced the appointee's nomination.

Richard Nixon

1st week	personal secretary; congressional liaison
2d week	chief of staff; press secretary; counsel
3d week	director of Office of Communications
4th week	chair of Council of Economic Advisers; national security assistant; science adviser
5th week	none
6th week	entire cabinet; director of Bureau of the Budget
7th week	United Nations representative
8th week	none
9th week	none

10th week	none
11th week	director of Central Intelligence Agency

Jimmy Carter

1st week	none
2d week	press secretary
3d week	none
4th week	none
5th week	secretary of state; director of Office of Management and Budget
6th week	secretaries of the treasury, transportation
7th week	secretaries of the interior, commerce, agriculture, defense, labor, housing and urban development; attorney general; national security assistant; United Nations representative; chair of Council of Economic Advisers
8th week	secretaries of health, education, and welfare, energy; director of Central Intelligence Agency
9th week	none
10th week	none
11th week	chief assistant and other top White House aides

Ronald Reagan

1st week	none
2d week	chief of staff; counselor
3d week	none
4th week	none
5th week	none
6th week	secretaries of commerce, the treasury, transportation, health and human services, defense, state, labor; attorney general; director of Office of Management and Budget; director of Central Intelligence Agency
7th week	congressional liaison; domestic policy adviser; secretaries of the interior, energy, housing and urban development, agriculture; national security assistant; United Nations representative
8th week	none
9th week	press secretary
10th week	secretary of education
11th week	none

George Bush

1st week	secretary of state; counsel
2d week	chief of staff; secretaries of the treasury, education, attorney general; director of Office of Management and Budget
3d week	press secretary; national security assistant
4th week	none
5th week	secretary of commerce; director of Central Intelligence Agency; United Nations representative; chair of Council of Economic Advisers; trade representative
6th week	secretaries of agriculture, defense, housing and urban development
7th week	secretaries of transportation, the interior, health and human services, veterans affairs, labor; director of Environmental Protection Agency
8th week	none
9th week	secretary of energy; director of drug policy
10th week	none

Bill Clinton

1st week	none
2d week	none
3d week	none
4th week	none
5th week	none
6th week	chief of staff; director of National Economic Council; secretaries of the treasury, labor, health and human services, commerce; director of Office of Management and Budget; chair of the Council of Economic Advisers; director of Environmental Protection Agency
7th week	secretaries of housing and urban development, veterans affairs, education, energy, defense, state; director of Central Intelligence Agency; United Nations representative; national security assistant
8th week	secretaries of the interior, agriculture, transportation; attorney general; trade representative
9th week	none
10th week	none
11th week	White House staff, including congressional liaison, press secretary, domestic policy adviser, counsel

George W. Bush

1st week	none (contested election, weeks 1 through 5)
2d week	none
3d week	none
4th week	chief of staff
5th week	none
6th week	secretary of state
7th week	national security adviser; counsel; White House counselor; secretaries of the treasury, commerce, housing and urban development, agriculture; attorney general; director of Environmental Protection Agency; director of Office of Management and Budget
8th week	secretaries of defense, the interior, education, veterans affairs, health and human services; press secretary
9th week	secretaries of energy, labor (withdrawn), transportation; economic adviser; director of Federal Emergency Management Agency
10th week	secretary of labor; trade representative
11th week	director of Central Intelligence Agency

Source: Data from Charles O. Jones, *Passages to the Presidency from Campaigning to Governing* (Brookings, 1998), pp. 94–95, and additional information.

Appendix 4B: Sequence of Cabinet Secretary Appointments

Dates listed are those on which the president announced the appointee's nomination.

Richard Nixon

December 11, 1968	entire cabinet

Jimmy Carter

December 3, 1976	Cyrus Vance (State)
December 14, 1976	Brock Adams (Transportation); Michael Blumenthal (Treasury)
December 18, 1976	Cecil Andrus (Interior)
December 20, 1976	Griffin Bell (Justice); Robert Bergland (Agriculture); Juanita Kreps (Commerce)
December 21, 1976	Harold Brown (Defense); Patricia Harris (Housing and Urban Development); Ray Marshall (Labor)

December 23, 1976	Joseph Califano (Health, Education, and Welfare); James Schlesinger (Energy)

Ronald Reagan

December 11, 1980	Malcolm Baldridge (Commerce); Drew Lewis (Transportation); Donald Regan (Treasury); Richard Schweiker (Health and Human Services); Caspar Weinberger (Defense); William French Smith (Justice)
December 16, 1980	Raymond Donovan (Labor); Alexander Haig (State)
December 22, 1980	James Edwards (Energy); Samuel Pierce (Housing and Urban Development); James Watt (Interior)
December 23, 1980	John Block (Agriculture)
January 7, 1981	Terrel Bell (Education)

George Bush

November 9, 1988	James Baker (State)
November 15, 1988	Nicholas Brady (Treasury)
November 21, 1988	Lauro Cavazos (Education); Richard Thornburgh (Justice)
December 6, 1988	Robert Mosbacher (Commerce)
December 14, 1988	Clayton Yeutter (Agriculture)
December 16, 1988	John Tower (Defense) Rejected by Senate March 9, 1989
December 20, 1988	Jack Kemp (Housing and Urban Development)
December 22, 1988	Manuel Lujan (Interior); Louis Sullivan (Health and Human Services); Samuel Skinner (Transportation)
December 24, 1988	Elizabeth Dole (Labor)
January 12, 1989	James Watkins (Energy)
March 10, 1989	Dick Cheney (Defense)

Bill Clinton

December 10, 1992	Lloyd Bentsen (Treasury)
December 11, 1992	Robert Reich (Labor); Donna Shalala (Health and Human Services)
December 12, 1992	Ronald Brown (Commerce)
December 17, 1992	Jesse Brown (Veterans Affairs); Henry Cisneros (Housing and Urban Development)
December 21, 1992	Hazel O'Leary (Energy); Richard Riley (Education)

December 22, 1992	Les Aspin (Defense); Warren Christopher (State)
December 24, 1992	Mike Espy (Agriculture); Federico Peña (Transportation); Zöe Baird (Justice), withdrawn January 22, 1993; Bruce Babbitt (Interior)
February 11, 1993	Janet Reno (Justice)
George W. Bush	
December 16, 2000	Colin Powell (State)
December 20, 2000	Paul O'Neill (Treasury); Donald Evans (Commerce); Melquiades Martinez (Housing and Urban Development); Ann Veneman (Agriculture)
December 22, 2000	John Ashcroft (Justice)
December 28, 2000	Donald Rumsfeld (Defense)
December 29, 2000	Gale Norton (Interior); Rod Paige (Education); Anthony Principi (Veterans Affairs); Tommy Thompson (Health and Human Services)
January 2, 2001	Spencer Abraham (Energy); Linda Chavez (Labor), withdrawn January 9, 2001; Norman Mineta (Transportation)
January 11, 2001	Elaine Chao (Labor)

Source: Data from Charles O. Jones, *Passages to the Presidency from Campaigning to Governing* (Brookings, 1998), p. 97, and additional information.

CHAPTER FIVE

The Senate: An "Obstacle Course" for Executive Appointments?

BURDETT LOOMIS

When you draw a line here and say, "no further," then you've basically stopped the work of the Senate. . . . It isn't a threat. . . . It's a reality.
Senator Larry Craig, June 2000

FUELED BY ANALYSES from both journalists and academics, the conventional wisdom has grown up that the Senate has become increasingly hostile to presidential appointees. Would-be judges, justices, ambassadors, commissioners, and executive branch officials are "Borked" by vicious interests and their Capitol Hill coconspirators. Appointees are "held hostage" by senators who seek substantive tradeoffs or the confirmation of their own favored candidates for judicial or regulatory posts. Senators place "holds" on nominations, thus delaying the process interminably. All in all, the Senate's performance, at least as commonly portrayed, does little to enhance the appointment confirmation process—quite the contrary. The Senate, to hark back to Robert Bendiner's description of more than thirty years ago, seems a major culprit in the lengthy and often distasteful politics of confirmation—a veritable "obstacle course on Capitol Hill."[1]

This characterization fits with our understanding of the Senate of the past twenty years. As detailed by Barbara Sinclair and her fellow congressional scholars, the Senate has become both highly individualized and highly partisan.[2] At first blush, this appears an unlikely pairing. After all, one notion of a highly partisan legislature would have senators subordinating their own desires to the good of the entire partisan caucus. Nevertheless, individualism has flourished to the point that the Senate, once a bastion of collegiality, has become progressively a less civil, less cordial place—sometimes almost rivaling the raucous House of the 1990s in its testiness.[3] The lengthy, increasingly bitter partisan standoff over the last year of the Clinton administration gives further credence to the belief that the Senate has evolved into a particularly hostile environment in which appointments from a president of the chamber's minority party would be harshly treated.

The early evidence on the Senate's treatment of George W. Bush's cabinet appointees illustrates how the politics of group mobilization continues to fuel hostility within the Senate, especially when a president makes an appointment that is perceived as confrontational (such as that of former senator John Ashcroft for attorney general). In the turmoil of the shifting balance of power in the narrowly divided Senate of the 107th Congress, the opportunities for delay and game playing are obvious.

Headlines, assumptions, and conventional wisdom, however, can be wrong, to a greater or lesser extent; and for this reason it might be wise to examine the data on confirmations. Does the Senate now take longer to confirm nominees than it used to, especially in the modern era? If so, how much longer? To the point of really making a difference? Are more nominations withdrawn? Or returned to the executive? Are some executive departments more inviting targets than others? Are some Senate committees especially difficult to navigate?

Second, it might well be asked how Senate processes might be altered in a partisan, individualistic era, especially given that the chamber usually operates through the mechanism of unanimous consent as opposed to the rule-dominated House. Are there any realistic prospects for "reform"? Even if the conventional wisdom proves accurate, and presidential appointments do often run into a congressional roadblock, there may be little that can be done within the legislative branch. Indeed, political scientist Chris Deering's assessment of Senate confirmation politics in 1986 bears repeating: "The relationship between the executive and legislative branches . . . remains essentially political. . . . The Senate's role in the review of executive personnel is but one example of that relationship. The Senate's role in the confirmation process was designed not to eliminate politics but to make possible the use of politics as a safeguard . . . , a protection against tyranny."[4] Given the rancor of the 1990s, one might well argue that more is going on than "the protection against tyranny," but exactly what remains open to question.

The following discussion focuses on appointments to top-level, policy-making positions in the executive branch that the Senate confirms. This excludes ambassadors, directors of regulatory commissions, military commissions, and federal attorneys. The emphasis here is placed on the 329 full-time positions in the fourteen executive departments that require presidential appointment and the approval of the Senate.[5] The positions typically include each department's secretary, deputy secretary, undersecretary, all the assistant secretaries, general counsels, and inspectors general and the heads of important units like the Food and Drug Administration, the Immigration and Naturalization Service, and the Bureau of the Census. The number of positions ranges from forty-eight at the State Department to fourteen in the Department of Veterans Affairs; only State and Defense (with forty-three) have more than thirty slots that require confirmation.

Executive Branch Appointments and the Senate

In the less-than-distant past, a president could expect that his appointments would be confirmed without much acrimony (or much scrutiny, to tell the truth). To the extent that senators examined the records of the nominees at all, they focused on financial conflicts of interest rather than policy issues or ideology.[6] Absent some scandal, the working assumption has been that presidents should have their nominees confirmed in a timely manner.

To understand the magnitude of any "problem" with Senate confirmations of executive branch appointments, we need to know the length of the Senate confirmation process and the extent to which some appointments take a disproportionately long time to be resolved; the number of withdrawals, returned appointments, and acting appointees; and the way in which appointments are processed under differing conditions, such as divided government and various periods of a presidency (especially in the transition as opposed to the remainder of a president's tenure). Unfortunately, the available data do not allow for systematic explorations before the Reagan administration, so comparisons over time are perforce limited.[7] Nevertheless, some trends do begin to appear that converge with the emergence of the modern, transformed Senate, replete with enhanced partisanship and greater individualism.

First, the confirmation process has grown longer. In 1981, the Republican Senate took an average of thirty days to confirm Ronald Reagan's first wave of top-level executive branch appointees; in 1993, the Democratic Senate took forty-five days to confirm Bill Clinton's initial set of nominees, an increase of 50 percent (see table 5-1).[8] Six years later, in the first session of the 106th Congress, the confirmation process had dragged out to eighty-seven days, almost twice the 1993 figure and almost three times the 1981 length. The comparisons are skewed somewhat by two factors: the Republican control of the Senate in 1999 and the less urgent, less visible nature of confirming appointees late in an administration compared with the initial round of appointments, which receive considerable attention within the context of the need to put a government in place a few weeks after the November election.

Nevertheless, the process has generally grown longer, both early and late in an administration. Although both George Bush and Bill Clinton obtained confirmation for their executive appointees within forty-five days in their first two years in office, the process lengthened for Clinton in the 104th through 106th Congresses, when he faced a Republican Senate. In the last two years of the Bush presidency (1991–92), the Democratic Senate took an average of sixty-one days to confirm his nominees. In contrast, the Republican Senate of the 1995–99 period took about eighty-six days—almost three months—to confirm the typical high-ranking Clinton nominee for an executive branch position.

Given that the median figures are somewhat lower than the averages, it becomes apparent that a substantial number of Clinton's appointees often faced extended periods of uncertainty as they waited for confirmation. During the Bush administration (1989–92), the confirmation process lasted one hundred days or more for only 25 of its 389 successful nominees. Conversely, in just one Congress (the 105th), 40 of Clinton's nominees waited at least 100 days before winning confirmation. Overall, almost 25 percent of Clinton's nominees faced at least a hundred-day confirmation period (and these were the successful nominees).

In addition, although the 1999 confirmation process averaged almost three months when the Congress was in session, these figures do not include the thirty-four days of late-summer congressional recess. In terms of the actual number of days, many of Clinton's 1999 appointees faced an average confirmation process of 121 days—almost exactly four months. This does not mean, of course, that positions remained vacant, because under the 1998 Federal Vacancies Reform Act, many slots were filled by

Table 5-1. *Average and Median Length of Senate Confirmations, by Congress, 1989–99*

Days

Department	*101st (1989–90)*	*102d (1991–92)*	*103d (1993–94)*	*104th (1995–96)*	*105th (1997–98)*	*106th (1999)*
Agriculture						
n	15	6	14	5	6	2
Average	42.1	58.5	25.9	60.0	37.7	75.5
Median	19	57	22	47	28	76
Commerce						
n	28	11	23	3	17	7
Average	64.8	68.0	58.9	97.7	87.5	109.1
Median	57	66	37	95	88	72
Defense						
n	39	13	53	8	25	8
Average	28.8	70.9	44.6	87.4	49.9	48.1
Median	33	63	46	52	36	39
Education						
n	14	11	15	3	4	3
Average	38.7	72.2	47.4	180.3	120.0	112.7
Median	43	69	38	164	127	108
Energy						
n	15	8	17	4	11	7
Average	48.6	79.5	41.3	135.0	74.1	82.0
Median	60	52	38	153	56	74
Health and Human Services						
n	16	4	19	2	10	...
Average	26.6	54.3	49.4	85.0	118.7	...
Median	32	51	37	85	109	...
Housing and Urban Development						
n	12	4	15	4	10	2
Average	56.8	90.5	28.0	124.8	79.2	79.0
Median	62	72	29	111	78	79
Interior						
n	14	2	14	5	9	1
Average	35.1	86.0	32.6	81.4	51.8	14.0
Median	36	86	29	90	35	14

(continued)

acting officials.[9] Nevertheless, the lengthening confirmation process in the Senate indicates that a problem does exist, and all the more so when this period is added to the increasing amount of time that the president has taken to make appointments.[10]

In a related vein, some Senate committees take a disproportionate time to process appointments. At the start of both the Bush and the Clinton

Table 5-1. *Average and Median Length of Senate Confirmations, by Congress, 1989–99 (Continued)*

Days

Department	*101st (1989–90)*	*102d (1991–92)*	*103d (1993–94)*	*104th (1995–96)*	*105th (1997–98)*	*106th (1999)*
Justice						
n	21	8	27	1	8	3
Average	54.6	94.6	71.2	42.0	91.8	83.7
Median	46	94	60	42	94	65
Labor						
n	14	8	19	3	10	5
Average	55.9	48.5	45.6	85.0	90.3	175.6
Median	29	49	47	83	76	115
State						
n	37	13	32	6	27	14
Average	35.8	37.8	29.2	81.7	77.2	73.3
Median	31	30	27	79	69	44
Transportation						
n	16	10	16	3	11	3
Average	41.8	29.8	56.4	162.0	60.8	102.3
Median	27	35	37	111	57	66
Treasury						
n	24	8	24	11	12	11
Average	38.2	27.5	41.8	68.4	87.9	81.9
Median	27	35	30	80	81	75
Veterans						
n	13	5	11	1	6	1
Average	61.2	74.9	34.1	92.0	129.2	80.0
Median	74	85	23	92	92	80
Total, by Congress	278	112	304	69	176	67
Overall Average	43.1	60.8	44.9	94.5	77.8	86.8
Overall Median	38	55	36	98	67	(66)

Source: Data from Biennial Congressional Research Service Reports, 1989 to 1999, compiled by Rogelio Garcia.

administrations the Commerce and Judiciary Committees extended their processes substantially beyond the average of all confirmations. In contrast, the Foreign Relations Committee expeditiously processed top State Department nominees as both administrations took shape. Although the Republican Senate systematically dragged its feet on Clinton's appointees in the 1995–2000 period, it did not single out any executive branch

Table 5-2. *Outcome of Executive Branch Nominations, by Administration, 1981–99*

Administration and year	Total	Confirmed		Returned		Withdrawn	
	Number	Number	Percentage	Number	Percentage	Number	Percentage
Bill Clinton							
1999	*85*[a]	*68*	*80*	*0*	*0*	*3*	*4*
1997–98	*207*[b]	*166*	*80*	*16*	*8*	*9*	*4*
1995–96	*61*	*59*	*75*	*1*	*24*	*1*	*2*
1993–94	323	310	96	9	3	4	1
George Bush							
1991–92	*136*	*111*	*82*	*21*	*15*	*4*	*3*
1989–90	*286*	*278*	*96*	*8*	*3*	*0*	*0*
Ronald Reagan							
1987–88	*159*	*131*	*83*	*24*	*15*	*4*	*3*
1985–86	182	165	91	14	8	3	2
1983–84	111	93	84	18	16	0	0
1981–82	269	260	97	6	2	3	1

Source: Data from Congressional Research Service studies, 1983 through 2000, compiled by Rogelio Garcia.
Note: Italicized items denote control of Senate by opposing party. Nine recess appointments were made in 1998.
a. Includes fourteen carryover appointments.
b. Includes sixteen carryover appointments.

departments—with one major exception. Education Department nominees have required exceptional patience in this era; confirmation of Education nominees took more than half again as long as the average for all appointees named by Clinton. Between 1995 and 1999, Education Department nominees required more than 130 days, on average, to win confirmation, and only two of ten appointees won approval in fewer than 100 days (excluding recess days).

A second set of indicators of whether a problem exists relates to the likelihood that a president's appointments will be confirmed (see table 5-2). How often does the Senate return appointments to the executive branch or successfully press for the withdrawal of nominations? Again, looking at the rates under differing circumstances is instructive. The president is more likely to do well with the appointments he makes in the year or two following his first election than at any other time during his administration, and divided government may make a difference in affecting confirmation rates.

Bill Clinton's 1993 record of cabinet appointments merits particular attention in that it demonstrates how quickly an administration can get its top initial appointees confirmed when his party also controls the

Senate. In 1993, the Senate held hearings and processed fourteen top Clinton appointments within a single day of the formal presentation of their nominations. This record is all the more impressive given the highly negative impression of the Clinton transition as a whole.

As illustrated in table 5-2, Presidents Reagan, Bush, and Clinton have fared similarly in winning confirmation for their nominees. They all won approval of more than 95 percent of their appointees in the first two years of their administrations, but the level of success tailed off for the remainder of their tenures in office. To the extent that a trend emerges, it reinforces the inference that the Senate has raised more obstacles over time. Ronald Reagan's nominees were confirmed at an 86 percent clip between 1983 and 1988, whereas Bill Clinton won approval for only 78 percent of his later appointments. Clinton faced a Republican Senate, however, for the entire six-year stretch, while Reagan dealt with a Democratic chamber only in the last two years of his administration, when his confirmation rate fell to 83 percent (very similar to George Bush's 82 percent success rate in 1991–92, under similar conditions).

Considering both the length of the process and the rate of confirmations, the picture becomes clearer. Especially with a Senate controlled by the opposition party, presidents can expect progressively longer confirmation processes that will frequently result in withdrawn or returned nominations. Adding insult to injury, many of these withdrawals and returns come after extended periods of waiting, which often drag out as long as or longer than many confirmations. Under Clinton, this was especially notable in the Justice Department. There, in mid-2000, ten of twenty-seven slots were filled with acting appointees, as the Senate and the Clinton administration fought out many of their postimpeachment differences within the confines of this department.

A summary view of confirmations over the past two decades indicates that the Senate process has grown longer, that divided government contributes a bit to lower rates of confirmation, and that there has been a modest overall decline in the president's capacity to win approval in the Senate for his top-level executive branch nominees. In addition, certain departments (Education, Justice under Clinton) may well be singled out for special attention by particular groups of Republican senators, working with or through the party leadership. At the same time, President Clinton did win confirmation of 96 percent of his nominees in the first two years of his administration, albeit with less dispatch than had Ronald Reagan in 1981. This leads us to consider whether the Senate is truly the culprit here and, if so, whether something might realistically be done to affect the way the chamber handles the confirmation of presidential nominees.

The Senate: Partisan, Individualistic, and Separate

Aside from anecdotal evidence of particular bitter confirmation fights, such as former senator John Tower's failure to win confirmation as secretary of defense in 1989, or ineptly handled appointments (for example, Lani Guinier and Zöe Baird in the Clinton transition), we have little systematic evidence of how the Senate affects confirmation politics in the post-1980 era of increased individualism and stronger partisanship.[11] Nevertheless, convincing evidence does exist that the Senate has become both more individualistic and more partisan. Sinclair, for example, reports steady growth in filibusters over the past forty years, and especially in the last twenty, and Sarah Binder and Steven Smith demonstrate that the use of filibusters continues to reflect the policy goals of individual senators, groups of senators, and, at times, the minority party.[12] Moreover, the Senate has increasingly come to consider itself an equal partner within the appointments process. As separation-of-powers scholar Louis Fisher observes, "The mere fact that the President submits a name for consideration does not obligate the Senate to act promptly."[13] Indeed, the Senate's willingness to sit on a nomination may reflect its status in a "separate-but-equal" system.

Nevertheless, it is the unlikely combination of individualism and partisanship that defines the contemporary Senate, as Sinclair notes:

> By the mid-1970s an individualist Senate had emerged. The Senate had become a body in which every member regardless of seniority considered himself entitled to participate on any issue that interested him for either constituency or policy reasons. Senators took for granted that they—and their colleagues—would regularly exploit the powers the Senate rules gave them. Senators became increasingly outward-directed, focusing on their links with interest groups, policy communities, and the media more than their ties with each other.
>
> By the late 1980s, another major change in senators' behavior became manifest. Senators were increasingly voting along partisan lines. In the late 1960s and early 1970s, only about a third of Senate roll call votes pitted a majority of Democrats against a majority of

> Republicans. By the 1990s, from half to two-thirds of roll calls were such party votes. The frequency with which senators voted with their partisan colleagues on party votes increased as well. By the 1990s a typical party vote saw well over 80 percent of the Democrats voting together on one side and well over 80 percent of the Republicans on the other.[14]

As with appropriations and other legislative processes, the confirmation of executive branch nominees has been affected by enhanced individualism and heightened partisanship. Every senator can place a "hold" on a nomination—delaying it, if not delivering to it a death sentence—though this tactic has been used more visibly on ambassadorial appointments than on executive branch choices.[15] Guarantees by the Senate leadership to the contrary, the practice of placing holds on legislation and nominations remains an option for any senator and especially those in the majority, who have the ear of their leader. Glen Krutz, Richard Fleischer, and Jon Bond argue that "negative entrepreneurs" in the Senate seek to build cases on ideological, ethical, and qualifications grounds that tend to change over time (for example, the so-called nanny problem—of hiring illegal aliens and not paying Social Security taxes—that has confronted Baird and others).[16] As one successful (but befuddled) nominee recounted, "It's very difficult to determine who is opposing the nomination and for what reasons."[17]

In addition, even noncontroversial nominations can fall victim to the highly partisan environment of Senate politics as nominees are "held hostage" to other nominations, to appropriations bills, or to substantive legislation. The most notable recent example of this interbranch tug-of-war came with Clinton's nomination of the veteran diplomat Richard Holbrooke to become U.S. ambassador to the United Nations. Aside from enduring extended attacks on his public record and personal finances, Holbrooke became a pawn in two ideological wars—the hostility of some senators toward the United Nations and the desire of other senators to see the Republican campaign finance scholar Bradley Smith appointed to the Federal Election Commission. Both Holbrooke and Smith were eventually confirmed, though not in a one-for-one exchange. Holbrooke's delay was seen as highly unusual by the Senate historian Richard Baker, and the Heritage Foundation congressional expert Marshall Wittman observed that although "there is a Senate tradition of holding Presidential nominees hostage for other ends, . . . what's unique is this one is at the level of the UN ambassador."[18] In short, where there is real controversy, as with the appointment of Bill Lann Lee to head the Justice Department's Civil Rights Division, partisan conflict increases and extends beyond the Congress to the Senate's relationship with the White House.[19]

The Senate's behavior on nominations has had the consequence of making potential nominees wary of considering a prospective appointment. Responding to a survey conducted between July and October 2000, one-half of an elite sample of possible top-level appointees concluded that the Senate is "too demanding, making [the] process an ordeal."[20] Thus the Senate's slow and sometimes highly political confirmation practices have an impact even before a candidate's name has been submitted. Moreover, perceptions of the process appear to have grown worse over time. In a survey of top-level officials who had been confirmed between 1984 and 1999, almost half the respondents (46 percent) judged the Senate process an ordeal. Moreover, 24 percent of those who were confirmed in the 1964–84 period felt that the Senate process took too long, but 39 percent of the later appointees came to this conclusion.[21]

Confirmation and the Senate

The great majority of presidential appointees to high-level executive positions win approval by the Senate, although the rate of confirmation success hovers at about 80 percent in the years after a newly elected president initially constructs his administration. Adding to their uncertainty, these later appointees must wait an average of four months for the Senate to act, once it has received the nomination. The process is long, and the outcome uncertain, for these nominees. Add to this the partisan politicking and the intense scrutiny that can occur, and it is no wonder that some potential officeholders decline the honor of nomination.

Is there any indication that the Senate might smooth the way for future nominees? Given the profound changes in the chamber over the past twenty-five years—the great latitude allowed individual members and the intense partisanship that dominates much decisionmaking—it seems unlikely that reformers would profit much from attempting to reshape Senate procedures. Nevertheless, some potential for change may exist. Former senator Nancy Kassebaum Baker, for example, has called for limiting holds to fourteen days and for mandating a confirmation vote in forty-five days, save for exceptional circumstances. There is little reason to believe, however, that an individualistic, closely divided, and highly partisan Senate will bow to such requests.

In terms of timely confirmation of presidential appointees, the best circumstance would be for the same party to control both the Senate and the presidency. Although the evidence is mixed, Ronald Reagan did better in the mid-1980s, with a Republican Senate, than did either George Bush or Bill Clinton, with opposing-party control of the Senate, in the 1990s. Striving to "govern together" by bridging the separate institutions may be more valuable than seeking to change an institution that has proved highly resistant to structural reforms.

Notes

1. Robert Bendiner, *Obstacle Course on Capitol Hill* (McGraw-Hill, 1964); see also, G. Calvin Mackenzie and Robert Shogan, *Obstacle Course* (New York: Twentieth Century Fund Press, 1996).

2. Barbara Sinclair, "Individualism, Partisanship, and Cooperation in the Senate," in Burdett A. Loomis, ed., *Esteemed Colleagues: Civility and Deliberation in the U.S. Senate* (Brookings, 2000), pp. 59–77; Barbara Sinclair, *Unorthodox Lawmaking*, 2d ed. (Washington: CQ Press, 2000).

3. Eric Uslaner, "Is the Senate More Civil than the House?" in Loomis, *Esteemed Colleagues,* pp. 32–55.

4. Christopher J. Deering, "Damned If You Do, and Damned If You Don't: The Senate's Role in the Appointments Process," in G. Calvin Mackenzie, ed., *The In-and-Outers: Presidential Appointees and Transient Government in Washington* (Johns Hopkins University Press, 1987), pp. 118–19.

5. Rogelio Garcia, "Presidential Appointments to Full-Time Positions in Executive Departments during the 106th Congress, 1999–2000," Congressional Research Service report, April 12, 2000, p. 1.

6. Norman J. Ornstein, "The Confirmation Clog," *Foreign Affairs*, vol. 79, no. 6 (November–December 2000), pp. 87–99; G. Calvin Mackenzie, *The Politics of Presidential Appointments* (New York: Free Press, 1981), p. 98 ff.

7. In the most systematic recent examination of confirmations, Glen S. Krutz, Richard Fleischer, and Jon R. Bond report on research going back to the 1960s, but they do not discuss the length of the process; see Krutz, Fleischer, and Bond, "From Abe Fortas to Zoe Baird: Why Some Presidential Nominations Fail in the Senate," *American Political Science Review*, vol. 92, no. 4 (December 1988), pp. 871–81. They find no differences under divided government, although their data stop before the Clinton-Republican battles of the 1995–2000 period.

8. Rogelio Garcia, "Senate Action on Nominations to Policy Positions in the Executive Branch, 1981–1992," *Congressional Research Services, April 28, 1993;* Roger Davidson and Colton Campbell, "The Senate and the Executive," paper presented at the Robert J. Dole Institute conference, "Civility and Deliberation in

the U.S. Senate," Washington, July 16, 1999, table 2 (drawn from data in a Congressional Research Service report by Rogelio Garcia).

9. Garcia, "Presidential Appointments to Full-Time Positions," p. 9.

10. Davidson and Campbell, table 2; Krutz, Fleischer, and Bond, "From Abe Fortas to Zoe Baird," suffers from a database that unfortunately stops at 1994.

11. On Guinier and Baird, see Stephen L. Carter, *The Confirmation Mess* (New York: Basic Books, 1994); on judicial confirmations, see Sarah A. Binder and Forrest Maltzman, "Holding Up the Senate: The Politics of Confirmation," paper presented at the annual meeting of the Midwest Political Science Association, Chicago, April 27–30, 2000.

12. Sinclair, "Individualism, Partisanship, and Cooperation in the Senate"; Sarah A. Binder and Steven S. Smith, *Politics or Principle? Filibustering in the U.S. Senate* (Brookings, 1997), p. 202.

13. Louis Fisher, *Constitutional Conflicts between Congress and the President*, 4th ed. (University Press of Kansas, 1997), p. 27.

14. Barbara Sinclair, "The 'Sixty-Vote Senate': Strategies, Processes, and Outcomes," paper presented to the Norman Thomas Conference on Senate Exceptionalism, Vanderbilt University, October 21–23, 1999. In fact, for the 105th Congress, Senate party loyalty scores slightly exceeded those of the House, which has been seen as the more partisan chamber.

15. See, for example, "A Nominee's Long Road to 'No,'" *Washington Post*, October 3, 2000, p. A3.

16. Krutz, Fleischer, and Bond, "From Abe Fortas to Zoe Baird."

17. Quoted in Paul C. Light and Virginia L. Thomas, *The Merit and Reputation of an Administration: Presidential Appointees on the Appointments Process* (Brookings and Heritage Foundation, 2000), p. 12.

18. Quoted in Eric Schmitt, "When Nomination Turns to Wrangling to Impasse," *New York Times,* July 28, 1999, p. A16.

19. "Clinton Defies GOP with Lee Recess Appointment," *Washington Times*, August 4, 2000, p. A3.

20. Paul C. Light and Virginia L. Thomas, *Posts of Honor: How America's Corporate and Civic Leaders View Presidential Appointments* (Brookings and Heritage Foundation, 2001), p. 29.

21. Light and Thomas, *The Merit and Reputation of an Administration*, pp. 28, 29.

CHAPTER SIX

The Senate as a Black Hole? Lessons Learned from the Judicial Appointments Experience

SARAH A. BINDER

FOR MANY A PRESIDENTIAL appointee, the Senate must loom like an institutional black hole—an abyss that engulfs even the most luminous nominee. That impression is, in fact, mistaken. Most presidential nominees survive the Senate confirmation process and are eventually confirmed. For many recent nominees, however, the experience has been long and unsettling.

Consider, for example, the plight of Richard Paez, a federal district court judge selected by President Bill Clinton to fill a vacancy in 1996 on the pivotal Ninth Circuit Court of Appeals. On paper, his confirmation by the Senate should have been a slam dunk. Paez had the highest rating possible from the American Bar Association, a group that in the past has routinely evaluated the competency of judicial appointees. Moreover, he had been confirmed just two years earlier by a Democratic Senate for his appointment to the lower district court seat, with his nomination sailing through in three months. Following a change in party control of the Senate, however, it was a full four years before the Republican Senate saw fit to confirm his elevation to the appellate bench.

Although Paez's landmark wait was hardly typical of the Senate confirmation process, the significant delay in getting judicial appointees onto the bench is a recurrent theme in the recent past: The average wait for judicial nominees over the past twenty years has increased nearly sixfold. Judicial appointees selected by President Ronald Reagan in his first term sailed through on average in just about a month. By Clinton's last term, the average judicial nominee took nearly half a year to negotiate the path to confirmation, and many waited a full two years with no Senate action.[1]

To be sure, judicial appointments differ significantly from executive branch appointees. The life tenure and broad policy jurisdiction of judges raise the stakes for senators concerned about the course of federal law and public policy. Nevertheless, both types of nominees face confirmation by the same Senate, a body charged with the constitutional duty of providing advice and consent to the president. Thus the more that is understood about the politics of confirming judicial nominees, the more accurate will be the forecast of the experiences likely to be encountered by the president's executive branch appointees.

Judicial nominees face predictable constraints in navigating their courses to confirmation. Some constraints are electoral in nature, created by the political or partisan context of the time. Others are institutional, erected by the Senate to protect its members' rights but then often exploited by senators for strategic advantage. Such constraints, of course, can be used to affect the course of both judicial and executive branch nominees. Thus delineating and explaining patterns in the Senate's treatment of judicial nominees provide a guidepost for all presidential appointees facing confirmation by the Senate. No nominee, I argue, can afford to ignore the significant institutional and electoral hurdles that the Senate erects against presidential appointees seeking public service.

Apples and Oranges?

In many respects, equating judicial and executive branch nominees is akin to comparing apples and oranges. Above all, judicial appointees serve for life, rather than for fixed terms or at the will of the president. Given judges' unlimited tenure, the policy consequences of confirming a judicial nominee are far more lasting than the consequences of accepting a president's choice for the typical executive branch position. Although a judge's behavior is not perfectly predictable over time and is not solely driven by his or her policy views, we know that judges and justices generally are guided by their ideological predispositions.[2] In confirming a judge for a particular court, senators are helping to shape the political and policy disposition of that court for the tenure of the judge.

Not only do judges have life tenure, but their jurisdictions tend to be much broader than the turf covered by the typical executive branch appointee. This is particularly so for appellate court judges, as their decisions are often unchallenged by the Supreme Court. As the Court has shrunk its docket considerably over the past decade or so, the broad policy reach of appellate court judges is increasingly likely to have an indelible impact on the shape of public policy and law. In contrast, a typical executive branch appointee has a narrow jurisdictional reach, and his or her decisions are subject to scrutiny and reversal by legislators. Decisions made by executive branch appointees are far less likely to have the type of policy impact made by federal judges. Although this is perhaps less pertinent to cabinet officials who preside over a broad swath of policymaking, executive branch appointees are in general more constrained than judges in their exercise of power. Centralization of decisionmaking authority within the White House over the past few decades, as well as the growth of budgetary constraints and regulatory review procedures, ultimately limits the policy discretion of executive branch appointees.[3] Although federal judges are conceptually subject to review by higher courts, many decisions of the appellate courts ultimately stand untouched because the Supreme Court wields discretionary authority to set its own docket.

The broad policy reach of judges also has consequences for the types of decisions they reach and thus for the way in which the Senate reviews judicial nominees. Because of the wide jurisdiction of the federal courts, contentious and ideological policy issues are bound to come before the courts, particularly as courts become more active in statutory interpretation and application of the law.[4] In contrast, not every executive branch department has jurisdiction over issues of ideological consequence. A presidential appointee within the Department of Transportation, for example, might never have to be involved in a contentious ideological matter. It follows that the Senate may in fact treat executive and judicial nominees differently, given the variation in the ideological stakes of each type of appointment.

Despite such differences between executive and judicial appointments, there is still good reason to compare the experiences of the two and to expect similarities in the way the Senate treats them. Most important, both types of appointees are considered by the Senate under a common political and institutional context. Understanding the political and structural environments shared by judicial and executive nominees is thus essential to understanding how the judicial confirmation experience can inform the confirmation of executive branch nominees.

A Shared Political Environment

Probably the most remarkable thing about the political environment of the Senate confirmation process is how little attention is paid to it. Only a small percentage of judicial nominees ever attracts media or public attention, and only the highest presidential appointees—usually at the cabinet level—invite sustained public or media interest. Of the 377 lower-court judges appointed by Clinton over his two terms in office, the names of no more than a handful were likely to have been recognized by even the most politically attentive. Not only do nominations fail to attract much public and media attention, they typically draw little attention within the Senate. Senate attention to both types of nominations is generally quite uneven, with intense interest in a particular nominee varying strongly among senators and across Senate committees.

The low visibility within and outside the Senate of all but the most important nominees—for cabinet or Supreme Court appointments—has important consequences for the fate of nominees. Such low salience creates a political environment in which senators holding the most intense interest in a nomination can exercise disproportionate influence over the fate of an appointee, generally free from intense public or media scrutiny. Moreover, the low and uneven salience of attention means that senators often target nominees to take them as hostages during unrelated political or policy battles with the president or the administration. Senator Charles Grassley (R-Iowa), for example, took hostage a highly salient nomination—the appointment of Richard Holbrooke as U.S. representative to the United Nations—as well as several low-visibility ambassadorial appointments in 2000, all because of an unrelated dispute with the State Department over its treatment of a department whistle-blower.[5] The Democrats in turn retaliated by holding up Grassley's preferred nominee for an appointment to the Internal Revenue Service Oversight Board. Not to be outmaneuvered, Republicans then held up the remaining six Clinton nominees to the Immigration and Naturalization Service Board.

Senators themselves will often admit that their willingness to delay a presidential nominee has little to do with the qualifications of the nominee. Richard Bryan (D-Nevada), for example, obstructed an appointee to a new agency within the Energy Department in 2000. He did so not because he disapproved of the president's choice but because he disliked the way the Republican majority had defined the jurisdiction of the new agency. Indeed Bryan was quoted as saying that he had "no reservations about the general."[6] Such political games are facilitated by the low and uneven salience of most presidential appointments. Operating below the radar screen of most media outlets and thus public attention, senators are quick to size up the political environment surrounding a nominee and adjust their procedural and political strategies accordingly.

Not all nominees are taken hostage for unrelated political demands, of course. Considerable foot-dragging can occur because of the policy views of the nominee. Certainly the drawn-out fight over Richard Paez was the result of Republican charges that he would tilt the Ninth Circuit Court too strongly in a liberal direction.[7] What is important to remember, however, is that such hostage-taking for ideological reasons is in large part made possible because of the political environment of the confirmation process: few senators within the chamber care intensely about any given nominee, and the media and public pay exceedingly little attention to most nominees. When ideological differences divide the parties, the political environment is particularly conducive to hostage-taking by ideological foes of the president.

A Shared Institutional Environment

In addition to a common political context, executive and judicial nominees also come before the Senate within a similar institutional environment. Although some unique rules affect the judicial confirmation process, both executive and judicial nominees must wend their way through an elaborate system of committee, party, and chamber rules and practices—all of which can affect the speed and outcome of the confirmation process for presidential appointees.

The first institutional hurdle for a nomination after it is announced by the president and referred to the Senate is consideration and approval by the relevant Senate committee. Committee approval is essential, as the Senate traditionally defers considerably to the judgment of its committees in considering presidential appointees. Indeed the low salience of most appointees almost guarantees that senators who do not sit on the relevant committee will have limited interest in any particular nomination. In essence, the Senate's institutional structure encourages logrolling across committees in terms of how they treat presidential appointees. Committees are given exclusive jurisdiction to review appointees headed to agencies or departments within each committee's purview, and thus each committee routinely defers to the judgment of the committee with jurisdiction over the particular appointment.

It is important to remember, however, that such deference between committees is cemented by the low visibility of most presidential appointees. In considering appointments at the highest levels of the cabinet or at the Supreme Court level, senators are unlikely to defer exclusively to the opinion of the relevant committee members. This was amply clear in senators' decisions on whether or not to support President George W. Bush's nomination of former senator John Ashcroft to be attorney general at the start of Bush's term. Despite the committee's approval of Ashcroft, a decision to confirm did not automatically follow for forty-two of the fifty Senate Democrats. Given the high salience and the contested and ideological character of the appointment, it made strong political sense for senators not simply to defer to the recommendation of the Senate Judiciary panel. This exception tends to confirm the rule, however: most appointments do not generate such public or media attention, and thus senators' incentives to challenge committee recommendations on routine nominations are dampened.

Although committees vary considerably in the formality of their confirmation process,[8] the basic contours of the process are similar for executive and judicial nominees. That is, all nominees must make it onto a committee's agenda to be considered and approved. The way in which committee rules distribute influence across the committee has a bearing on the speed and fate of each nominee in committee. Essentially, support of a committee's chair is required for a nomination to make it onto the committee's agenda. Although a majority of a committee can call a committee hearing without the chair's consent, the chair still wields considerable discretion over the committee's agenda, making it impossible for any nominee to circumvent a recalcitrant chair. William Weld's 1997 effort to be confirmed as Clinton's ambassador to Mexico comes to mind: a majority of the committee voted to proceed to his confirmation hearing, but in the face of opposition from Jesse Helms (R-North Carolina), the chair of the Senate Foreign Relations Committee, the nomination proceeded nowhere.[9]

Often, however, there is a fair amount of variation within a committee on how nominations are handled.[10] Executive branch nominees at the lowest rungs are not always given a hearing but nevertheless can proceed to committee approval. Even those nominees receiving a hearing are hardly likely to encounter the type of media show generated by the hearings held for Robert Bork and Clarence Thomas on their nominations to the Supreme Court. More likely, nominees will be considered in a group, with some or all of the nominees then proceeding together to a committee vote. Nor is the full complement of a committee's members likely to show up for such low-salience nominees. Across committees, there is also significant variation, as Senate panels differ considerably in the level of background investigation required for each nominee, although all committees have their own forms for nominees to complete that are independent of forms required by the White House, the Office of Government Ethics, and the Federal Bureau of Investigation.

On one dimension of committee consideration, there is in fact a stark difference between executive and judicial nominations. According to Judiciary panel procedures, senators are afforded the opportunity to "blue-slip" the president's judicial choice for federal judicial vacancies within their home states. Allowed to register objections to judicial nominees, the home-state senators wield disproportionate power during the committee stage of confirmation. Although Senate Judiciary panel chairs might once have automatically adhered to the preferences of the home-state senator, today such deference is not automatic. Instead, as Edward Kennedy (D-Massachusetts) established upon taking up the gavel of the Judiciary panel in 1979, blue-slip objections tend to weigh heavily on the chair's assessment of whether to proceed with a nomination but do not confer on the home-state senator an automatic veto right.[11]

Although Congress grants no comparable blue-slip right for executive branch appointments, certainly the support of a home-state senator can go a long way toward ensuring smooth sailing for presidential nominees. By securing such senatorial support, a nominee in essence transforms the visibility of his or her appointment, at least to that particular senator. However, because salience of nominations is so uneven across senators—thus encouraging logrolls among senators—even the strong support of a single senator or a Senate state delegation may be insufficient for securing swift consideration in committee. Home-state support might not always be sufficient to ensure confirmation, but it certainly reduces some of the institutional obstacles faced by unknown nominees pending before an often indifferent Senate committee.

Once approved by committee, nominations must clear a second broad institutional hurdle: making it onto the Senate's crowded agenda. Again, Senate rules and precedents regarding floor proceedings affect both executive and judicial nominees. Given the ways in which Senate rules structure floor proceedings in the chamber, the assent of both the majority and the minority party leaders is usually critical for gaining a spot on the

Senate's executive session calendar. The Senate majority leader traditionally holds the right of first recognition on the Senate floor, meaning that by custom the presiding officer gives the majority leader priority in being recognized to speak. Such a right of first recognition confers a significant advantage on the majority party over the floor agenda,[12] particularly as regards the majority leader's ability to control the agenda of executive business during the Senate's executive session—the forum in which both executive and judicial branch nominees are considered by the full chamber.

The majority leader in effect wields veto power over the executive session agenda. The implication is clear: absent support of the majority leader, a nominee is unlikely to be confirmed. To be sure, the support of the leader can often be the result of strategic bargaining over a set of nominees rather than an expression of his or her sincere support. But without the *de facto* support of the majority leader, it is all but impossible for nominees to secure floor consideration.[13] Such procedural advantages clearly enhance the importance of support from the majority leader in shaping the fate of presidential appointees.

The majority leader's discretion over the executive session agenda is not wielded without challenge, however, because nominations can be filibustered. True, presidential appointees—at least those below the highest ranks of appointments to the cabinet and Supreme Court—are rarely filibustered. When a nomination is filibustered, the majority party needs to muster sixty votes in the chamber, a threshold sufficiently large under most conditions to require support from the minority party as well. Rather than face a potentially disruptive filibuster on the floor, however, the majority leader usually seeks unanimous consent of the full chamber before bringing up a nomination. Such consent agreements result from negotiation between the majority and minority party leaders, with each party's rank-and-file members given the chance to withhold his or her consent. Once consent is reached, nominations tend to be considered en bloc on the Senate floor, with the names of most nominees never even mentioned.[14]

As a result, despite the majority party's control of the agenda, the minority party wields considerable influence over the fate of presidential appointees. Confirmation is unlikely, in other words, without the tacit consent of the minority party. Given the de facto requirement of minority party assent, the party opposing the president retains power to affect the fate of nominees even when it does not control the Senate. Thus Republicans opposed to Clinton nominees during the brief period of unified Democratic control in 1993–94 did not sit back and idly watch the Democrats confirm the president's nominees. The need for bipartisan consent significantly empowered minority party Republicans seeking to stall the new president's nominees from taking public office.

The routine practice of securing unanimous consent provides a tremendous opportunity for senators to obstruct nominations pending before the Senate. Such obstruction is usually termed a "hold," and it is yet another procedural tactic that affects equally the fate of executive and judicial branch nominees. Technically, a senator places a hold by refusing to grant unanimous consent at a leader's request. A few decades ago, senators placed holds simply to ensure that the leader heeded special scheduling concerns in the consideration of a measure or nomination.[15] In more recent times, holds have been wielded as unilateral vetoes by senators seeking to detail measures or nominations otherwise headed to the Senate floor.[16] There is no formal reason why the majority or minority leader would observe a hold coming from within his or her ranks, except that leaders constantly rely on the cooperation of senators to proceed through the Senate's agenda. Ignoring a colleague's hold—whether from the majority or minority party's ranks—puts the leader at future risk when a far more salient and important measure or nomination might be slated to come to the floor.

Holds gain much of their force from the strategic leverage they afford senators, given leaders' frequent need for unanimous consent. Holds are especially attractive tools for another reason, as well: by and large, they can be placed in secret, with other senators, the media, and the public never knowing the identity of the senator or senators who placed the hold. Secrecy lends itself to gamesmanship by senators, because it enables them to pursue their political or policy goals without engendering Senate or public discontent. Indeed on some occasions senators engage in what might be called "tag-team" holds or, more commonly, "rolling holds": as one senator lifts an anonymous hold, another senator takes his or her place. Thus no single senator can be blamed for the delay, as no one knows at any given moment just which senator has placed the hold. At other times, senators employ what are known as "blanket holds," placing a hold simultaneously on a block of measures of nominations. Senator James Inhofe (R-Oklahoma), although not doing it anonymously, placed such a blanket hold on thirty-some judicial nominees in January 2000, making it clear that he would refuse to grant consent to President Clinton's nominees until his other unrelated demands were met.

In the 106th Congress (1999–2000), some progress was made toward reforming the practice of holds when majority leader Trent Lott (R-Mississippi) and minority leader Tom Daschle (D-South Dakota) announced that they would no longer honor holds placed anonymously.[17] Any senator wishing to place a hold would instead have to notify the bill's sponsor and the committee with jurisdiction over the issue, as well as provide written notification to party leaders. By striking at the secrecy of the hold, reformers hoped to reduce senators' incentives to place holds: no longer shielded by anonymity, senators would face a higher political cost for exploiting the rules at the expense of their colleagues' legislative goals.

Despite the heralded reform of holds in March 1999, by July of that year several anonymous holds were pending on the nomination of Richard Holbrooke as ambassador to the United Nations.[18] Senators, as it turns out, had discovered some convenient loopholes in the reform. First, the agreement held that senators had to inform the committee chair with jurisdiction and the party leader when placing a hold. Nothing in the agreement, however, required either the chair or the leader to reveal publicly who had placed the hold. In the case of Holbrooke, Jesse Helms (R-North Carolina) was happy to honor the secret hold, as Helms himself opposed the nominee. Nor did Lott feel compelled to reveal the identify of the senators obstructing Holbrooke, because one of the holds was placed by Lott himself, as became clear within a few days.[19]

Second, the agreement required senators to notify the sponsor of a measure when a hold was placed. Nominations have no sponsor as such, and thus senators seeking to obstruct a nominee could do so in secrecy without violating the letter of the agreement. Holbrooke was eventually confirmed, at the cost of conceding to the demands of Lott and a second senator—both of whom sought a commitment from Clinton to nominate a particular candidate for a seat on the Federal Election Commission.[20] Once again, holds were placed for reasons tangential to the qualifications of the pending nominee.

Although judicial and executive branch appointees may seem at first glance like apples and oranges—thus hardly justifying the drawing of lessons from one to the other—both types of nominees face confirmation by the same Senate. As such, despite apparent differences in judicial and executive appointments, indelible features of the Senate and its members shape the fate of both types of nominees. Senators' uneven attention to the president's nominees and the Senate's unique institutional rules and practices together ensure that the two types of nominees will face similar hurdles in seeking confirmation by the Senate. Understanding how politics and institutions interact to shape the fate of nominees is thus essential to explaining the logic of the confirmation process for judicial and executive appointees alike.

Historical and Recent Trends

Most judicial appointees are eventually confirmed. Over the past half century, on average 90 percent of presidential appointees to the federal bench have been confirmed in the Congress in which they were nominated. To be sure, significant variation in confirmation rates exists across the Congresses of the postwar period (see table 6-1). Although rates were generally lower in the 1990s than had been typical of earlier decades, not all presidential nominees encountered smooth sailing before the 1990s. Harry S Truman's contentious relationship with a Republican Congress in 1947 and 1948 is evident in the relatively low approval rate for his judicial nominees, reaching only 78 percent in the 80th Congress. Even within presidential administrations significant variation in confirmation often occurs. At the end of his first term, Dwight D. Eisenhower managed a perfect 100 percent approval rate for his nominees. In contrast, by the end of his administration his record had fallen to 88 percent. So too do we see variation within administrations in recent years, as Clinton fared significantly worse during the 104th Congress (1995–96), with only 73 percent of his nominees confirmed, than during the 105th (1997–98), during which the approval rate rose to 82 percent. Ultimately, however, an overwhelming majority of nominees do get confirmed, as seen in the generally high confirmation rates presidents have achieved over the past fifty years.

The Senate rarely rejects judicial nominees outright by chamber vote. Over the past fifty years, only forty-four recorded floor votes have been taken on judicial nominees; more than half of those occurred on Clinton nominees in the late 1990s after the Senate Republican conference made recorded votes on nominees routine, in contrast with the Senate's historical treatment of nominees.[21] More often, judicial nominees fail because time runs out. There are, in other words, exceedingly few "quick" rejections. This pattern is in keeping with the tendency of senators to pay little attention to most nominations. Because attention is so uneven and salience so low for the typical nominee, it is relatively easy for a senator

Table 6–1. *Rate of Confirmation of Federal Judicial Nominees, by Congress, 1947–98*

Congress	*Years*	*Nominees confirmed (mean percentage)*
80	1947–48	78
81	1949–50	95
82	1951–52	85
83	1953–54	93
84	1955–56	100
85	1957–58	94
86	1959–60	88
87	1961–62	98
88	1963–64	97
89	1965–66	99
90	1967–68	93
91	1969–70	95
92	1971–72	100
93	1973–74	97
94	1975–76	81
95	1977–78	97
96	1979–80	92
97	1981–82	99
98	1983–84	86
99	1985–86	96
100	1987–88	82
101	1989–90	96
102	1991–92	69
103	1993–94	90
104	1995–96	73
105	1997–98	82

Source: Data from Sarah A. Binder and Forrest Maltzman, "Stacking the Bench: The Logic and Politics of Senate Confirmation," unpublished manuscript.

to kill a nomination simply by dragging out the nomination. True, a large proportion of failed nominees are eventually confirmed in a subsequent Congress, but certainly the vacancy that results from significant delays during the confirmation process carries personal costs for the nominee and policy costs for the court.

How severe or widespread are such delays? In one sense, Judge Paez's four-year wait before the Republican Senate is extreme. Only a handful of nominees have had their nominations dragged out for more than a single Congress, and many with long waits are simply not renominated by the president in a subsequent Congress. Nevertheless, Paez's experience does reflect a broader trend under way in recent years. Figure 6-1 illustrates the

Figure 6-1. *Average Length of Confirmation Process for Successful Judicial Nominees, 1947–98*

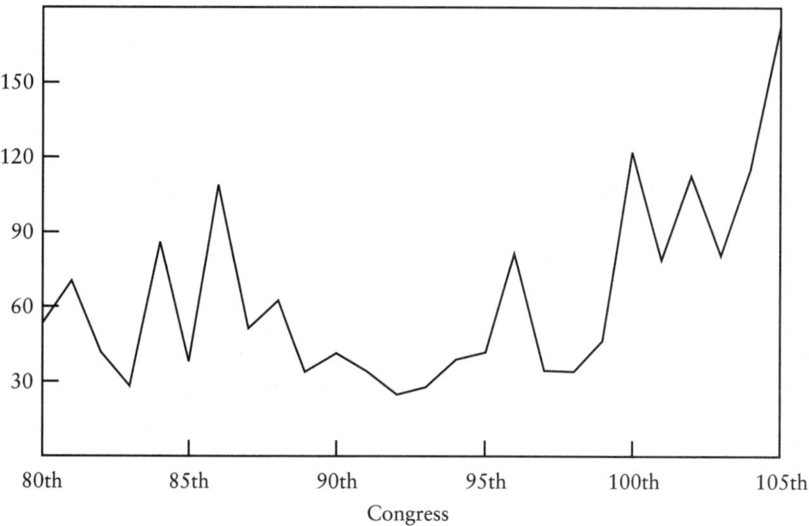

Source: Sarah A. Binder and Forrest Maltzman, "Stacking the Bench: The Logic and Politics of Senate Confirmation," unpublished manuscript.

a. Average length of time each successful nomination for the lower federal courts was pending before the Senate (from nomination to final confirmation).

lengthening of the confirmation process over the last half of the twentieth century for all judicial nominees eventually confirmed by the Senate. Whereas the Senate took just one month to confirm the average judicial nominee during Ronald Reagan's first term (the 97th Congress), by the end of Clinton's second term the average wait had grown sixfold. At least one-third of Clinton's judicial nominees in the 105th Congress (1997–98) waited more than six months to be confirmed, with the longest wait for a confirmed nominee stretching nearly the entire length of the two-year Congress.

The delays Clinton weathered in getting his nominees confirmed to the bench are not simply a reflection of his polarized relations with a conservative Republican Senate. During the mid-1980s a Democratic Senate took an average of nearly four months to confirm judicial nominees of Presidents Reagan and Bush, and during 1993 and 1994 a Democratic Senate averaged three months in confirming Clinton's nominees.

Indeed, although the politics of recent confirmations might be especially polarized, contentious relations between the Senate and the president go a long way back. During Eisenhower's last term, for example, it took the Democratic Senate led by Lyndon Johnson an average of four months—and sometimes as long as seven months—to confirm judicial nominees. Although lengthy delays are more typical of recent years, foot-dragging over judicial appointments is hardly a brand-new development.

The Politics of Senate Delay

By any measure, the Senate's performance in dispensing advice and consent regarding judicial nominees varied widely over the last half of the twentieth century. What accounts for the uneven performance? A number of alternative explanations have been offered for the variation in the Senate's treatment of judicial nominees, and in this section I review them, with an eye to establishing a broader logic that might make sense of the ways and means of Senate confirmation.[22]

Do Elections Matter?

Pundits assessing the Senate's treatment of Clinton's nominees typically point first to poisoned relations between conservative Republicans and Clinton. It is often suggested that personal and political antagonisms between Clinton and conservatives led Republican senators to slow confirmation of even the most highly qualified nominees. This may account for some of the delay, but hardly for all, given that the trend toward lengthy confirmation proceedings was well under way before Clinton took office in 1993 and Republicans gained control of the Senate only after the 1994 elections.

Others suggest that the extreme delays encountered by judicial nominees in the 106th Congress owed much to the approaching presidential election. With control of both the Senate and the White House up for grabs in November 2000, it was natural for Republican senators to approach their confirmation duties with particular caution. Rather than confirming the last judicial nominees of an outgoing Democratic president, pragmatic politics would dictate that Republicans save these lifetime appointments for a president of their own party. Not surprisingly, at the end of the 106th Congress forty judicial nominees remained in limbo. Most had not even received a hearing before the Senate Judiciary panel.

The historical record confirms that an approaching presidential election affects the politics of advice and consent. Over the past fifty years, the Senate has treated judicial nominations submitted or pending during a presidential election year differently from others. First, it has taken longer to confirm nominees pending before a presidential election than those submitted earlier in a president's term. Second, and more notably, those nominated during a presidential election year are much less likely to be confirmed, even controlling for the presence of divided government and the quality of the nominee. For all judicial nominations submitted between 1947 and 1998, nominees pending in the Senate before a presidential election were 25 percent less likely to be confirmed than nominees submitted earlier in a president's term.

Elections that result in divided party control of the White House and Senate also slow the confirmation process. Judges are policymakers as well as judicial arbiters with life tenure, giving senators good cause to scrutinize the views of all potential federal judges. Because presidents overwhelmingly seek to appoint judges from their own party, Senate scrutiny of judicial nominees should be particularly intense when different parties control the White House and the Senate. It should come as no surprise, then, that the Senate has taken nearly 60 percent longer to confirm nominees during periods of divided government than during unified control. Judicial nominees are also less likely to be confirmed during divided government, even controlling for the quality of the nominee and other relevant factors.[23]

Party politics also affects the course of nominations when presidents seek to fill vacancies on appellate circuits whose judges are evenly balanced between the two parties. Senate majorities are especially reluctant to confirm nominees to such courts when the appointment would tip the balance of the court in favor of a president from the opposing party. One of the hardest-hit such courts in recent years has been the Sixth Circuit Court of Appeals, straddling populous midwestern states such as Michigan and Ohio. At the close of the Clinton presidency, a quarter of the bench was vacant, including one seat declared a judicial emergency after sitting empty for five years. The Senate slowdown on appointments to the Sixth Circuit Court was most likely motivated by the strategic importance of the circuit, since confirming Clinton's nominees would have deprived a Republican president of the opportunity to move a balanced court into the conservative camp. In short, electoral and partisan dynamics strongly shape the Senate's conduct of advice and consent, making it difficult for presidents to stack the federal courts as they see fit.

Institutional Culprits

If elections alone were to blame for slow confirmations, presidential appointees might have little opportunity to hasten matters along. However, the process of advice and consent is equally affected by an array of Senate rules, each of which distributes power in a unique way across the institution. Committee and chamber rules in particular cast a long shadow on the fate of judicial nominees, as senators are often quite willing to exploit the rules available in pursuit of policy or political gain. Understanding how institutional rules interact with senators' ideological and political incentives is thus critical to unraveling the logic of the confirmation process.

As has already been discussed, Judiciary Committee rules and practices affect the fate of nominees in several ways. First, by tradition senators from the home state of each nominee cast first judgment on potential appointees. The veto power of home-state senators is institutionalized in Judiciary panel procedures, which allow them to register blue-slip objections to judicial nominees referred to the committee. Although "negative" blue slips no longer kill a nomination outright, they do enter into the chair's decisions on whether and when to proceed with a nominee.[24]

Historically, significant ideological differences between the president and the home-state senator have led to longer confirmation proceedings than normal, at least for appellate nominees—a trend that confirms the power of home-state senators to affect panel proceedings. In practical terms, the strong support of a nominee's home-state senator is essential in gaining committee approval. Given the often fractured attention of the Senate and the willingness of senators to heed the preferences of the home-state senator, a strong advocate in the Senate with an interest in seeing the nomination proceed is critical to a nominee's confirmation. Although home-state senators for executive branch nominees lack the leverage of a "blue slip" veto, securing a strong Senate sponsor can go a long way in greasing the skids in committee.

Second, as we have seen, Senate rules grant considerable procedural powers to committee chairs. Because of the generally low salience of most judicial nominations, the Senate largely defers to the Judiciary Committee's judgment on whether and when to proceed with a nomination. The committee chair, who has the power to convene hearings and to schedule a vote to report a nomination to the chamber, wields great discretion over the fate of each nominee. Not surprisingly, ideological differences between the Judiciary panel chair and the president affect discernibly the course of judicial nominations. The greater the ideological differences, the longer it takes the committee to act. Because all committee chairs retain agenda-setting powers, executive branch appointees are well served by establishing rapport with and support from the relevant panel chair.

Rules and practices governing proceedings on the executive calendar of nominations also affect the speed with which judicial nominees are confirmed. Given the majority leader's advantage in being recognized first on the floor—and the restriction on debate for motions to go into executive session—the majority party is afforded an opportunity to slow down the confirmation process if it so desires. The impact of such rules is seen vividly in a comparison of the fates of nominees during periods of unified and divided control of government. When the president's party controls the Senate, nominations are confirmed more quickly, as the majority leader can take advantage of his scheduling leverage to call up nominations in a timely manner. Under divided control, the majority leader can again reap advantage from his modicum of agenda-setting powers, albeit this time by delaying consideration of presidential appointees by the full Senate. Empirical evidence for such strategic maneuvering is strong: nominations made during periods of divided control take longer than those pending during unified control, controlling for a host of other factors that might affect the speed of confirmation.[25]

The majority leader's discretion over the executive session agenda is limited, however, as became clear in exploring the impact of unanimous consent rules in the chamber. Because majority and minority party leaders must negotiate with each other—as well as with their respective rank and file—before most nominations are brought to the floor, senators or a party with an incentive to slow down a nominee have ample institutional opportunity for doing so. Predicting when individual senators will exploit their procedural rights to delay nominees for often unrelated purposes is fraught with error, as senators often hold up nominations for reasons entirely tangential to the nominee or the position being filled. Predicting when party coalitions are likely to stretch out the confirmation is far easier. The critical ingredient again seems to be ideological disagreement between pivotal institution coalitions. This time, ideological differences between the two party coalitions have a strong bearing on the timing of confirmation. As ideological differences increase, the speed of confirmation decreases; and as such differences recede, nominations move more swiftly through the Senate. Such effects are robust even after controlling for the myriad of other factors likely to affect the confirmation process.[26]

Presidents and the Senate

Although presidents lack formal means of pushing nominations through to confirmation, they are not powerless in shaping how the Senate dispenses advice and consent. In the first place, better-qualified nominees tend to sail more quickly through the Senate. At least in recent decades, a higher rating from the American Bar Association has often cut the time it takes judicial nominees to get confirmed and increased the probability of confirmation. The quality of a president's nominee, in other words, helps smooth the way to confirmation.

Presidents can also have tremendous impact on the fate of a nomination by strategically timing its referral to the Senate. As already noted, nominations made earlier in a president's term tend to move more swiftly than those made in a presidential election year. Nominations also take longer as the Senate gets mired in considering scores of appointees. In general, the fewer nominees pending, the more quickly a nominee will be confirmed.

Perhaps surprisingly, there is little evidence that more-popular presidents are able to get their nominees approved more quickly. That may be why presidents only rarely use their bully pulpit to draw attention to the plight of their nominees. Alternatively, the limited ability of presidents to shape the course of confirmation may be a consequence of the generally low level of presidential attention to most lower-rung appointments after they are made. In short, presidents have some influence over the speed of advice and consent, but their influence is exercised only at the margins of the legislative arena, a finding consistent with much of what we know about presidential influence in Congress.[27]

One Hundred Atomic Bombs?

It has been said that the Senate is composed of a hundred atomic bombs, each of which can be triggered on a second's notice. Perhaps—though the dozens of judicial nominees detained in recent years by senators in pursuit of assorted policy and political goals would suggest that a hostage-taking metaphor would be equally apt. Senator James Inhofe certainly set a new standard in the wars of advice and consent when he held more than thirty judicial nominees hostage in a battle with the president over an unrelated recess appointment early in the year 2000. Whether nominees are taken hostage as each party seeks action on blocs of nominees hanging in limbo before the Senate or whether they are simply used as pawns by senators trying to influence other matters of import to themselves, the low and uneven salience of most nominations encourages hostage-taking. Simply put, senators rarely pay a political cost for holding up presidential appointees.

Is significant reform of the confirmation process possible? Although several independent groups have called for reform of the process in recent years, there are good reasons to be skeptical that meaningful reform is forthcoming. First, recommendations for reform often take the form of exhorting the Senate to do better. One such report, issued in 1999 by Citizens for Independent Courts, advocates that the Senate adopt as its goal a strict outside limit on the length of the confirmation process. Nominations should be made within 180 days of a vacancy, and the nominee must then be confirmed within 60 days. As a mechanism for enforcing such a timetable, the report calls on the president and Senate "to commit themselves more accurately."[28] Similarly, the Miller Center of Public Affairs issued a high-profile report in 1996 also exhorting the Senate to do better, in part encouraging the Judiciary Committee to hire more lawyers to investigate nominees and to forgo holding hearings on nominees deemed uncontroversial.[29] Exhorting the Senate to do better is unlikely ever to produce the desired results, however, as long as basic electoral and institutional incentives remain in place that encourage senators to hold nominees hostage in a bargaining game with the president and fellow senators. Absent a graver crisis, senators' political and policy incentives are unlikely to be altered by outside pleas for reform.

Second, even raising the stakes of the confirmation mess has proved insufficient for effecting Senate reform. No less a voice than Chief Justice William Rehnquist, in his year-end report on the state of the judiciary, rebuked a Republican Senate for foot-dragging on Clinton's nominees in 1997.[30] In the summer of 2000, presidential candidate George W. Bush also called on the Senate to speed up the nominations process (though he suggested that such efforts were unnecessary until a new administration had taken office).[31] The *New York Times* has also called on the Senate to reform its confirmation politics—in editorials as far back as 1959 bemoaning the state of affairs in the Senate.[32] Clearly, neither well-intentioned outside voices nor high-level public voices are sufficient for effecting Senate reform.

Although it may be extremely tough to alter the political incentives that encourage Senate foot-dragging on the confirmation of presidential nominees, an alternative would be to streamline senators' institutional opportunities to engage in such behavior. One possibility would be to expedite nominations, just as the Senate "fast-tracks" consideration of budget reconciliation and many trade agreements. If fast-track procedures were applied to presidential appointee confirmation, nominations would be afforded expeditious committee action, senators would be prohibited from filibustering nominees, and nominees could be moved through executive session by majority vote (rather than unanimous consent). Fast-tracking would reduce the chances for senators to place holds on nominations and would help ensure swift floor consideration for all nominees.

Convincing the Senate to reform its rules of debate and privilege is, of course, difficult. Unless a significant majority of senators agree that the political costs of ignoring reform are too steep a price to pay, reform of Senate rules is unlikely to occur.[33] Perhaps a new president eager to have nominees confirmed might convince the Senate that a national crisis is at hand and the Senate to blame by stalling his or her nominees, but absent such extraordinary circumstances significant reform will most likely come slowly, if at all.

Concluding Thought

Although the Senate's pattern of advice and consent may at times seem encumbered neither with rhyme nor with reason, more careful scrutiny suggests that Senate rules widely and predictably allocate influence across the Senate. With senators often willing to exploit their procedural rights, swift confirmation of presidential appointees, however well qualified, is rare. For nominees navigating the shoals of the chamber, understanding the ways and means of Senate institutions is essential. Committee chairs, pivotal senators, and majority and minority party leaders alike wield considerable influence over the fate of presidential nominees. Cultivating support from these critical institutional players is essential in building a deliberate path toward confirmation—and a little help from the stars would not hurt one bit.

Notes

1. The author acknowledges a grant from the National Science Foundation (SBR #9805772) for the collection of data on the fate of lower federal court judicial nominees.

2. On the impact of ideology on judicial decisionmaking, see Jeffrey Segal and Harold J. Spaeth, *The Supreme Court and the Attitudinal Model* (New York: Cambridge University Press, 1993); on the impact of more strategic factors, see Forrest Maltzman, James F. Spriggs, and Paul J. Wahlbeck, *Crafting Law on the Supreme Court: The Collegial Game* (New York: Cambridge University Press, 2000).

3. Terry M. Moe, "The Politicized Presidency," in John E. Chubb and Paul E. Peterson, eds., *The New Direction in American Politics* (Brookings, 1985), pp. 235–71.

4. R. Shep Melnick, *Between the Lines: Interpreting Welfare Rights* (Brookings, 1994).

5. "In the Loop: Hollywood Dress Code," *Washington Post*, May 24, 2000, p. A35; "Lott and McConnell Also Have 'Hold' on Holbrooke," *Washington Post*, July 7, 1999, p. A4.

6. "Nominee Is Held Up in Energy Dept. Fight," *Washington Post*, May 31, 2000, p. A25.

7. Close observers of judicial nominations, however, have noted that Clinton moderated his appointments after Republicans took control of the Senate in 1995; see Sheldon Goldman and Elliot Slotnick, "Clinton's Second-Term Judiciary: Picking Judges under Fire," *Judicature,* vol. 82 (May–June 1999), pp. 265–84.

8. Christopher J. Deering, "Damned If You Do and Damned If You Don't: The Senate's Role in the Appointments Process," in G. Calvin Mackenzie, ed., *The In-and-Outers: Presidential Appointees and Transient Government in Washington* (Johns Hopkins University Press, 1987).

9. Donna Cassatta, "Helms Lashes Back at Critics, Holds Firm on Blocking Weld," *Congressional Quarterly Weekly Report*, vol. 55, no. 36 (September 13, 1997), pp. 2159–60.

10. Deering, "Damned If You Do."

11. Sheldon Goldman, *Picking Federal Judges* (Yale University Press, 1997).

12. Steven S. Smith, "Forces of Change in Senate Party Leadership and Organization," in Lawrence C. Dodd and Bruce I. Oppenheimer, eds., *Congress Reconsidered*, 5th ed. (Washington: CQ Press, 1993), pp. 259–90.

13. Nor can senators offer nominations as nongermane amendments to other business, a technique often used by senators outside of executive session to challenge the majority party's agenda control; Steven S. Smith, *Call to Order* (Brookings, 1989); Smith, "Forces of Change."

14. Deering, "Damned If You Do," p. 225n. Instead, according to Deering, the majority leader usually asks for unanimous consent to a series of calendar numbers, with the minority leader responding as to whether or not they have been cleared by his conference colleagues.

15. Smith, *Call to Order.*

16. Barbara Sinclair, *The Transformation of the U.S. Senate* (Johns Hopkins University Press, 1989); Smith, *Call to Order.*

17. "Senate Lifts Veil on Bill 'Holds,'" *Washington Post*, March 4, 1999, p. A8.

18. "Senate Has a 'Hold' on Holbrooke," *Washington Post*, July 3, 1999, p. A5.

19. "Lott and McConnell Also Have 'Hold' on Holbrooke," *Washington Post*, July 7, 1999, p. A4.

20. Ibid.; to place the power of the hold in perspective, that candidate had once written that Clinton's administration "may be the most corrupt White House in American history." The eventual nominee, Bradley Smith, was himself the target of holds from Democrats later in 2000, when Republicans moved to confirm him.

21. The decision to require recorded votes is discussed in Ed Henry, "His Power Being Judges, Hatch Beats Back Leaders," *Roll Call*, May 1, 1997.

22. The findings in this section are discussed in greater methodological detail in Sarah A. Binder and Forrest Maltzman, "Senatorial Delay in Confirming Federal Judges, 1947–1998," *American Journal of Political Science* (forthcoming).

23. Such a finding is consistent with previous work exploring the confirmation of executive branch and Supreme Court appointees; see, for example, G. Calvin Mackenzie, *The Politics of Presidential Appointments* (New York: Free Press, 1981); Nolan McCarty and Rose Razaghian, "Advice and Consent: Senate Responses to Executive Branch Nominations, 1885–1996," *American Journal of Political Science*, vol. 43, no. 4 (October 1999), pp. 1122–43; Jeffrey A. Segal "Senate Confirmation of Supreme Court Justices: Partisan and Institutional Politics," *Journal of Politics*, vol. 49, no. 4 (November 1987), pp. 998–1015.

24. Goldman, *Picking Federal Judges.*

25. See Binder and Maltzman, "Senatorial Delay in Confirming Federal Judges." Binder and Maltzman's results are based on data about the fate of only appellate court nominees between 1947 and 1998. Extending the data to include federal district court judges yields similar results for the effect of divided control.

26. Such factors are delineated in detail in Binder and Maltzman, "Senatorial Delay in Confirming Federal Judges," and include variables such as party control of the White House and Senate, differences between the chair and the president, the timing of the nomination, the workload of the Senate, and the quality of the nominee.

27. See, for example, George C. Edwards, *At the Margins: Presidential Leadership of Congress* (Yale University Press, 1989).

28. Citizens for Independent Courts, "Justice Held Hostage: Politics and Selecting Federal Judges" (Washington: The Century Foundation, 1999), pp. 10–11.

29. Miller Center of Public Affairs, *Improving the Process of Appointing Federal Judges: A Report of the Miller Center Commission on the Selection of Federal Judges* (Charlottesville: Miller Center of Public Affairs, University of Virginia, 1996), p. 9.

30. "Senate Imperils Judicial System, Rehnquist Says," *New York Times*, January 1, 1998, p. A1.

31. Dana Milbank, "Bush Aims at 'Discord' in Capital," *Washington Post*, June 9, 2000, p. A1.

32. "Congress and the Judges," *New York Times*, August 30, 1959, pt. 4, p. 10.

33. Sarah A. Binder and Steven S. Smith, *Politics or Principle? Filibustering in the U.S. Senate* (Brookings, 1997).

CHAPTER SEVEN

Repetitiveness, Redundancy, and Reform: Rationalizing the Inquiry of Presidential Appointees

TERRY SULLIVAN

THE WHITE HOUSE wants to know what real estate the nominee now owns or the properties now owned by the nominee's spouse. It also wants a list of properties the nominee and spouse have owned in the past six years but do not now own. The Federal Bureau of Investigation (FBI) wants to know only about properties that the nominee currently owns or has an interest in. Presumably, the properties in which the nominee might have an interest include more than those the nominee owns outright. The FBI drops holdings of the spouse and drops holdings of the past six years. The U.S. Office of Government Ethics then wants the nominee to report those properties the nominee has sold or bought. Elsewhere on the ethics office form, the nominee would list real estate assets currently held and any others that had made at least two hundred dollars. Drop income for the past six years in favor of the past two.[1] Skip the properties the nominee owns but did not buy recently. Return the nominee's spouse to the mix of reporting on ownership. Then add to the ownership report any dependent children the nominee may have who own property in their own names. Then set the values of the transactions within one of fifteen ranges.

After answering the demands of these three organizations, what else might a nominee face? Well, the Senate committee wants to return to the White House question of ownership by dropping the spouse and the dependent children. Because it uses the FBI's time frame, it drops the past six years, and it then drops the past two years. It ignores sales and acquisitions. It ignores information on the value ranges of properties. On the other hand, the Senate committee requires the nominee to post a specific value for each of the properties reported. Hence, nominees must muster information on real estate property over four forms in three different time periods, designating three separate classes of ownership, sorting according to at least two separate types of transactions, and in some cases indicating values across fifteen distinct categories.

Fixing the Inquiry Mess

Although he had chaos in mind, the Irish poet W. B. Yeats surely presaged the inquisition presidential appointees face in securing a post when he penned the phrase "fabulous formless darkness." Over the past thirty years, confirming the president's nominees has become an increasingly convoluted fen of executive and Senate forms, strategic entanglements, and "gotcha" politics. According to the 1996 Task Force on Presidential Appointments assembled by the Twentieth Century Fund, the appointments process has discouraged and demoralized many of those who would work in the administration. A recent survey of former appointees from the past three administrations released by the Brookings Institution's Presidential Appointee Initiative concludes that "a quarter [of those surveyed] were so unhappy with the nomination and confirmation process that they called it embarrassing, and two-fifths said it was confusing. . . . Almost half described it as 'a necessary evil.'"[2] The study concludes that "the Founders' model of presidential service is near the breaking point. Not only is the path into presidential service getting longer and more tortuous, it leads to ever-more stressful jobs. Those who survive the appointments process often enter office frustrated and fatigued."[3]

The process may seem broken along a number of dimensions, but several studies have noted the task of filing forms as one of the major flaws of the appointments process. Appointees find the inquiries they must face intrusive and burdensome. Both the Twentieth Century Fund Task Force and the Presidential Appointee Initiative report call for finding ways to restrain the intrusiveness of the inquiries and diminish the burdens of form filings.

Taking Measure of the Darkness

Nominees to presidential appointments must file four forms.[4] The Personal Data Statement (PDS), which originates with the White House, covers some forty-three questions (in some versions the "nanny-tax" question is included) laid out in paragraphs of text. If the White House permits them to go on to the vetting stage, applicants fill out three additional forms. The Standard Form (SF) 86 develops information for a national security clearance, commonly known as the FBI background check. The SF 86 contains two parts: the standard questionnaire and a "supplemental questionnaire," which repackages some previous questions from the standard questionnaire into broader language often similar, though not identical, to questions asked on the White House PDS. The SF 278, which comes from the U.S. Office of Government Ethics (OGE), gathers information for financial disclosure. This form also doubles as an annual financial disclosure report for all federal employees above the rank of GS-15.[5] For most nominees, the third form comes from the Senate committee of jurisdiction.[6] After returning each of these forms, some nominees will receive a fifth form, another from the Senate committee of jurisdiction, asking for responses to more specific questions. These additional questions typically refer to specific issues before the nominee's agency.

Although they complain about several characteristics of the process, nominees regularly and uniformly underscore their frustration with the repetitive nature of questions. Indeed, nominees leave the impression that the forms contain nothing but repetitive inquiries. That degree of repetitiveness does not exist, but the kinds of questions on which nominees must report repetitive information do pose an undue burden. Take, for example, the questions asked about ownership of real property in the various financial disclosure sections mentioned at the beginning of this chapter.

A Passing Note on Intrusiveness

In filing forms, nominees must build databases on a number of subjects. Some argue that these inquiries unnecessarily invade a nominee's privacy and secure information that plays no significant role in determining their qualifications. While securing information on their property holdings, for example, the government asks nominees not only to reveal the value of these properties but also to report those values with unnecessary precision. On the SF 278, the Office of Government Ethics requires nominees to "place a value on assets owned by spouse or dependent children up to 'over $1,000,000.' For assets owned by the nominee, place a value on assets up through 'over $50,000,000.'" The categories are as follows:

—$1,001 to $15,000
—$15,001 to $50,000
—$50,001 to $100,000
—$100,001 to $250,000
—$250,001 to $500,000
—$500,001 to $1,000,000
—Over $1,000,000
—$1,000,001 to $5,000,000
—$5,000,001 to $25,000,000
—$25,000,001 to $50,000,000.

The use of these narrowly defined categories (indeed the categories derive from statutory language) draws a distinction between properties worth $99,999 and those worth $100,001, as if the movement from the one category to the next reflects some definable increase in apparent conflicts of interest. This approach to potential conflicts of interest clearly reflects an assumption that disclosure of these specific values will dissuade potential nominees from developing such conflicts. On its face, this regulatory assumption seems flawed.[7]

Measuring Repetitiveness

The degree to which nominees must muster varied information to answer repetitive inquiries serves as a surrogate measure of the unnecessary burdens placed on nominees by the government's inquiry. The analysis that follows assumes that no good purpose results from requiring nominees to vary their responses to similar questions. In table 7-1, the questions asked of nominees are distributed into three categories of repetitiveness. To assess repetitiveness, the analysis distinguishes between questions on the basis of how much common information they require. Those questions that inquire into the same subject without varying the information constitute identical questions (for example, "last name").[8] Those questions that request information on the same subject but vary the information along at least one dimension constitute similar questions (for example, the questions on real property mentioned earlier). Those that seek different information from other questions constitute unique questions (for example, the "nanny-tax" question asked only on the White House PDS).

Across the four forms, including a representative Senate committee questionnaire,[9] nominees must respond to approximately 233 inquiries. Nominees must answer 116 unique questions (those without an analog).

Table 7-1. *Repetitiveness of Questions on Executive Forms*

Type of question	*Number*	*Percent repetitive*[a]
Identical	18	8
Similar	99	42
Unique	116	50
Total	233	. . .

Source: Compiled by author from PDS, SF 86, Supplement to SF 86, SF 278, and a representative Senate confirmation questionnaire.

a. The category "repetitive" includes both similar and identical questions.

They answer another 99 similar questions (those with analogs); and they regularly repeat the answers to 18 identical questions. Thus, by these estimates, half of the questions nominees must answer are repetitive, having some analog elsewhere.

The Distribution of Repetitiveness

Table 7-2 summarizes the distribution of questions across seven topics used to organize the White House Personal Data Statement: personal and family background, profession and education, tax and financial information, employment of domestic help, participation in public activities, legal involvements, and miscellaneous information.[10] Based on the figures reported in the table, more than one-quarter of the questions asked of nominees cover personal contact information and family background. This large proportion of questions derives primarily from the detailed background information required on the SF 86. Following personal and family information, the bulk of the remaining questions focus on the professional and educational achievement or legal entanglements of nominees. Given that the OGE form does not cover legal involvement, the preponderance of these kinds of questions indicates that both the PDS and the FBI background check place a great deal of emphasis on legal issues.

Table 7-2 also reports the degree to which a topic includes repetitive questions (combining identical and similar questions). Given this summary, one result is misleading: 34 percent of the questions regarding personal and family background are repetitive. Yet because most of the identical questions across all four forms fall into this category (fifteen of the eighteen asked) and solicit basic personal identification and contact information (for example, name and phone number), the questions on personal and background information, though repetitive, do not constitute the kind of real burden about which nominees complain. This category

Table 7-2. *Repetitiveness of Questions on Executive Forms, by Topic*
Number unless otherwise specified

Topic	*Unique*	*Repetitive*[a]	*Totals*	*Percent repetitive*
Personal and family background	42	22	64	34
Professional and educational background	21	39	60	65
Tax and financial information	11	21	32	66
Domestic help issue	1	0	1	0
Public and organizational activities	2	7	9	78
Legal and administrative proceedings	9	25	34	74
Miscellaneous	30	3	33	9
Total	116	117	233	...
Average repetitiveness	...	...	...	50

Source: Compiled by author from PDS, SF 86, Supplement to SF 86, SF 278, and a representative Senate confirmation questionnaire.
a. The category "repetitive" includes both similar and identical questions.

also accounts for the largest number of unique questions (forty-two). As one prescription for reducing repetitiveness in this category, then, reformers could merely limit the amount of contact information required of nominees.[11]

The greatest proportion of the burden generated by genuinely repetitive questions occurs on three topics: professional and educational background (65 percent of sixty questions), tax and financial information (66 percent of thirty-two questions), and legal and administrative proceedings (74 percent of thirty-four questions). Association with employers and potential conflicts of interest constitute classic examples of repetitiveness among the professional and educational questions. All four institutions involved in vetting nominees have an interest in describing potential conflicts of interest embedded in the nominee's professional relationships. Patterns of repetitiveness in reporting conflicts of interest resemble those patterns found in reporting property (under the tax and financial information topic): multiple reporting periods, multiple subjects, and multiple types of information.

The level of repetitiveness across questions on legal and administrative proceedings seems particularly impressive given that, as noted earlier, the OGE form asks no questions about legal entanglements. The high proportion of repetitive questions on this topic results almost exclusively from the FBI's tendency to disjoin questions from the PDS into several specialized variations. For example, whereas the White House asks about arrests, charges, convictions, and litigation all in one question, the FBI asks a series of questions covering separate classes of offenses and case dispositions: felonies, firearms violations, pending charges on felonies, courts martial, civil investigations, agency procedures, and so on. In addition, the FBI background check uses a different time period from that explored on the PDS.

Strategies for Rescuing Nominees

Ameliorating the current situation for presidential appointees rests on reducing the intrusiveness of inquiry and the burdens that repetitiveness places on these nominees. Reducing the degree of intrusiveness would require a range of policy decisions on the part of institutions reluctant to give up the leverage over the process they believe their forms generate. Relieving the burden of unnecessary inquiry, on the other hand, requires the sacrifice of little in the way of control. Hence practical reform of the process more reasonably rests on one of three alternative ways of reducing repetitiveness: reducing the number of questions asked, increasing redundancy, or exercising the strategic imperative of a single institution.

Reducing the Number of Questions

Given that repetitive questions make up only half of all questions asked of nominees, reform efforts could properly focus on reducing the number of unique questions asked of nominees. This approach most closely resembles an attempt at reforming the level of intrusiveness because, of the 116 questions having no counterpart elsewhere, a few more than half (60) occur on the FBI background check. More than half of those (40), or a bit more than one-third of the total number of individual questions, relate to personal and family background. These questions establish a host of background characteristics presumably necessary to trace an individual's identity, including basic descriptors like height, hair color, and citizenship of spouse. The only questions in this group that might seem superfluous require information on the nominee's previous marriages and the descriptions required of adults who reside with the nominee but are not part of the immediate family. This approach to reform is problematic, however, because the questions generated by both the FBI, in the SF 86, and the OGE, in the SF 278, have substantial institutional justification. The FBI might argue that it needs to generate sufficient data on such topics to discover security risks, and the OGE has a substantial statutory basis for its inquiries on the SF 278. In effect, it seems unlikely that trying to reduce the scope of inquiry by truncating these kinds of questions will reduce the burden on nominees, except where authorities challenge the basic techniques used in carrying out a security background investigation.

As one possible reform in this area, the federal government could transfer basic background information on a nominee to the FBI before it begins its investigation. The administration would request a name search on the nominee from the government's files and then electronically transfer the results to the appropriate forms. The administration could then return these forms, partially completed, to the nominee to check, amend, and complete. Those forms having been completed, the background check would begin in earnest. In addition to effectively reducing the burden on nominees, this approach would reduce the amount of time the FBI spends retracing earlier investigations.

Increasing Redundancy

Without reducing the number of issues covered, reform could accommodate nominees by reducing repetitiveness and transforming the similar questions into identical questions, thereby increasing redundancy across the four forms. Among the repeated questions, three-quarters have similarities with other questions but require nominees to significantly reshape their earlier answers. The questions on real property, which ask nominees six separate though similar questions, constitute a perfect example. Settling on a single question, using the OGE approach, for example, would reduce the number of questions on real property by five (of six) and cut the percentage of repetitiveness in the tax and financial category by almost one-half, from 66 percent to 35 percent, while reducing the number of questions in this category by almost one-half (from thirty-two to seventeen) (see table 7-3).

Another approach would be to create such a common question by combining the broadest range of information required on any dimension involved in a topic. On the real property question, for example, all institutions could agree to the longer time designation used by the White House, the FBI's broader definition of subjects, and the broader notion of ownership inherent in the FBI's term "interest." In the end, this reform would reduce the burden on nominees by affording them a standard format within which to provide information.

Table 7-3. *Reduction in Repetitiveness by Increasing Redundancy*
Number unless otherwise specified

Topic	*Unique*	*Repetitive*[a]	*Totals*	*Percent repetitive*
Personal and family background	41	18	59	31
Professional and educational background	22	14	36	39
Tax and financial information	11	6	17	35
Domestic help issue	1	0	1	0
Public and organizational activities	2	2	4	50
Legal and administrative proceedings	7	6	13	46
Miscellaneous	30	1	31	3
Total	114	47	161	...
Average repetitiveness	...	...	...	29

Source: Compiled by author from PDS, SF 86, Supplement to SF 86, SF 278, and a representative Senate confirmation questionnaire.
a. The category "repetitive" includes both similar and identical questions.

Similar reductions in repetitiveness could result from reducing the number of different questions requiring information on professional relationships. At least ten separate questions ask about the nominee's connections with corporations and other institutions. Like those on property, these questions differ from one another only in detail: varying time periods or the type of organizations involved, the level of connection to an organization that must be reported, the level of compensation triggering a report, and so on. Reform in this topic could reduce the number of questions on conflict of interest from ten to, say, three.[12] Other changes in this topic would lower the number of questions concerning educational attainment, plans for postgovernment compensation, and foreign representation. Consolidation among these groups could result in a further reduction from eight questions to three. In all, reformulation in the topic of professional relationships could lower the level of repetitiveness from 65 percent to 39 percent.

Under the last topic with serious repetitiveness, legal and administrative proceedings, reformulation could eliminate all but six repetitive questions. That would reduce the repetitiveness in the topic from 74 percent to 46 percent. Overall, reformulating questions in the forms required by the executive branch could reduce repetitiveness from half of all questions to fewer than one-third. By normal standards, that reduction would constitute a reduction of 42 percent, a substantial improvement. In the end, using this reform approach would reduce the level of inquiry from

233 questions to 161, a total reduction in burden of 31 percent.[13] Appendix 7A lists, by topic, those questions that remain when redundancy is increased without challenging intrusiveness.

Taking Strategic Imperatives Seriously

Under one further reform strategy, one of the four institutions would unilaterally surrender control over information, relying on the information gathered by the others. This reform could guarantee a significant reduction in information requirements on nominees and repetitiveness.

The White House has the best opportunity to take this reform approach on two accounts. First, because it initiates the process, it can afford to limit its own information requirements by securing the information delivered to the other agencies. Instead of offering its own form, the White House could import information from an applicant's SF 86 and SF 278 as part of the initial negotiations process conducted pursuant to identifying eventual nominees. Based on those drafts, then, the White House would determine whether to carry through with its intent to nominate, thereby triggering the appointment vetting process. Because a number of the PDS questions are repeated on other forms, this strategy would reduce repetitiveness to around 28 percent, a slightly greater improvement over the more complicated strategies outlined earlier.

Appendix 7B identifies four categories of questions asked on the White House Personal Data Statement, ranging from those asked nowhere else (unique) to those that are identical to questions asked on other forms. In designating questions for deletion, this analysis assumes that the former category of questions should remain, because they occur nowhere else, whereas the White House could obtain the information sought by the latter from other questionnaires.[14]

Two categories remain in between these two extremes. The first group includes questions that ask for different information, usually of a more general nature, from that found on the other questionnaires. According to this analysis, the White House should retain these questions, assuming that more information is better than less. The other category also involves questions that obtain different information from other questionnaires; typically, however, these questions request less information than those on other forms, or variants on information found on other forms, and they could therefore be dropped.

In developing an inventory of those questions that should remain on a revised White House Personal Data Statement, the analysis simply drops those questions that elicit information required elsewhere in a more general form. It also eliminates, as irrelevant, two questions on the Personal Data Statement about the employment of the nominee's spouse. Appendix 7C presents a proposed revision of the White House Personal Data Statement that reduces information in almost every category, with the exception of the "specialty questions" on domestic help and child support. Further reductions of the Personal Data Statement could result by eliminating the questions on legal and administrative proceedings altogether. The FBI's background check, using the SF 86, could suffice to investigate legal entanglements, although the questions asked on that form seem less clear-cut than those asked on the Personal Data Statement.

The Relative Ease of Reform

As is clear from this assessment of the inquiry nominees must face, reforming the process seems overdue. Regardless of one's assessment of the level of or necessity for intrusiveness, surely the government cannot justify the burdensome repetitiveness of the process. The elaborate systems of inquiry needlessly confuse the nominees and represent an unnecessary burden on those so willing to serve. That attempts to change the situation, both inside and outside of government and across institutions, have been uniformly unsuccessful attests to the diligence and entrenchment of the forces of confusion and burden in this particular process.

Each of the institutions involved in vetting administration nominees plays a role in this affliction. Few have any special justification for placing that burden unfairly on the nominee, yet they all stand unyielding in reforming the process. Although they seem promising, even the most recent statutory requirements for study and analysis that the Congress has imposed on the president and, in turn, the president has assigned to the OGE have the familiar ring of past attempts. For this reason, sidestepping direct reform and relying instead on modification and increased redundancy seems to be the approach most likely to yield results.

Although it is the least challenging reform, improving redundancy constitutes a great improvement over the current situation. Make no mistake about that: nominees and those professionals who must assist them in filing forms would welcome a 30 percent reduction in the number of inquiries they must face, even if the remaining questions ask more of them than any of the previous three questions alone. To face a single inquiry, however broad, has its advantages.

Of course, improving the questionnaires will not rein in the range of other practices that have made the nomination process so difficult in recent times. The innovative and comprehensive empirical research of Nolan McCarty and Rose Razaghian, based on their data covering all nominations since 1885, clearly demonstrates that over time, the process has suffered much more from corrosive partisanship and leadership disarray in the Senate. They conclude that "political conflict induced by divided government and polarization clearly leads to a more drawn-out confirmation process. . . . The ease with which . . . dilatory tactics can be employed is likely to give the opposition much more leverage over the process than they would have in a more majoritarian body."[15] Obviously, then, a real reform movement must focus on developing a more viable and resilient common ground on presidential appointments—one that moves beyond repairs to redundancy and toward a collective, majoritarian agreement on the proper constitutional balance on nominations and the president's team.

Notes

1. Submitting their forms at the administration's beginning (say on January 4, 2001), nominees report only properties owned as of that moment and transactions on the second question that have occurred only in the past two calendar years: 1999 and 2000; see instructions to SF 278.

2. Paul C. Light and Virginia L. Thomas, *The Merit and Reputation of an Administration: Presidential Appointees on the Appointments Process* (Brookings and Heritage Foundation, 2000), p. 10. In a separate survey of those who had not held presidential appointments, 81 percent of these "neophytes," responding to the same question, said they thought filling out the various forms would "not be difficult" (Paul C. Light and Virginia L. Thomas, *Posts of Honor: How America's Corporate and Civic Leaders View Presidential Appointments* [Brookings and Heritage Foundation, 2001], p. 18). The authors concluded that detailed familiarity with the forms and their contents greatly altered for the negative the opinions of those who brave the process.

3. Ibid., p 1.

4. Actually, appointees must fill out several additional forms granting permissions for various background and Internal Revenue Service checks; but for purposes of analysis these do not represent much of a burden on nominees, and no one considers them noxious.

5. Below the rank of GS-15, federal employees report on a simplified financial disclosure form, the SF 450.

6. Many Senate committees will ask the nominee to fill out a standard questionnaire for the committee and then, based on answers to that questionnaire and with the help of policy experts in the General Accounting Office, will require answers to a second, more tailored questionnaire covering specific policy questions before the agency involved. In addition, an appointee to a position as agency inspector general will fill out the committee questionnaire from the substantive committee and another questionnaire from the Senate Committee on Governmental Affairs, which has joint jurisdiction over inspectors general for all agencies.

7. 5 U.S.C., appendix §102(a)(1)–(3). The disclosure of specific amounts rests on a "principal/agent" theory of control inherent to representative democracy. A representative avoids conflicts of interests by anticipating the adverse reaction of an aroused and informed public who will in turn judge and vote on the representative's qualifications. Disclosing such minutiae, therefore, acts as a deterrent to potentially undesirable behavior. Yet presidential nominees face a different situation. They come into government from the private world, where they may not have lived their lives in anticipation of governing. They cannot set their behavior in response to future restrictions they could not properly anticipate. Thus they enter public service with likely conflicts of interests inadvertently acquired. In response, the government must find a resolution rather than a deterrent for these extant conflicts. For the purposes of resolution, then, detailed figures provide no particular guidance because they do not necessarily supply any useful information about the nature of potential resolutions.

8. Many of these "identical" questions do not appear on all forms. For example, although the title of the position to which the nominee is appointed appears in identical syntax when it does appear, it does not appear on each of the four forms appointees must fill out. Some institutions apparently have no interest in that particular question. Despite the lack of universal usage, this analysis considers these questions as similar in form to those that do appear in identical form across all four forms (for example, last name).

9. The analysis presented here uses the form required by the Senate Committee on Commerce. It has exactly the median number of inquiries (seventy-three) across the twenty-one questionnaires used by the various Senate committees.

10. In table 7-3, identical and similar questions are conflated into the more general category, "repetitive."

11. For example, the OGE requires very little contact information on the SF 278. Instead, it relies on the agency to maintain contact with the nominee.

12. The reduced number would include a single question on the SF 86 outlining the nominee's employment history and two separate questions distinguishing between employment-related relationships and adviser relationships.

13. The analysis uses a scale of 0 to 100 percent, thus one with fixed upper and lower bounds; change is measured in terms of the remaining distance. So, a change from 50 percent to 25 percent equals a change of 50 percent, as it travels half the distance available between 50 and 0. Similarly a change from 50 percent

to 75 percent travels half the remaining distance to 100 percent and so also equals a change of 50 percent.

14. The White House should retain some basic identifying information on its form, including name, birth date and place, and social security number.

15. Nolan McCarty and Rose Razaghian, "Advice and Consent: Senate Responses to Executive Branch Nominations, 1885–1996," *American Journal of Political Science,* vol. 43, no. 4 (October 1999), pp. 1122–43.

Appendix 7A: Proposed General Questionnaire, Designed to Increase Redundancy

Personal and Family Background

—First name, middle name, last name, Jr., II, etc.
—Other names used and dates of use
—Home address
—Home telephone number
—Office address
—Office telephone number
—Date of birth
—Place of birth
—Citizenship
—Social security number
—Height
—Weight
—Hair color
—Eye color
—Sex
—Mother's maiden name
—Naturalization certificate: where were you naturalized?
—Citizenship certificate
—State Department Form 240: Report of Birth Abroad of a Citizen of the United States
—U.S. passport
—Dual citizenship
—Current marital status
—Date married
—Place married
—Spouse's name
—Spouse's other names
—Spouse's date of birth
—Spouse's place of birth
—Spouse's social security number
—Spouse's citizenship
—Spouse's occupation
—Spouse's current employer
—If separated, date of separation
—If legally separated, record of separation
—Address of current spouse (if different from your own)
—Former spouse's name
—Former spouse's date of birth
—Former spouse's place of birth
—Address of former spouse
—Former spouse's citizenship (countries)
—Former spouse: date married
—Former spouse: place married
—Former spouse: date of divorce or death
—Former spouse: if divorced, record of divorce
—Names of children
—Ages of children

—List the places where you have lived, beginning with the most recent and working back 7 years. All periods must be accounted for in your list. Be sure to indicate the actual physical location of your residence: do not use a post office box as an address, do not list a permanent address when you were actually living at a school address, etc. Be sure to specify your location as closely as possible: for example, do not list only your base or ship, list your barracks number or home port. You may omit temporary military duty locations under 90 days (list your permanent address instead), and you should use your APO or FPO address if you lived overseas.

—For any address in the past 5 years, list a person who knew you at that address, and who preferably still lives in that area (do not list people for residences completely outside this 5-year period, and do not list your spouse, former spouses, or other relatives). Also for addresses in the past five years, if the address is "General Delivery," a Rural or Star Route, or may be difficult to locate, provide directions for locating the residence on an attached continuation sheet.

—Give the full name, correct code (specified below), and other requested information for each of your relatives and associates, living or dead.

1 – Mother
2 – Father
3 – Stepmother
4 – Stepfather
5 – Foster parent
6 – Child (adopted also)
7 – Stepchild
8 – Brother
9 – Sister
10 – Stepbrother
11 – Stepsister
12 – Half-brother
13 – Half-sister
14 – Father-in-law
15 – Mother-in-law
16 – Guardian
17 – Other relative*
18 – Associate**
19 – Adult currently living with you

*Code 17 (Other relative): include only foreign national relatives not listed in codes 1–16 with whom you or your spouse are bound by affection, obligation, or close and continuing contact.

**Code 18 (Associates): include only foreign national associates with whom you or your spouse are bound by affection, obligation, or close and continuing contact.

—If your mother, father, sister, brother, child, or current spouse or person with whom you have a spouselike relationship is a U.S. citizen by other than birth or an alien residing in the United States, provide the nature of the individual's relationship to you (spouse, spouselike, mother, etc.) and the individual's name and date of birth on the first line.

—Provide the individual's naturalization certificate or alien registration number and use one of the document codes below to identify proof of citizenship status. Provide additional information as requested.

1 – Naturalization certificate: Provide the date issued and the location where the person was naturalized (court, city, and state).

2 – Citizenship certificate: Provide the date and location issued (city and state).

3 – Alien registration: Provide the date and place where the person entered the United States (city and state).

4 – Other: Provide an explanation in the "Additional information" block.

—List three people who know you well and live in the United States. They should be good friends, peers, colleagues, college roommates, etc., whose combined association with you covers as well as possible the past 7 years. Do not list your spouse, former spouses, or other relatives, and try not to list anyone who is listed elsewhere on this form.

—Please identify any adults (18 years or older) currently living with you who are not members of your immediate family. Provide the names of those individuals, dates and places of birth, and whether or not they are United States citizens.

—In the past 7 years, have you had an active passport that was issued by a foreign government? If so, provide inclusive dates, names of firms and governments involved, and an explanation of your involvement.

—Do you have any medical conditions that could interfere with your ability to fulfill your duties? Please explain.

Professional and Educational Background

—Title of position

—Department or agency

—Date of appointment, candidacy, election, or nomination

—Reporting status

—Name of congressional committee considering nomination (presidential nominees subject to Senate confirmation)

—Calendar year covered

—Termination date

—Selection: (a) Do you know why you were chosen for this nomination by the president? (b) What do you believe in your background or employment experience affirmatively qualifies you for this particular appointment?

—If confirmed, do you expect to serve out your full term or until the next presidential election, whichever is applicable?

—Please list each high school, college, and graduate school you attended, the dates of attendance, and the degrees awarded.
—Employment record: List all jobs held since college, including the title or description of job, name of employer, location of work, and dates of employment.
—Has any of the following happened to you in the past 7 years?

1. fired from a job
2. quit a job after being told you would be fired
3. left a job by mutual agreement following allegations of misconduct
4. left a job by mutual agreement following allegations of unsatisfactory performance
5. left a job for other reasons under unfavorable circumstances

If so, please provide the date, the employer's name and address, and the reason (from the previously mentioned list).
—Government experience: List any advisory, consultative, honorary, or other part-time service or positions with federal, state, or local governments, other than those listed above.
—Have you had any military service? If so, give particulars, including the dates, branch of service, rank or rate, serial number, and type of discharge received.
—Memberships: List all memberships and offices held in professional, fraternal, scholarly, civic, business, charitable, and other organizations.
—Report sources of more than $5,000 compensation received by you or your business affiliation for services provided directly by you during any one year of the reporting period. This includes the names of clients and customers of any corporation, firm, partnership, or other business enterprise, or any other nonprofit organization when you directly provided the services generating a fee or payment of more than $5,000. You need not report the U.S. government as a source.
—Please list all corporations, partnerships, trusts, or other business entities with which you have ever been affiliated as an officer, director, trustee, partner, or holder of a significant equity or financial interest (i.e., any ownership interest of more than 5 percent) or whose decisions you have the ability to influence. Please identify the entity, your relationship to the entity, and dates of service and affiliation.
—Please provide the names of all corporations, firms, partnerships, trusts, or other business enterprises and all nonprofit organizations and other institutions with which you are now or during the past five years have been affiliated as an adviser, attorney, or consultant. It is only necessary to provide the names of major clients and any client matter in which you and your firm are involved that might present a potential conflict of inter-

est with your proposed assignment. Please identify the entity, your relationship or duty with regard to each, and dates of service.

—Report your agreements or arrangements for (1) continuing participation in an employee benefit plan (e.g., pension, 401(k), deferred compensation); (2) continuation of payment by a former employer (including severance payments); (3) leaves of absence; and (4) future employment. See instructions regarding the reporting of negotiations for any of these arrangements or benefits.

—If you performed any work for or received any payments from any foreign government, business, or individual in the past ten years, please describe the circumstances and identify the source and dates of services and payments.

—Please list any registration as an agent for a foreign principal, or any exemption from such registration. Please provide the status of any and all such registrations and/or exemptions (i.e., whether active and whether personally registered).

—Have you ever registered as a lobbyist or other legislative agent to influence federal or state legislation or administrative acts? If yes, please supply details including the status of each registration.

—Published writings: List the titles, publishers, and dates of books, articles, reports, or other published materials you have written.

—Identify each instance in which you have testified before Congress in a nongovernmental capacity, and specify the subject matter of each testimony.

—If you are a member of any licensed profession or occupation (such as lawyer, doctor, accountant, insurance or real estate broker, etc.), please specify the present status of each license and whether such license has ever been withdrawn, suspended, or revoked and the reason therefore.

—Do you have any significant interest in any relationship with the government through contracts, consulting services, grants, loans, or guarantees? If yes, please provide details.

—Does your spouse or any family member or business in which you, your spouse, or any family members have a significant interest have any relationship with the government through contracts, consulting services, grants, loans, or guarantees? If yes, please provide details.

—Are you a male born after December 31, 1959?

—Have you registered with the Selective Service System? If "Yes," provide your registration number. If "No," show the reason for your legal exemption below.

—Honors and awards: List all scholarships, fellowships, honorary degrees, and honorary society memberships that you believe would be of interest to the Committee.

—Speeches: Provide the Committee with two copies of any formal speeches you have delivered during the past 5 years which you have copies of on topics relevant to the position for which you have been nominated.
—Do you agree to have written opinions provided to the Committee by the designated agency ethics officer of the agency to which you are nominated and by the Office of Government Ethics concerning potential conflicts of interest or any legal impediments to your serving in this position?
—Explain how you will resolve any potential conflict of interest, including any that may be disclosed by your responses to the above items. (Please provide a copy of any trust or other agreements.)

Tax and Financial Information

—For you, your spouse, and dependent children, report each asset held for investment or the production of income which had a fair market value exceeding $1,000 at the close of the reporting period or which generated more than $200 in income during the reporting period, together with such income.
—For yourself, also report the source and actual amount of earned income exceeding $200 (other than from the U.S. Government). For your spouse, report the source but not the amount of earned income of more than $1,000 (except report the actual amount of any honoraria over $200 of your spouse).
—Report liabilities over $10,000 owed to any one creditor at any time during the reporting period by you, your spouse, or dependent children. Check the highest amount owed during the reporting period. Exclude a mortgage on your personal residence unless it is rented out; loans secured by automobiles, household furniture, or appliances; and liabilities owed to certain relatives listed in instructions. See instructions for revolving charge accounts.
—Please describe all real estate held in your name or in your spouse's name during the past six years. Please include real estate held in combination with others, held in trust, held by a nominee, or held by or through any other third person or title-holding entity. Please also include dates held.
—Provide the identity and a description of the nature of any interest in an option, mineral lease, copyright, or patent held, directly or indirectly, during the past 12 months and indicate which, if any, have been divested and the date of divestment.
—Do you have any foreign property, business connections, or financial interests? If so, provide inclusive dates, names of firms and/or governments involved, and an explanation of your involvement.
—Do you intend to create a qualified diversified trust?

—Has a tax lien or other collection procedure ever been instituted against you or your spouse by federal, state, or local authorities? If so, describe the circumstances and the resolution of the matter.

—Have you and your spouse filed all federal, state, and local income tax returns?

—Have you or your spouse ever filed a late income tax return without a valid extension? If so, describe the circumstances and the resolution of the matter.

—Has the Internal Revenue Service ever audited your federal tax return? If so, what resulted from the audit?

—Have you or your spouse ever paid any tax penalties? If so, describe the circumstances and the resolution of the matter.

—Have you ever had any contact with a foreign government, its establishments (embassies or consulates), or its representatives, whether inside or outside the United States, other than on official U.S. government business? (Does not include routine visa applications and border crossing contacts.) If so, provide inclusive dates, names of firms and/or governments involved, and an explanation of your involvement.

—For you, your spouse, and dependent children, report the source, a brief description, and the value of (1) gifts (such as tangible items, transportation, lodging, food, or entertainment) received from one source totaling more than $260, and (2) travel-related cash reimbursements received from one source totaling more than $260. For conflicts analysis, it is helpful to indicate a basis for receipt such as personal friend, agency approval under 5 U.S.C.§4111 or other statutory authority, etc. For travel-related gifts and reimbursements, include travel itinerary, dates, and the nature of expenses provided. Exclude anything given to you by the U.S. government; given to your agency in connection with official travel; received from relatives; received by your spouse or dependent child totally independent of their relationship to you; or provided as personal hospitality at the donor's residence. Also for purposes of aggregating gifts to determine the total value from one source, exclude items worth $104 or less. See instructions for other exclusions.

—Describe the terms of any beneficial trust or blind trust of which you, your spouse, or your dependents may be a beneficiary. In the case of a blind trust, provide the name of the trustee(s) and a copy of the trust agreement.

—Provide a description of any fiduciary responsibility or power of attorney which you hold for or on behalf of any other person.

—In the past 7 years, have you been over 180 days delinquent on any debt(s)? If so, provide the date incurred, the date satisfied, the amount, the type of loan or obligation and account number, and the name and address of the creditor or obligee.

—Are you currently over 90 days delinquent on any debt(s)? If so, provide the date incurred, the date satisfied, the amount, the type of loan or obligation and account number, and the name and address of the creditor or obligee.

Domestic Help

—Do you presently have or have you in the past had domestic help (i.e., housekeeper, babysitter, nanny, or gardener)? If yes, please indicate years of service for each individual and also give a brief description of the services rendered.

Public and Organizational Activities

—Political affiliations and activities

a. List all offices with a political party which you have held or any public office for which you have been a candidate.

b. List all memberships and offices held in and services rendered to all political parties or election committees during the past 10 years.

c. Itemize all political contributions to any individual, campaign organization, political party, political action committee, or similar entity of $500 or more for the past ten years.

d. Have any complaints been lodged against you or your political committee with the Federal Election Commission or state or local election authorities? If so, please describe.

—Have you or your spouse at any time belonged to any membership organization, including but not limited to those described in the preceding paragraph, that as a matter of policy or practice denied or restricted affiliation (as a matter of either policy or practice) based on race, sex, ethnic background, or religious or sexual preference?

—Have you ever been an officer or a member or made a contribution to an organization dedicated to the violent overthrow of the United States government and which engages in illegal activities to that end, knowing that the organization engages in such activities with the specific intent to further such activities?

—Have you ever knowingly engaged in any acts or activities designed to overthrow the United States government by force?

Legal and Administrative Proceedings

—Have you ever been involved in civil or criminal litigation, or in administrative or legislative proceedings of any kind, either as a subject of investigation or arrest, plaintiff, defendant, respondent, witness, or party in interest? Give full details identifying dates, issues litigated, and the location where the civil action is recorded.

—Have you or any business of which you are or were an officer ever been involved as a party in interest in an administrative agency investigation, proceeding, or civil litigation? If so, please provide details.

—Have you or any firm, company, or other entity with which you have been associated ever been convicted of a violation of any federal, state, county, or municipal law, regulation, or ordinance? If so, please provide full details.

—Please list any bankruptcy proceeding in which you or your spouse have been involved as a debtor.

—Have you or your spouse ever been accused of or found guilty of any violations of government or agency procedure (specifically including security violations and/or any application or appeal process)?

—Please list any complaint ever made against you by any administrative agency, professional association, or organization or federal, state, or local ethics agency, committee, or official.

—Please list any and all judgments rendered against you including the date, amount, name of the case, subject matter of the case, and the date of satisfaction. Please include obligations of child support and alimony and provide the status of each judgment and/or obligation, paying special attention to report any late payments or outstanding obligations. Please note if any motions or court actions for modification of child support or alimony have been filed or instituted. Note if any motions or court actions have been filed or instituted to compel late payments or past due amounts. Note if any writs of garnishment have been issued. Please provide details.

—The following questions pertain to the illegal use of drugs or drug activity. You are required to answer the questions fully and truthfully, and your failure to do so could be grounds for an adverse employment decision or action against you, but neither your truthful responses nor information derived from your responses will be used as evidence against you in any subsequent criminal proceeding.

—Since the age of 16 or in the past 7 years, whichever is shorter, have you illegally used any controlled substance, for example, marijuana, cocaine, crack cocaine, hashish, narcotics, amphetamines, depressants, hallucinogens, or prescription drugs? If yes, provide the date, identify the controlled substance and/or prescription drugs used and the number of times each was used.

—Have you ever illegally used a controlled substance while employed as a law enforcement officer, prosecutor, or courtroom official, while possessing a security clearance, or while in a position directly and immediately affecting the public safety? If yes, provide the date, identify the controlled substance and/or prescription drugs used and the number of times each was used.

—In the past 7 years, have you been involved in the illegal purchase, manufacture, trafficking, production, transfer, shipping, receiving, or sale of any narcotic, depressant, stimulant, hallucinogenic, or cannabis for your own intended profit or that of another? If yes, provide the date, identify the controlled substance and/or prescription drugs used and the number of times each was used.

—In the past 7 years, has your use of alcoholic beverages such as liquor, beer, and wine resulted in any alcohol-related treatment or counseling? If yes, provide the date of treatment and the name and address of the counselor or doctor below. Do not repeat information reported in the response to the drug questions.

—Has the United States government ever investigated your background and/or granted you a security clearance? If yes, use the codes that follow to provide the requested information below. If yes, but you can't recall the investigating agency and/or the security clearance received, enter Other agency code or clearance code as appropriate, and Don't know or Don't recall under the Other agency heading below. If your response is no or you don't know or can't recall if you were investigated and cleared, check the No box.

1. Defense Department
2. State Department
3. Office of Personnel Management
4. FBI
5. Treasury
6. Other

Codes:
0 – Not required
1 – Confidential
2 – Secret
3 – Top Secret
4 – Sensitive Compartmented Information
5 – Q
6 – L
7 – Other

—To your knowledge, have you ever had a clearance or access authorization denied, suspended, or revoked or have you ever been debarred from government employment? If yes, give date of action and agency. Note: an administrative downgrade or termination of a security clearance is not a revocation.

Miscellaneous

—Please provide any other information, including information about other members of your family, that could suggest a conflict of interest or be a possible source of embarrassment to you, your family, or the president.

—Have you ever had any association with any person, group, or business venture that could be used, even unfairly, to impugn or attack your character and qualifications for a government position?

—Do you know anyone or any organization that might take any steps, overtly or covertly, fairly or unfairly, to criticize your appointment, including any news organization? If so, please identify and explain the basis for the potential criticism.

—List foreign countries you have visited, except on travel under official government orders, beginning with the most current and working back 7 years. (Travel as a dependent or contractor must be listed.) Use one of these codes to indicate the purpose of your visit:

1 – Business 3 – Education
2 – Pleasure 4 – Other

Include short trips to Canada or Mexico. If you have lived near a border and have made short (one day or less) trips to the neighboring country, you do not need to list each trip. Instead, provide the time period, the code, the country, and a note ("Many Short Trips"). Do not repeat travel covered in earlier items.

—Why do you wish to serve in the position for which you have been nominated?

—What goals have you established for your first two years in this position, if confirmed?

—What skills do you believe you may be lacking which may be necessary to successfully carry out this position? What steps can be taken to obtain those skills?

—Please discuss your philosophical views on the role of government. Include a discussion of when you believe the government should involve itself in the private sector, when society's problems should be left to the private sector, and what standards should be used to determine when a government program is no longer necessary.

—Describe your department's or agency's current mission, major programs, and major operational objectives.

—Describe your working relationship, if any, with the Congress. Does your professional experience include working with committees of the Congress? If yes, please describe.

—Will you ensure that your department or agency complies with deadlines for information set by congressional committees?

—Will you ensure that your department or agency does whatever it can to protect congressional witnesses and whistle-blowers from reprisal for their testimony and disclosures?
—Will you cooperate in providing the committee with requested witnesses, to include technical experts and career employees with firsthand knowledge of matters of interest to the committee?
—Please explain how you will review regulations issued by your department or agency, and work closely with Congress, to ensure that such regulations comply with the spirit of the laws passed by Congress.
—Are you willing to appear and testify before any duly constituted committee of the Congress on such occasions as you may reasonably be requested to do so?
—Please describe how your previous professional experience and education qualify you for the position for which you have been nominated.
—What forces are likely to result in changes to the mission of this agency over the coming five years?
—What are the likely outside forces which may prevent the agency from accomplishing its mission? What do you believe to be the top three challenges facing the board or commission and why?
—What factors, in your opinion, have kept the board or commission from achieving its mission over the past several years?
—Who are the stakeholders in the work of this agency?
—What is the proper relationship between your position, if confirmed, and the stakeholders identified in the previous item?
—The Chief Financial Officers Act requires all government departments and agencies to develop sound financial management practices similar to those practiced in the private sector. (a) What do you believe are your responsibilities, if confirmed, to ensure that your agency has proper management and accounting control? (b) What experience do you have in managing a large organization?
—The Government Performance and Results Act requires all government departments and agencies to identify measurable performance goals and to report to Congress on their success in achieving these goals. (a) Please discuss what you believe to be the benefits of identifying performance goals and reporting your progress in achieving those goals. (b) What steps should Congress consider taking when an agency fails to achieve its performance goals? Should these steps include the elimination, privatization, downsizing, or consolidation of departments and/or programs? (c) What performance goals do you believe should be applicable to your personal performance, if confirmed?

—Please describe your philosophy of supervisor-employee relationships. Generally, what supervisory model do you follow? Have any employee complaints been brought against you?

—Please explain what you believe to be the proper relationship between yourself, if confirmed, and the inspector general of your department or agency.

—Please explain how you will work with this Committee and other stakeholders to ensure that regulations issued by your board or commission comply with the spirit of the laws passed by Congress.

—In the areas under the department or agency's jurisdiction, what legislative action(s) should Congress consider as priorities? Please state your personal views.

—Within your area of control, will you pledge to develop and implement a system that allocates discretionary spending based on national priorities determined in an open fashion on a set of established criteria? If not, please state why. If yes, please state what steps you intend to take and a time frame for their implementation.

Appendix 7B: Information Requirements of the White House Personal Data Statement

This appendix analyzes the questions posed to nominees on the White House Personal Data Statement by identifying the degree to which each question asks for unique information in the vetting process. Each question carries one of four possible descriptions:

—Identical information: The question has an exact analog among the other three forms required of presidential appointees for jobs that require Senate confirmation and should therefore be dropped.

—More information: The question elicits more general information than similar questions on the other questionnaires and should therefore be retained.

—Less-general information: The question elicits different information, and usually less-general information, from that sought on other executive branch forms. Because the White House could obtain this information from the other forms, this question could be dropped.

—Unique information: The question elicits information that is not asked for on any of the other forms. Under most circumstances these questions should remain on the Personal Data Statement.

Question topic	Level of repetitiveness
Personal and Family Background	
—First name	Identical information
—Middle name	Identical information
—Last name	Identical information
—Home address	Identical information
—Home telephone number	Identical information
—Office address	Identical information
—Office telephone number	Identical information
—Date of birth	Identical information
—Place of birth	Identical information
—Citizenship	Identical information
—Social security number	Identical information
—Current marital status	Identical information
—Spouse's name	Identical information
—Spouse's citizenship	Identical information
—Names of children	Identical information
—Ages of children	Identical information
—Do you have any medical conditions that could interfere with your ability to fulfill your duties? Please explain.	More information
—Spouse's occupation	Unique information
—Spouse's current employer	Unique information
Professional and Educational Background	
—Please list each high school, college, and graduate school you attended, the dates of attendance, and the degrees awarded.	Identical information
—Please chronologically list activities, other than those on your resume, from which you have derived earned income (e.g., self-employment, consulting activities, writing, speaking royalties, and honoraria) since age 21.	Less-general information
—Please list all corporations, partnerships, trusts, or other business entities with which you have ever been affiliated as an officer, director, trustee, partner, or holder of a significant equity or financial interest (i.e., any ownership interest of more than 5 percent) or whose decisions you have the ability to influence. Please identify the entity, your relationship to the entity, and dates of service and/or affiliation.	Less-general information

Question topic	Level of repetitiveness
—Please provide the names of all corporations, firms, partnerships, trusts, or other business enterprises and all nonprofit organizations and other institutions with which you are now or during the past five years have been affiliated as an adviser, attorney, or consultant. It is only necessary to provide the names of major clients and any client matter in which you and your firm are involved that might present a potential conflict of interest with your proposed assignment. Please identify the entity, your relationship or duty with regard to each, and dates of service.	Less-general information
—Other than the entities identified in the previous item, please provide the names of any organization with which you were associated which might present a potential conflict of interest with your proposed assignment. For each entity you identify in your response to this question, please provide your relationship or duty with regard to each and the dates of service.	Less-general information
—Please describe any contractual or informal arrangement you may have made with any person or any business enterprise in regard to future employment or termination payments or financial benefits that will be provided you if you enter government employment.	Less-general information
—If you performed any work for and/or received any payments from any foreign government, business, or individual in the past 10 years, please describe the circumstances and identify the source and dates of services and/or payments.	Less-general information
—Please list any registration as an agent for a foreign principal or any exemption from such registration. Please provide the status of any and all such registrations and/or exemptions (i.e., whether active and whether personally registered).	Less-general information
—Have you ever registered as a lobbyist or other legislative agent to influence federal or state legislation or administrative acts? If yes, please supply details, including the status of each registration.	More information

Question topic	Level of repetitiveness
—Please list each book, article, column, or publication you have authored, individually or with others.	Unique information
—Identify each instance in which you have testified before Congress in a nongovernmental capacity, and specify the subject matter of each testimony.	Unique information
—If you are a member of any licensed profession or occupation (such as lawyer, doctor, accountant, insurance or real estate broker, etc.), please specify the present status of each license and whether such license has ever been withdrawn, suspended, or revoked and the reason therefore.	Unique information
—Do you have any significant interest in any relationship with the government through contracts, consulting services, grants, loans, or guarantees? If yes, please provide details.	Unique information
—Does your spouse or any family member or business in which you, your spouse, or any family members have a significant interest have any relationship with the government through contracts, consulting services, grants, loans, or guarantees? If yes, please provide details.	Unique information
Tax and Financial Information	
—As of the date of this questionnaire, please list all assets with a fair market value in excess of $1,000 for you and your spouse, and provide a good faith estimate of value.	Less-general information
—As of the date of this questionnaire, please list all liabilities in excess of $10,000 for you and your spouse. Please list the name and address of the creditor, the amount owed to the nearest thousand dollars, a brief description of the nature of the obligation, the interest (if any), the date on which due, and the present status (i.e., is the obligation current or past due).	Less-general information
—Please describe all real estate held in your name or in your spouse's name during the past six years. Please include real estate held in combination with others, held in trust, held by a nominee, or held by or through any other third person or title-holding entity. Please also include dates held.	More information

Question topic	Level of repetitiveness
—Has a tax lien or other collection procedure ever been instituted against you or your spouse by federal, state, or local authorities? If so, describe the circumstances and the resolution of the matter.	More information
—Have you and your spouse filed all federal, state, and local income tax returns?	More information
—Have you or your spouse ever filed a late income tax return without a valid extension? If so, describe the circumstances and the resolution of the matter.	More information
—Have you or your spouse ever paid any tax penalties? If so, describe the circumstances and the resolution of the matter.	Unique information
Domestic Help	
—Do you presently have or have you in the past had domestic help (i.e., housekeeper, babysitter, nanny, or gardener)? If yes, please indicate years of service for each individual and also give a brief description of the services rendered.	Unique information
Public and Organizational Activities	
—Have you ever run for public office? If yes, does your campaign have any outstanding campaign debt? If so, are you personally liable? Please also provide complete information as to the amount of debt and creditors.	More information
—Please list current and past political party affiliations.	More information
—Have you or your spouse at any time belonged to any membership organization, including but not limited to those described in the preceding paragraph, that as a matter of policy or practice denied or restricted affiliation based on race, sex, ethnic background, or religious or sexual preference?	Less-general information

Question topic	Level of repetitiveness
—Please list each membership you have had with any civic, social, charitable, educational, professional, fraternal, benevolent or religious organization, private club, or other membership organization (including any tax-exempt organization) during the past 10 years. Please include dates of membership and any positions you may have had with the organization.	More information
Legal and Administrative Proceedings	
—Please list any lawsuits you have brought as a plaintiff or which were brought against you as a defendant or third party. Include in this response any contested divorce proceedings or other domestic relations matters.	Less-general information
—Please list and describe any administrative agency proceeding in which you have been involved as a party.	Less-general information
—Please list any bankruptcy proceeding in which you or your spouse have been involved as a debtor.	More information
—Have you or your spouse ever been arrested for, charged with, or convicted of violating any federal, state, or local law, regulation, or ordinance (excluding traffic offenses for which the fine was less than $100)? If so, please identify each such instance and supply details, including date, place, law enforcement agency, and court.	More information
—Have you or your spouse ever been accused of or found guilty of any violations of government or agency procedure (specifically including security violations and/or any application or appeal process)?	More information
—Please list any complaint ever made against you by any administrative agency, professional association or organization, or federal, state, or local ethics agency, committee, or official.	More information
—Please list any and all judgments rendered against you, including the date, amount, name of the case, subject matter of the case, and the date of satisfaction. Please include obligations of child support and alimony and provide the status of each judgment and/or obligation.	More information

Question topic	Level of repetitiveness
—With regard to each obligation of child support and/or alimony, state the following: Have any payments been made late, or have there been any lapses in payment? Have any motions or courts actions for modification of child support or alimony been filed or instituted? Have any actions or motions to compel payment or initiate collection of late payments and/or past due amounts been filed or threatened? Have any writs of garnishment been issued? If your response was yes to any of the above questions, please provide details.	More information
—Have you or your spouse ever been investigated by any federal, state, military, or local law enforcement agency? If so, please identify each such instance and supply details, including date, place, law enforcement agency, and court.	Unique information
Miscellaneous	
—Please provide any other information, including information about other members of your family, that could suggest a conflict of interest or be a possible source of embarrassment to you, your family, or the president.	More information
—Have you ever had any association with any person, group, or business venture that could be used, even unfairly, to impugn or attack your character and qualifications for a government position?	Unique information
—Do you know anyone or any organization that might take any steps, overtly or covertly, fairly or unfairly, to criticize your appointment, including any news organization? If so, please identify and explain the basis for the potential criticism.	Unique information

Appendix 7C: Proposed White House Personal Data Statement

Personal and Family Background

—First name, middle name, last name

—Date of birth

—Place of birth

—Social security number

—Do you have any medical conditions that could interfere with your ability to fulfill your duties? Please explain.

Professional and Educational Background

—Have you ever registered as a lobbyist or other legislative agent to influence federal or state legislation or administrative acts? If yes, please supply details, including the status of each registration.

—Please list each book, article, column, or publication you have authored, individually or with others.

—Identify each instance in which you have testified before Congress in a nongovernmental capacity, and specify the subject matter of each testimony.

—If you are a member of any licensed profession or occupation (such as lawyer, doctor, accountant, insurance or real estate broker, etc.), please specify the present status of each license and whether such license has ever been withdrawn, suspended, or revoked and the reason therefore.

—Do you have any significant interest in any relationship with the government through contracts, consulting services, grants, loans, or guarantees? If yes, please provide details.

—Does your spouse or any family member or business in which you, your spouse, or any family members have a significant interest have any relationship with the government through contracts, consulting services, grants, loans, or guarantees? If yes, please provide details.

Tax and Financial Information

—Please describe all real estate held in your name or in your spouse's name during the past six years. Please include real estate held in combination with others, held in trust, held by a nominee, or held by or through any other third person or title-holding entity. Please also include dates held.

—Has a tax lien or other collection procedure ever been instituted against you or your spouse by federal, state, or local authorities? If so, describe the circumstances and the resolution of the matter.

—Have you and your spouse filed all federal, state, and local income tax returns?

—Have you or your spouse ever filed a late income tax return without a valid extension? If so, describe the circumstances and the resolution of the matter.

—Have you or your spouse ever paid any tax penalties? If so, describe the circumstances and the resolution of the matter.

Domestic Help

—Do you presently have or have you in the past had domestic help (i.e., housekeeper, babysitter, nanny, or gardener)? If yes, please indicate years of service for each individual and also give a brief description of the services rendered.

Public and Organizational Activities

—Have you ever run for public office? If yes, does your campaign have any outstanding campaign debt? If so, are you personally liable? Please also provide complete information as to the amount of debt and creditors.

—Please list current and past political party affiliations.

Legal and Administrative Proceedings

—Please list any bankruptcy proceeding in which you or your spouse have been involved as a debtor.

—Have you or your spouse ever been arrested for, charged with, or convicted of violating any federal, state, or local law, regulation, or ordinance (excluding traffic offenses for which the fine was less than $100)? If so, please identify each such instance and supply details, including date, place, law enforcement agency, and court.

—Have you or your spouse ever been accused of or found guilty of any violations of government or agency procedure (specifically including security violations and/or any application or appeal process)?

—Please list any complaint ever made against you by any administrative agency, professional association or organization, or federal, state, or local ethics agency, committee, or official.

—Please list any and all judgments rendered against you, including the date, amount, name of the case, subject matter of the case, and the date of satisfaction. Please include obligations of child support and alimony and provide the status of each judgment and/or obligation.

—With regard to each obligation of child support and/or alimony, state the following: Have any payments been made late, or have there been any lapses in payment? Have any motions or courts actions for modification of child support or alimony been filed or instituted? Have any actions or motions to compel payment or initiate collection of late payments and/or past due amounts been filed or threatened? Have any writs of garnishment been issued? If your response was yes to any of the above questions, please provide details.

—Have you or your spouse ever been investigated by any federal, state, military, or local law enforcement agency? If so, please identify each such instance and supply details, including date, place, law enforcement agency, and court.

Miscellaneous

—Please provide any other information, including information about other members of your family, that could suggest a conflict of interest or be a possible source of embarrassment to you, your family, or the president.

—Have you ever had any association with any person, group, or business venture that could be used, even unfairly, to impugn or attack your character and qualifications for a government position?

—Do you know anyone or any organization that might take any steps, overtly or covertly, fairly or unfairly, to criticize your appointment, including any news organization? If so, please identify and explain the basis for the potential criticism.

CHAPTER EIGHT

Appointments Past and Future: How Presidential Appointees View the Call to Service

JUDITH M. LABINER
PAUL C. LIGHT

THE UNITED STATES has always depended on citizen servants to lead its government. The Founding Fathers believed their young country would not survive long as a representative democracy without leaders whose patriotism and love of justice would help their fragile nation heal the divisions of the day.

These hopes extended to what Philadelphia's Benjamin Franklin called "posts of honor" in the executive branch.[1] Worried that some fair-weather patriots would be drawn to government in search of profit, Franklin proposed that executive officers receive "no salary, stipend, Fee or reward whatsoever for their service."[2] Although the Constitutional Convention quietly tabled his proposal without debate, Franklin's proposal reflected the young republic's desperate need for leaders motivated by public interest, not private gain.

As the federal agenda has expanded over the past two hundred years to keep pace with public demand, so has the need for highly talented presidential appointees who are committed to the idea of citizen service. Results from two recent surveys of past and potential appointees offer mixed news about the likelihood that the nation's most talented citizens will be drawn to this kind of service. The surveys provide an extended look backward at the actual experiences of past appointees as they moved through the process and a unique look forward at whether some of the nation's most talented citizens are likely to accept a president's invitation to serve.

The surveys offer a mixed portrait of the presidential appointments process. On the one hand, they suggest that both past and potential appointees see great honor in serving their country. The vast majority of past appointees would recommend a presidential post to their friends and family, and the vast majority of potential appointees believe that service generates a host of long-term benefits. On the other hand, past and potential presidential appointees alike view the process of entering office with disdain, describing it as embarrassing, confusing, and unfair. They see the process as far more cumbersome and lengthy than it needs to be and place the blame at both ends of Pennsylvania Avenue.

More troubling, both surveys suggest that the presidential appointments process may be failing at its most basic task. It does not give appointees the information they need to act in their own best interest throughout the process, it does not move fast enough to give the departments and agencies of government the leadership they need to faithfully execute the laws, and it produces a less-than-enviable pool of actual appointees. More than three-quarters of the appointees nominated by presidents Ronald Reagan, George Bush, and Bill Clinton who were interviewed for the Presidential Appointee Initiative rated their colleagues as a "mixed lot," whereas only 11 percent considered their colleagues "the best and the brightest."

Fortunately the nominees surveyed suggested a range of simple solutions for redressing the most destructive of the problems facing the presidential appointments process and building a more persuasive case for service. In brief, they urged the president and Congress to simplify the appointments process and make it easier for appointees to return to their previous careers after service. Although these changes would not guarantee a yes when the president makes the call to service, they would eliminate some of the most significant burdens that confront the nation's most talented citizens as they make the choice between accepting a post of honor and just staying home.

The Surveys

The two surveys that produced the data presented in this chapter were conducted by Princeton Survey Research Associates on behalf of the Presidential Appointee Initiative, a project of the Brookings Institution funded by the Pew Charitable Trusts. Both surveys were completed by telephone.

The survey of former appointees, conducted in the winter of 1999–2000, was designed to examine the actual experience of 435 executive-level 1 to 4 appointees (secretary to assistant secretary) during the Reagan, Bush, and Clinton administrations (1984 through 1999). The sample was limited to those serving in a cabinet department or one of six independent agencies: the Environmental Protection Agency, the Federal Emergency Management Agency, the National Aeronautics and Space Administration, the Small Business Administration, the United States Agency for International Development, and the United States Information Agency. These six agencies were selected to assure comparability with a project conducted in 1985 by the National Academy of Public Administration, which surveyed appointees who had gone through the process from 1964 to 1984. In all, 107 Reagan, 127 Bush, and 201 Clinton appointees were interviewed for the first Presidential Appointee Initiative survey, yielding a 59 percent response rate of those contacted for the study. The respondents were mostly men (81 percent), and most were over fifty years of age (76 percent).

The survey of potential appointees, conducted during the summer and fall of 2000, focused on civic and corporate leaders. The survey was designed to examine the willingness to serve among individuals who might be, perhaps even should be, asked to serve. The study targeted six elite groups of likely appointees:

—executives of Fortune 500 companies

—presidents of the nation's top three hundred colleges and universities, as ranked by the 2000 *U.S. News and World Report*

—executive directors of the nation's largest nonprofit organizations, as measured by donations

—scholars at the nation's nine leading think tanks, as identified in a survey of impact and credibility

—registered lobbyists at the nation's 117 largest lobbying firms, as measured by revenues

—senior state and local officials

Interviews were completed with 100 *Fortune* 500 executives, 100 university presidents, 85 nonprofit chief executive officers, 95 think-tank scholars, 100 lobbyists, and 100 state and local government officials. The overall response rate was 29 percent of those sampled and eligible. The demographics of the potential appointees were similar to those of the former appointees surveyed: most were male (81 percent), over fifty years of age (66 percent), and white (92 percent).

Together these two surveys provide a unique opportunity to judge the state of the presidential appointments process today. To the extent that it leaves appointees exhausted, embittered, and unprepared for the rigors of service or discourages talented Americans from ever serving in the first place, the process is failing in its most basic obligation to help the president fill some of the most important jobs in the world. The Founding Fathers clearly understood that the quality of a president's appointments is as important to the public's confidence in government as the laws that its leaders enact. "There is nothing I am so anxious about as good nominations," Thomas Jefferson wrote at the dawn of his presidency in 1801, "conscious that the merit as well as reputation of an administration depends as much on that as on its measures."[3] Unfortunately, the merit and reputation of future administrations appear to be imperiled by a process that has calcified and corroded beyond any reasonable justification.

The Motivation to Serve

The nation's founders did more than just hope for a government led by its most talented leaders. They also accepted the call to service themselves. Most had served in public office before traveling to Philadelphia for the Constitutional Convention, and most served afterward. Having argued so passionately for a republic led by citizens, the founders willingly left their farms, small businesses, law firms, newspapers, and colleges to bring their new government into being.

The two surveys clearly suggest that America's most talented citizens continue to be motivated to serve. Even as they recognize the sacrifices inherent in service, past and potential appointees have an overwhelmingly positive view of their impact while in office. Indeed, 83 percent of past appointees said they would recommend an appointment to a close friend (see table 8-1), while the same percentage of potential appointees had a favorable impression of serving as a presidential appointee (see table 8-2). An overwhelming majority of potential appointees (78 percent) said they would find serving an enjoyable experience, and almost all (97 percent) considered an appointment an honor. More than half (57 percent) of these potential appointees think they would gain more respect from family, friends, and neighbors by serving as a presidential appointee than in a senior post outside government.

Table 8-1. *Former Appointees' Recommendation to Consider Presidential Service*

If you had a good friend who was considering an appointment, would you strongly recommend, somewhat recommend, somewhat discourage, or strongly discourage your friend from considering it?

Recommendation	*Percentage*
Strongly recommend	54
Somewhat recommend	29
Somewhat discourage	7
Strongly discourage	1
N	435

Source: Survey of presidential appointees who served between 1984 and 1999 conducted for the Brookings Institution's Presidential Appointee Initiative by Princeton Survey Research Associates, 2000.

The Benefits of Service

The decision to accept the call to service is more than just an assessment of the rewards of service in the short term. It also involves a calculation of the benefits and costs of service that follow a term in office. Potential appointees clearly recognize the balance. Most (77 percent) felt that they would be able to return to their careers after their appointments ended and were not concerned about losing out on promotions in their fields (74 percent). Moreover, 83 percent of potential appointees predicted that their service would make them more attractive for future leadership posts. Lobbyists (95 percent), state and local government officials

Table 8-2. *Potential Appointees' Initial Impressions of Serving as a Presidential Appointee*

What first comes to mind when you think about the possibility of serving as a presidential appointee? Is your initial impression very favorable, somewhat favorable, somewhat unfavorable, or very unfavorable?

Impression	*Percentage*
Very favorable	41
Somewhat favorable	42
Somewhat unfavorable	12
Very unfavorable	4
N	580

Source: Survey of potential presidential appointees conducted for the Brookings Institution's Presidential Appointee Initiative by Princeton Survey Research Associates, 2001.

(93 percent), and think-tank scholars (84 percent) were most inclined to equate service for a president with later career advancement. Almost all of the potential appointees (97 percent) said they would make valuable contacts, which could also be profitable in the future.

Although many potential appointees (42 percent) expected that their salaries would be much lower while serving than in their current jobs, these valuable contacts and the opportunity to advance in their fields may help explain why 61 percent thought serving a president would increase their earning power outside government. Lobbyists (80 percent), local government officials (79 percent), and think-tank scholars (72 percent) were most likely to believe that serving a president would increase earning potential later in their careers. Not surprisingly, all three sets of chief executive officers (CEOs)—corporate (46 percent), academic (41 percent), and nonprofit (46 percent)—saw less potential for increased earning power than the other groups. They are, after all, already at the top of the salary scales in their fields.

These calculations are confirmed in part by the experiences of past appointees. Whereas 46 percent of the former appointees had earned higher salaries before their appointments than while serving, only 8 percent felt their service decreased their earning power over their careers. Twenty percent of the former appointees left their appointments for higher-paying jobs in the private sector.

It is important to note that not all potential appointees saw the benefits of service. Only 26 percent of potential appointees felt that their ability to make a difference through their work would be much enhanced by serving as a presidential appointee. Nonprofit CEOs (11 percent), university presidents (20 percent), and corporate CEOs (20 percent) were least inclined to think presidential service would significantly increase their ability to make an impact. One respondent who declined an offer to serve explained, "I felt I was doing more important work as editor-in-chief." Said another, "I was at a critical point in my prior company's development and I would have been leaving a bit of work in the change of the company which I thought was quite important."

The Costs of Service

As much as they saw the benefits of service, both past and potential appointees acknowledged that presidential service has burdens that are often heavier than a temporary decline in salary. Nineteen percent of past appointees said burnout or stress was the reason they left service. Of the

Table 8-3. *Former Appointees' Assessment of the Stress of Presidential Service, Compared with Work in Other Senior Positions*

Compared with other places you have worked, on a 1-to-5 scale, how would you rate the stress level of your work as a presidential appointee? One means very stressful, and 5 means not stressful at all.

Rating	*Percentage*
1 (Very stressful)	36
2	32
3	20
4	7
5 (Unstressful)	2
N	435

Source: Presidential Appointee Initiative's 2000 survey of presidential appointees who served between 1984 and 1999.

former appointees, 68 percent found their positions stressful compared with other places they had worked (table 8-3). Because they most likely came from challenging, senior leadership positions, their comparative assessment of the level of stress as a presidential appointee is particularly troublesome.

Potential appointees also saw presidential service as highly disruptive. Seven in ten said that an appointment would be more disruptive to their personal lives than a senior position outside government (table 8-4). This sentiment was held most firmly among think-tank scholars, almost half of whom (47 percent) perceived presidential service as much more disruptive, compared with 25 percent of university presidents and 29 percent of lob-

Table 8-4. *Potential Appointees' Assessment of the Perceived Impact of Presidential Service on Personal Life, Compared with Work in Other Senior Positions*

Compared with senior posts that you might be offered outside government, do you think serving as a presidential appointee would be much more disruptive to your personal life, somewhat more, about the same, somewhat less, or much less disruptive?

Rating	*Percentage*
Much more disruptive	32
Somewhat more disruptive	37
Equally disruptive	28
Somewhat less disruptive	2
Much less disruptive	less than 1
N	580

Source: Presidential Appointee Initiative's 2001 survey of potential presidential appointees.

byists and corporate and nonprofit CEOs. As one potential appointee who declined an offer to serve explained, "I had a daughter entering high school, and I knew the time commitment would have taken away from that."

Living in the Washington, D.C., area is another barrier to service. Of the Reagan, Bush, and Clinton appointees living outside of Washington before their appointment, 36 percent found living in the area a lot more expensive, and another 24 percent found it somewhat more expensive. Only 13 percent found the Washington area less expensive than the area they lived in before serving.

More than half of the potential appointees who lived outside Washington at the time of the survey rated the nation's capital city a much less or somewhat less favorable place to live than their current residence. Although this negative impression is almost certainly linked to the high cost of living and real estate in what has become one of the nation's most expensive places to live, it is also driven by worries about relocating one's spouse or partner to a new city. Fifty percent of potential appointees said that relocating their spouse or partner would be somewhat or very difficult.

To those who have served and those who may be asked to serve, presidential service requires great sacrifices balanced with great rewards. Taking into account all of the trade-offs, America's leaders still seem to value presidential appointments. Unfortunately, their strongly negative views of the confirmation process may cause some to bow out before they have a chance to think about what it would be like to serve.

Views of the Process

The function of the presidential appointment process is to recruit and confirm talented citizens for presidential service. As such, the components of a successful process are relatively easy to describe. It should give nominees enough information to enable them to act in their best interest throughout the process, move fast enough to give departments and agencies the leadership they need to faithfully execute the laws, and be open enough to draw talented people into service while rigorous enough to ensure that individual nominees are fit for their jobs. Unfortunately, this is not the process former and potential appointees describe.

The Burdens of Review

Past appointees view the process as unnecessarily burdensome at virtually every step. The confirmation process is viewed by those who

Table 8-5. *Former and Potential Appointees' General Description of Appointments Process (percentage)*

Asked of former appointees: How well does [each word] describe the process? Asked of potential appointees: How well do you think [each word] describes the process?

Percent

Description	*Former appointees*	*Potential appointees*
Necessary evil	47	57
Unfair	24	50
Embarrassing	23	51
Confusing	40	59
N	435	580

Source: Presidential Appointee Initiative's 2000 survey of presidential appointees who served between 1984 and 1999; Presidential Appointee Initiative's 2001 survey of potential presidential appointees.

endured it as, at best, a necessary evil (47 percent); at worst, it was seen as unfair (by 24 percent) (table 8-5). Twenty-three percent of former appointees described the nomination and confirmation process as embarrassing, and another 40 percent as confusing. Half of the Clinton appointees described the process as confusing, compared with just a third of the Bush and Reagan appointees.

This judgment is particularly unsettling given the apparent skill with which former appointees were able to master their jobs following their confirmation. Much as they felt challenged by the confirmation process, few past appointees found any of the substantive aspects of their positions difficult. More than two-thirds found the details of the policies they dealt with and directing career employees fairly easy. More than half found the decisionmaking procedures of their departments and the requirements of managing a large government organization relatively simple.

As troubling as the nomination and confirmation process was for those who actually went through it, the perception among America's potential appointees sounds an even louder alarm. Fifty-seven percent considered the process a necessary evil, and 50 percent viewed it as unfair. The majority (51 percent) of the civic and corporate leaders surveyed described the appointments process as embarrassing, and even more (59 percent) thought it was confusing.

Some of these opinions were almost certainly based on a lack of adequate information. Just over half of the past appointees said they had received enough (40 percent) or more than enough (16 percent) information about the process from the White House or other official sources. Roughly four in ten said they did not get enough information (28 percent) or got no information at all (11 percent). Women (51 percent) were more likely than men (37 percent) to report that they did not get enough information. An overwhelming 78 percent of the Reagan, Bush, and Clinton appointees surveyed found the financial disclosure forms less than straightforward.

It is no surprise, therefore, that so many past appointees sought help in the process, thereby compounding the less tangible burdens of being confirmed with the all too real monetary costs. Sixty-two percent of the Reagan, Bush, and Clinton nominees said they had sought outside help with the legal aspects of the process, and 48 percent said they had sought help with the financial aspects. One in five respondents had hired help of this kind, and, of those willing to share its cost, 38 percent spent more than one thousand dollars.

Delays in the Process

These frustrations are multiplied by a process that is filled with what past and potential appointees view as unnecessary delays. A nomination and confirmation process lasting more than six months was nearly unheard of between 1964 and 1984. Just 5 percent of those appointees who served during that time reported that more than six months had elapsed from the time they were first contacted by the White House to the Senate's confirmation of them.

But times have changed. Nearly one-third (30 percent) of the appointees who served between 1984 and 1999 reported that their confirmations took more than six months. By the same token, whereas almost half (48 percent) of the 1964–84 cohort said the process took one to two months, only 15 percent of the 1984–99 cohort said the same. Although the delays have increased with each successive administration since 1960, the jump was particularly significant during the Clinton administration. On average, it took Clinton appointees two months longer to enter office than Reagan or Bush appointees. Fifty-four percent of the second-term Clinton appointees reported their confirmations took more than six months.

Past appointees were particularly frustrated by the Senate confirmation process. Almost two-fifths of the appointees who served between 1984

Table 8-6. *Former Appointees' Assessment of Sources of Delay in the Appointments Process*

Asked of appointees who served 1964–84: Thinking about your most recent confirmation as a full-time, Senate-confirmed presidential appointee, which of the following steps, if any, seem to you to have taken longer than necessary to complete? Asked of appointees who served 1984–99: We are interested in whether you think any aspects of your appointment could have been processed more quickly. What about [stage]? Did this take longer than necessary or not?

Percent

Stage took longer than necessary	*Former appointees (1964–84)*	*Former appointees (1984–99)*
Senate confirmation process	24	39
Filling out financial disclosure and other forms	13	34
FBI full-field investigation	24	30
White House review	15	27
Initial clearance with members of Congress	7	18
Conflict-of-interest review	6	17
N	532	435

Source: Survey of presidential appointees who served between 1964 and 1984 conducted for the Presidential Appointee Project, National Academy of Public Administration, 1985; Presidential Appointee Initiative's 2000 survey of presidential appointees who served between 1984 and 1999.

and 1999 felt that the Senate confirmation process was too lengthy, an increase from less than a quarter of respondents who had served between 1964 and 1984 (table 8-6).

The Senate was hardly the only problem, however. A third of the Reagan, Bush, and Clinton appointees also complained that filling out the financial disclosure and other personal information forms (34 percent), the FBI full investigation (30 percent), and the White House review, excluding the president's personal approval (27 percent), took too long. One former appointee described the frustration of the delays this way: "Everybody says, 'Oh, it's two months, maximum.' Turned out to be six months. And that's pretty off-putting because your whole private life is on hold kind of while this is going on."

The delays did not affect all levels of nominees equally. Secretaries, deputy secretaries, and under secretaries reported fewer frustrations than assistant secretaries. Higher-level appointees were less likely to say the White House review (19 versus 31 percent), initial clearance with members of Congress (10 versus 20 percent), or Senate confirmation (28 versus 43 percent) dragged on too long.

Placing Blame

Past appointees found problems in the process at both ends of Pennsylvania Avenue. Forty-six percent said the Senate was too demanding and made the process more of an ordeal than was necessary. The frustration has risen over time. Only 33 percent of the Reagan appointees and 40 percent of the Bush appointees saw the Senate as too demanding, compared with 55 percent of first-term Clinton appointees and 62 percent of second-term Clinton appointees.

Past appointees also found fault with the White House. Thirty percent of past appointees thought the White House was too demanding and made the process more of an ordeal than was necessary (table 8-7). Frustration toward the White House has also risen over time. Only 15 percent of the Reagan appointees and 24 percent of Bush appointees saw the White House as too demanding, compared with 36 percent of first-term Clinton appointees and 44 percent of second-term Clinton appointees. Potential appointees also found fault with both the Senate and the White House. Of the potential appointees surveyed, two-thirds felt the Senate asks for too much and 42 percent perceived the White House as too demanding.

Together, these burdens, delays, and pressures have created an appointments process that appears to favor Washington insiders. Half of the 1984–99 appointees were working inside the beltway at the time of their nomination, and more than a third (35 percent) were working in another position in the federal government when they were chosen to serve the president.

Living in Washington does more than provide an easy transition into office. It also provides the kind of experience and information needed to survive the current process. Roughly half (52 percent) of the Washington residents among the past appointees surveyed said they knew a great deal about the process at the outset, compared with just a third (31 percent) who lived outside Washington. Forty-nine percent of those whose most recent job was in the federal government knew a great deal about the process, compared with 23 percent of those coming from other industries. Although Washington experience allows appointees to more skillfully and smoothly take control of the functions of government, the nation's founders clearly hoped that presidents would draw upon a talent pool that extended well beyond the nation's capital city. They wanted a government led not by a class of semiprofessional appointees but rather by

Table 8-7. *Former and Potential Appointees' Assessment of Senate and White House Processes*

Some people think the White House acts reasonably and appropriately in the way it processes potential presidential nominees. Others think it has become too demanding and thus makes the nomination process an ordeal. Which statement do you agree with more? and *Does the Senate as a whole act reasonably and appropriately in the way it processes presidential nominees, or has it become too demanding and thus makes the confirmation process an ordeal? Which statement do you agree with more?*

Percent

Assessment	*Former appointees*	*Potential appointees*
Senate is too demanding	46	66
White House is too demanding	30	42
N	435	580

Source: Presidential Appointee Initiative's 2000 survey of presidential appointees who served between 1984 and 1999; Presidential Appointee Initiative's 2001 survey of potential presidential appointees.

citizens from every corner and occupation. To the extent the current process favors candidates with the resources and knowledge that come from living within a few miles of the White House, a citizen government becomes more an abstract notion than a real possibility.

Explaining the Decline in Timeliness

The Founding Fathers did not intend the presidential appointments process to be easy. If they had, they would not have required Senate confirmation as part of their complex system of checks and balances. The question is whether the recent increase in appointee complaints is an appropriate expression of such constitutional obligations or a sign that presidential appointments have become hostages to a process run amok or to political disputes that are better solved through other means.

These studies cannot offer a definitive answer, if only because the impact of divided government from 1984 to 1999 has been decidedly mixed (table 8-8). In fact, former appointees reported that some delays were actually longer when the Democrats controlled both the presidency and the Senate, in part because the only moment of unified control during the period happened to come during one of the most haphazard presidential transitions in recent history. Just because divided government did not have a strong impact on delays does not mean the Senate confirmation process is working well. To the contrary, it suggests that the delays may have become part of the institutional norms within the Senate that will govern future presidential appointments regardless of party control.

Table 8-8. *Former Appointees' Assessment of Impact of Divided Government on Delays at Various Stages of the Appointments Process*

We are interested in whether you think any aspect of your appointment could have been processed more quickly. What about [stage]? Did this take longer than necessary or not?

Percent

Stage did not take longer than necessary	*1984–86 (divided)*	*1987–92 (divided)*	*1993–94 (one party)*	*1995–99 (divided)*
President's personal approval of nomination	73	79	59	71
Other White House review of nomination	69	68	47	50
Filling out financial disclosure and other forms	70	67	67	50
Initial clearance of selection with Congress	78	75	71	63
Conflict-of-interest reviews	84	78	86	66
Senate confirmation process	67	59	59	50
FBI full-field investigation	67	68	57	57
N	67	123	58	102

Source: Presidential Appointee Initiative's 2000 survey of presidential appointees who served between 1984 and 1999.

Clinton appointees bore the consequences of two events that were unique to their administration. First, the initial Clinton appointees entered office following an extraordinarily difficult transition. Whereas appointees from the second Reagan administration benefited from the administrative smoothing that had occurred in the first, and the Bush appointees benefited from a same-party transition, the first wave of Clinton appointees bore the brunt of one of the most confusing transitions in recent history.

Second, the last wave of Clinton appointees entered office during a period of intense scandal, including an impeachment trial and ongoing campaign finance investigations. As table 8-9 suggests, these two events created a roller coaster of inefficiency in the presidential appointments process. Whereas almost four out of five appointees (77 percent) who served between 1984 and 1992 thought the president's personal approval of their nomination was handled efficiently, about three in five (59 percent) during the Clinton transition, four in five (81 percent) from 1995 to 1997, and three in five (63 percent) from 1998 to 1999 felt similarly. A notable decline in the perceived timeliness of the FBI full-field investigation also occurred during the latter part of the Clinton administration.

Table 8-9. *Clinton Effect on Delays at Various Stages of the Appointments Process, 1984–99*

We are interested in whether you think any aspect of your appointment could have been processed more quickly. What about [stage]? Did this take longer than necessary or not?

Percent

Stage did not take longer than necessary	*1984–92 (before Clinton)*	*1993–94 (Clinton: transition)*	*1995–97 (Clinton: some stability)*	*1998–99 (Clinton: scandal)*
President's personal approval of nomination	77	59	81	63
Other White House review of nomination	68	47	62	42
FBI full-field investigation	68	57	69	48
Filling out financial disclosure and other forms	68	67	64	40
Initial clearance of selection with Congress	76	71	57	67
Conflict-of-interest reviews	80	86	67	65
Senate confirmation process	62	59	40	57
N	190	58	42	60

Source: Presidential Appointee Initiative's 2000 survey of presidential appointees who served between 1984 and 1999.

It would be a mistake to assume that Clinton's departure from office made all the delays and frustrations just cited disappear. Although Clinton's departure could improve White House and Senate relations, it could not in itself make the financial disclosure forms easier to master, the FBI field investigations shorter, or the Senate review more efficient. Nor could it do anything to make information more available to appointees or reduce the need for outside help. The delays have been increasing since 1960 and will continue to increase in the future.

A Note on Financial Disclosure Requirements and Conflict-of-Interest Laws

The Reagan, Bush, and Clinton appointees surveyed were divided over the problems associated with financial disclosure requirements and conflict-of-interest laws. Two in five appointees (41 percent) saw the laws as reasonable measures to protect the public interest, and almost as many (37 percent) thought they were unreasonable. On the other hand, nearly a third of Reagan, Bush, and Clinton appointees described the financial disclosure process as somewhat or very difficult.

Table 8-10. *Former and Potential Appointees' Assessment of Financial Disclosure Requirements and Conflict-of-Interest Laws*

Thinking generally about the financial disclosure requirements and conflict-of-interest laws, on a 1-to-5 scale what is your view of them? One means the current requirements go too far, and 5 means the current requirements are reasonable measures to protect the public interest.

Percent

Rating	*Former appointees*	*Potential appointees*[a]
1 (Go too far)	18	5
2	19	14
3	19	22
4	14	27
5 (Are reasonable)	27	30
N	435	572

Source: Presidential Appointee Initiative's 2000 survey of presidential appointees who served between 1984 and 1999; Presidential Appointee Initiative's 2001 survey of potential presidential appointees.

a. The sample of potential appointees was limited to those who were aware of the financial disclosure requirements and conflict-of-interest laws.

Potential appointees were much less likely than actual appointees to rate the financial disclosure requirements and conflict-of-interest laws as burdensome (table 8-10). The vast majority (81 percent) of potential appointees did not believe it would be difficult to collect and report the information needed to complete the financial disclosure forms, relatively few (16 percent) believed the conflict-of-interest laws would have much of an impact, and only 19 percent thought either unreasonable.

The think-tank scholars and lobbyists surveyed clearly understood enough about the disclosure forms to recognize the burdens involved, and the corporate CEOs sensed the potential problems embedded in disclosing their financial holdings. Among potential appointees, only 68 percent of think-tank scholars and 65 percent of lobbyists thought filling out the financial disclosure forms would be easy, compared with 94 percent of state and local government officials and 89 percent of nonprofit CEOs. Only 34 percent of lobbyists and 41 percent of corporate CEOs thought the conflict-of-interest laws would have little or no impact, compared with 83 percent of government officials and 81 percent of nonprofit CEOs. The state and local officials were unconcerned (only 9 percent found these rules unreasonable)—one suspects in part because in their current employment they were governed by similar statutes that they already knew well, and they had been spared the problems involved in the acquisition of great wealth.

At least compared with the actual experiences of former appointees, as a group, the potential appointees clearly underestimated the difficulties associated with financial disclosure requirements and conflict-of-interest laws. This mistaken impression may be the reason potential appointees did not rank these areas as a high priority for reform.

Prescriptions for Reform

The president and Congress can only do so much to improve the odds that talented Americans will accept the call to serve. They cannot move Washington, D.C., to San Francisco, for example, and most certainly should not eliminate the constitutional requirement for Senate confirmation or the basic conflict-of-interest protections embedded in federal statutes. Moreover, the Founding Fathers clearly expected—indeed, intended—that government service would be viewed as inconvenient and as a sacrifice, lest elected and appointed officials become so enamored of their jobs that they never go home. "I will not say that public life is the line for making a fortune," Thomas Jefferson wrote in 1808, just before leaving the presidency. "But it furnishes a decent and honorable support, and places one's children on good grounds for public favor."[4] Certainly both the president and Congress can redress some of the drawbacks of service, however, while accentuating its draws.

Past and potential appointees largely agreed on ways to improve the system, starting with providing basic information on how the process works. As already noted, the desire among past and potential appointees for more information is undeniable: 39 percent of the Reagan, Bush, and Clinton appointees said they either did not get enough information from the White House or got none at all, while 47 percent of the potential appointees said they knew little or nothing about how the process works. The impact of information, or a lack thereof, is also unmistakable. Past appointees who said they had enough information about the process were more likely than those with little or no information to describe the process as fair and not embarrassing.

Past and potential appointees also agreed on the need for a simpler, faster process. When asked what could be done to make the process easier, 37 percent of the Reagan, Bush, and Clinton appointees focused on streamlining the collection of information, and 28 percent on accelerating action (table 8-11). Similarly, 73 percent of the potential appointees said that simplifying the process would make a presidential appointment

Table 8-11. *Former Appointees' Suggestions for Making the Appointments Process Easier, by Administration*

In your opinion, what one thing could be done to make the appointments process easier?

Percent

Improvement	*Total*	*Reagan*	*Bush*	*Clinton (first term)*	*Clinton (second term)*
Make collection of information more efficient	37	19	38	33	40
Make process faster	28	31	23	40	31
Make process nonpartisan	11	6	9	9	17
Improve communication with White House and congressional staff	7	6	4	12	12
Improve communication between White House and Senate	2	4	4	0	1
N	435	67	123	58	102

Source: Presidential Appointee Initiative's 2000 survey of presidential appointees who served between 1984 and 1999.

either somewhat or much more attractive (table 8-12). The potential appointees also pointed to other reforms that might increase the odds of service, most notably increases in pay and help in returning to their previous jobs once their presidential appointments come to an end.

Where potential appointees stand on reform depends in part on where they sit. Lobbyists were the most supportive of higher pay (77 percent said the change would make a presidential appointment more attractive, compared with just 57 percent of corporate CEOs and 69 percent of university presidents). Nonprofit executives were the most supportive of return rights to their previous careers (76 percent said that option would make an appointment more attractive, compared with just 56 percent of state and local government officials).

Although roughly half of the potential appointees said their employers would strongly or somewhat encourage them to take a presidential appointment, the percentages were not uniform across the six groups of civic and corporate leaders. Only 18 percent of the nonprofit executives and just 10 percent of the corporate and university executives said their employers would strongly encourage them to take a presidential appointment, suggesting that were they to leave, it might not be with the support of their employers. Unfortunately, the majority in all three groups would find service more appealing if returning afterward to their previous jobs were a likely option. Both former and potential appointees agreed that simple reforms, like removing unnecessary bureaucracy, improving access to information, better communication, and working with employers to let their employees serve and return, may help to ensure that the nation's most talented leaders do not exit the process before it even begins.

In addition, the survey of past appointees presents clear evidence that the White House Office of Presidential Personnel often creates more problems than it solves in handling the onslaught of candidates for appointment. This office is often the first point of contact for lower-level appointees and handles most of the paperwork at key points in the process. If it is not working well, the entire process suffers.

Unfortunately, the office received mixed grades from their primary customers, the former appointees themselves (table 8-13). Asked to grade the helpfulness of the White House Office of Presidential Personnel staff on a range of issues from competence to staying in touch during the process, half or fewer awarded As or Bs. Although appointees gave the office high grades both for competence (50 percent As or Bs) and for personally caring whether the appointee was confirmed (46 percent), half gave the office a C (21 percent) or lower (30 percent) for staying in touch during what has become a long relationship.

There were significant differences in the assessment of performance across the three administrations, however. Clinton appointees were much more critical of the personnel office than either Reagan or Bush appointees, giving the office average or below-average grades on all of the questions asked. More than 40 percent of the Clinton appointees gave the office a D or an F on staying in touch with them during the process.

Making the Case for Service: A Statistical Analysis

Given all the opinions summarized here, it is useful to ask which, if any, of them factor into a potential appointee's willingness to serve. Do views of the confirmation process matter? Are individuals who see the honor in service more likely to be favorably inclined toward the president's call than those who do not? Do concerns about relocating family make potential appointees less willing to accept an appointment? One way to answer these questions is to subject the data to more sophisticated statistical analysis, using a regression model. Simply summarized, regression allows the researcher to test competing explanations for a greater or lesser willingness to serve.

Table 8-12. *Potential Appointees' Suggestions for Making Appointments More Attractive, by Sector of Current Employment*

For each of the following [suggested improvements], please tell me if it would make taking a full-time position as a presidential appointee seem much more attractive to you, somewhat more attractive, or not really have an effect.

Percent

Improvement	*Total*	*Fortune 500 CEOs*	*University presidents*	*Nonprofit CEOs*	*Think-tank scholars*	*Lobbyists*	*Government officials*
Simplify the process	73	80	74	72	78	79	58
Offer better pay	71	57	69	75	72	77	74
Allow appointees easier return to previous jobs	67	68	70	76	64	70	56
Make conflict-of-interest laws easier to satisfy	36	53	30	18	29	62	20
Make financial disclosure requirements easier to meet	35	47	33	24	34	46	23
N	580	100	100	85	95	100	100

Source: Presidential Appointee Initiative's 2001 survey of potential presidential appointees.

Table 8-13. *Former Appointees' Assessment of the White House Office of Presidential Personnel*

What grade would you give [the White House presidential personnel staff who helped you through the process] for [characteristic]? A means excellent, B good, C average, D poor, and F very poor.

Percent

Characteristic	A *(excellent)*	B *(good)*	C *(average)*	D *(poor)*	F *(very poor)*
Caring whether nominee was confirmed	26	20	18	13	7
Competence	21	29	23	9	3
Responding quickly to nominee's questions	20	23	20	12	4
Devoting sufficient time to nominee's appointment	19	24	23	11	6
Staying in touch with nominee during the process	13	21	21	21	9

Source: Presidential Appointee Initiative's 2000 survey of presidential appointees who served between 1984 and 1999.

A regression analysis of eleven different measures discussed here clearly suggests that some considerations are more important than others. The eleven measures involved are a mix of impressions about the effects of serving (the extent to which potential appointees saw both the honor in serving and a greater impact from that service), impressions of the process (the extent to which potential appointees described the process as fair, confusing, or embarrassing), demographics (gender, age, race, political ideology, and whether a potential appointee had actually been considered for an appointment in the past), and the ease or difficulty associated with relocating a spouse or partner to the Washington, D.C., area. The variables were tested for significance at a 95 percent confidence level. The regression analysis shows four significant predictors of greater favorability toward service: a sense that the process of appointment is fair, a sense that service would allow an individual to have an impact, a sense that service would be an honor, and the ease with which the potential appointee's spouse or partner could relocate to Washington.

Although it may be impossible to ease the challenges of relocating families to Washington, D.C., the regression suggests several ways the government could improve the image of service. First, presidents and the Senate should reassure candidates that they are committed to building an appointments process that is both reasonable and fair, including visible, substantial reform in how the process works. Second, presidents should strongly emphasize the impact of presidential appointees on the nation. Doing so would highlight one of the great advantages of public, as compared with private or nonprofit, service: it enhances the ability of one person to make a very large difference, indeed. As mentioned earlier, only 26 percent of civic and corporate leaders surveyed believe that their ability to make a difference through their work would be greatly enhanced by serving as a presidential appointee. People tapped for presidential appointments are likely to be at the top of their fields, steering major universities, directing nonprofits and businesses they believe in, advocating for the issues they care about, doing research they feel is important, and providing leadership in their state or local governments. It is not surprising that these leaders would need to be convinced they could have a more meaningful impact through government service.

Third, presidents should remind appointees of the honor involved in service to one's country. Old-fashioned though it may seem, patriotism and the love of country are still powerful motivators for public service.

Conclusion

There is much to admire in the views of the former and potential appointees inventoried in this chapter. America's most talented citizens remain ready to accept the call to serve and are still motivated by the old-fashioned values of patriotism and honor embedded in the constitutional system created more than two hundred years ago. The nation can be proud—even relieved—of this deep reservoir of readiness to serve in the wake of what has been one of the most partisan, intensely divided periods in recent American history.

Yet if the spirit of service is willing, the process for nominating and confirming America's most senior government leaders is weak. To the extent that the nation wants leaders who represent the great talent and wisdom that resides across all sectors of society and regions of the nation, it must address the growing toll the presidential appointments process takes on nominees for office. Not only must America's civic and corporate institutions be more willing to "let their people go" to Washington for service, but the president and Congress must work harder to "let those people come" by creating a simpler, fairer, and faster appointments process.

Notes

1. Max Farrand, ed., *The Records of the Federal Convention of 1787* (Yale University Press, 1966), vol. 1, p. 82.

2. Ibid., p. 78.

3. Thomas Jefferson to Archibald Stuart, 1801, in Andrew A. Lipscomb and Albert Ellery Bergh, eds., *The Writings of Thomas Jefferson* (Washington, 1903–04), vol. 10, p. 257.

4. Thomas Jefferson to William Wirt, 1808, ibid., vol. 11, p. 424.

CHAPTER NINE

"Political Hacks" versus "Bureaucrats": Can't Public Servants Get Some Respect?

E. J. DIONNE JR.

THE MOST MOVING moment at either party's national convention in 2000 was a resolutely nonpartisan speech that evoked a moment when taking a job in government was seen as far more than, well, just taking a job. "When my brother John and I were growing up," said Caroline Kennedy Schlossberg, "hardly a day went by when someone didn't come up to us and say, 'Your father changed my life. I went into public service because he asked me.'"[1]

Note that lovely phrase, "public service." Schlossberg was not exaggerating or being unduly romantic about the spirit of John F. Kennedy's New Frontier, which both shaped its time and reflected it. Serving in a new administration, whether on the White House staff, in the cabinet, or in a less grand post, was not simply an obligation or, in the current ugly phrase, "a ticket to punch." It was also a source of excitement. And so, as Godfrey Hodgson put it in his biography of Daniel Patrick Moynihan, "a varied population of political and intellectual adventurers" descended on Washington in the winter of 1960 and 1961."[2]

"They came," Hodgson writes, "from New York and San Francisco law firms, from state and city politics across the nation, from the growing world of foundations and pressure groups, and of course from the great graduate schools, swollen by the postwar demand for academic manpower." Hodgson understood that this crowd of adventurers were not saints, but neither were they mere opportunists: "The mood," he says, "was strangely blended from ambition and idealism, aggressive social climbing and a sense of youthful adventure."[3]

The Diminished Promise of Citizen Service

No doubt many entered the Bush administration in 2001 with that same sense of vigor and adventure. Long lists of Republican office seekers, out of executive power for eight years, testified to the continuing lure of executive positions, from the highest posts to the lowest. Still, it is difficult to hear Schlossberg's speech and to read Hodgson's account and not sense a shift in the spirit of the times. Forty years after that winter of the New Frontier, public service in the executive branch retains its allure, but not quite the same sense of glamour or promise.

As columnist Mark Shields pointed out at an event at the Brookings Institution in late December 2000, most politicians who have won the presidency over the past quarter century did so by running against "the government in Washington." Bush was no exception. As a result, expressing an open desire to serve in that very government and an open belief that it might accomplish large things flies in the face of what is now deeply ingrained conventional wisdom. Those who want to serve in government in Washington have to bash government to get there. That cannot make a life in government service very attractive to those not yet committed to the venture.

Yet no country is as dependent as ours on "citizen service" in its national administration. None relies so heavily on people who might be called amateurs, as against career civil servants, to govern. From the beginning of the republic we have operated on the assumption that a professional ruling class is problematic and to be avoided. Government, according to this view, should be refreshed periodically by tides of new leaders with new ideas and untapped energy—the very spirit captured so well by Hodgson and Schlossberg. The assumption continues to prevail that citizen service is essential to the health of civil society—in this case, citizen service at the very highest levels—because citizen service links the government to the rest of the society in a way a purely professional bureaucracy could not.

Professionalism versus Politics

That is the theory, anyway. In truth, our attitude toward those citizen servants reflects an odd balance of ideas. Our history is one of ambivalence as between professionalism on the one side and politics on the other. We admire the independence and expertise of professionals, yet we regularly denounce them when they work for the government. It is no accident that the famous Republican campaign commercial of 2000 in which the word "rats" appeared ever so briefly on our television screens—conveying or not conveying a "subliminal" message, depending on whom you believed—was in fact depicting the word "bureaucrats" at that critical and controversial moment. However honored they might occasionally be, the day-to-day civil servants who make the American government run do not enjoy the honor or prestige of their counterparts in France or Germany, Britain or Japan.

Yet if we denounce bureaucrats, we also denounce political appointees. This is obvious from the normal parlance of politics and journalism. We condemn certain agencies of government as patronage dumping grounds. We say we dislike the political spoils system. We insist on praising independent, nonpartisan government. Indeed, this was the impetus behind the civil service reform that, from the 1880s forward, took the awarding of tens of thousands of jobs out of politics. The premise, as James Q. Wilson puts it in his classic work *The Amateur Democrat*, was that "the merit system and open competition should be extended to insure, insofar as is feasible, that general principles rather than private advantage govern the awarding" of government benefits.[4]

These two traditions—a preference for political appointees over bureaucrats and a preference for civil servants over the beneficiaries of political patronage—are deeply rooted in our history. To understand the contradictions in our history is to understand our ambivalence today.

Jacksonian Rotation in Office

It is worth remembering that the idea of wholesale changes in the government following the defeat of an incumbent party in an election was originally seen as a "reform" by the advocates of Jacksonian democracy in the 1820s and 1830s. The followers of Andrew Jackson referred not to a spoils system but to a principle they held up as admirable and called "rotation in office." The Jacksonians believed their political foes had come to regard holding the appointive offices of government as a right that could not be disturbed even by the electorate. That is what Andrew Jackson was against. "Office is considered as a species of property," Jackson declared, "and government rather as a means of promoting individual interests than as an instrument created solely for the service of the people."[5]

As Harry L. Watson summarizes Jackson's views in *Liberty and Power*, his admirable book on Jacksonian democracy, "No one in a republic had an inherent right to public office—so no one could complain if he lost a public job in favor of someone more honest, more competent, or more in agreement with elected officials who carried a popular mandate." Jackson, as Watson notes, emphatically rejected the views of his former Federalist and soon-to-be Whig foes that "no one except a tiny elite had the training or experience to qualify for public office." As Jackson himself put it, "The duties of all public officers are, or admit to being made, so plain and simple that men of intelligence may readily qualify themselves for their performance." Jackson, as Watson notes, was not arguing for the hiring of incompetents, but he did demand "that public duties be shared among the large body of qualified citizens to avoid the creation of an entrenched and corrupt bureaucracy."[6]

The notion that rotation in office was a mighty weapon in the larger battle against privilege is nicely captured by historian Robert V. Remini in his study of Martin Van Buren. Remini notes that the Democrats' 1828 campaign placed heavy stress on the words "people" and "reform." "The precise direction all this 'reform' was to take," he writes, "was not explained. There was no need to. The people were simply banding together to take the national government out of the hands of the favored few. They were claiming what belonged to them. They were dispossessing 'the wise, the good, and the well born.'"[7]

"Rotation in office" was more than just an excuse to appoint one's friends. "To Jackson the principle of rotation directly addressed the problem of how and by whom government should be run," Remini writes in *The Revolutionary Age of Andrew Jackson*. "Jackson believed that through rotation the federal government in Washington could be made to respond directly to the changing demands of the American people as expressed by their ballots. Thus, each new administration, elected by the people, should bring in its own corps of supporters to make sure the policies of that administration were honestly and fairly implemented."[8]

Prefiguring, perhaps, the New Left's emphasis on participatory democracy, the Jacksonians thought, as Remini puts it, that "rotation meant that a great many more people would get an opportunity to serve the government. The more people actively involved in the affairs of the nation, the more democratic the system, and the more the problems of the nation get to be widely known and understood."[9] The idea came from Jefferson: "Greater participation by the electorate in government safeguards the nation from arbitrary and dictatorial rule."[10]

In other words, America's tradition of political appointments is rooted in a philosophical view of how democratic government can work best—and become more democratic in the process. If European democracies have a much shallower tradition of political nominations and a larger reverence for a career civil service, it is in part because none of the Western European democracies—many of which were not terribly democratic at the time—went through anything that quite resembled the Jacksonian revolution. Hard as it was for reformers to accept the idea later, the creation of a system of political patronage was originally seen as a way to foil both corruption and elitism. Despite abuses, Watson is correct in seeing rotation in office as "a solidly democratic principle that brought greater openness to government."[11]

Civil Service Reform: Depoliticizing Public Service

But there were, indeed, abuses, and they grew over time. The Jacksonian system was "susceptible to political manipulation," as Watson acknowledges.[12] As Remini, a sympathetic student of the Jacksonian principle, puts it, rotation "can be an easy excuse and justification for political head chopping, for regarding political jobs as 'spoils' won in a war in which enemies are punished and friends rewarded. . . . When rotation is administered by incompetents or thieves, then everyone suffers and the democratic system is dangerously compromised."[13] It is precisely that sense of incompetence and thievery that helped unleash the other great American public service tradition—civil service reform combined with a preference for expertise. It reached high tide between the 1880s and 1920.

The historian Robert H. Wiebe picks up this thread in his excellent study of the period, *The Search for Order*. In contrast with the Jacksonians, the new reformers saw the removal of government jobs from the political realm as "democracy's cure." Wiebe notes that "by denying politicians the spoils of office, the argument ran, civil service would drive out the parasites and leave only a pure frugal government behind. The nonpartisanship inherent in civil service would permeate politics, and as party organizations withered away, the men of quality now excluded by the spoilsmen and unscrupulous businessmen would resume their natural posts of command."[14]

It is also important to see that civil service reform and enhanced faith in a professionalized bureaucracy arose at a moment of growing faith in scientific rationality and a belief in the importance of expertise. The professionals of the period, Wiebe observes, "naturally conceived of science as a method for their disciplines instead of a set of universal principles."[15] As the sociologist Max Weber expresses it in his famous essay on bureaucracy, "Naturally, bureaucracy promotes a 'rationalist' way of life, but the concept of rationalism allows for widely differing contents. Quite generally, one can only say that the bureaucratization of all domination very strongly furthers the development of 'rational matter-of-factness' and the personality type of the professional expert."[16]

The importance of this view to American public life is described well by Moynihan himself in his famous 1965 essay, "The Professionalization of Reform." Moynihan cites Wesley C. Mitchell, of the National Bureau of Economic Research, who offered an almost perfect statement of the faith that Weber describes: "Our best hope for the future lies in the extension to social organization of the methods that we already employ in our most progressive fields of efforts. In science and industry . . . we do not wait for catastrophe to force new ways upon us. . . . We rely, and with success, upon quantitative analysis to point the way; and we advance because we are constantly improving and applying such analysis."[17]

Still a Healthy Tension?

Alas, it is not so clear how much we have advanced when it comes to making a joy in public service part of our political ethic. Where do our dueling traditions of political appointments and professionalized bureaucracy leave us today?

The professional view suffered body blows during the 1960s from left, right, and center. Moynihan predicted this in his original essay on the professionalization of reform: "a certain price will be paid and a considerable risk will be incurred." The price, said the man who journeyed to the New Frontier with such hope, "will be a decline in the moral exhilaration of public affairs at the domestic level."[18] And so there was.

The rise of the idea of participatory democracy on the New Left suggested that the distant bureaucrat claiming vastly more knowledge than average citizens needed to be taken down a peg or two. The goal of Lyndon Johnson's War on Poverty, "maximum feasible participation," suggested that real expertise could be found only on the streets and in the neighborhoods. On the right, George Wallace's attacks on "pointy-headed bureaucrats with thin briefcases full of guidelines" nicely captured the conservative rebellion against experts—and, in the case of Wallace and his followers, especially those pushing for new programs of racial inclusion. But the resentments could not be explained simply by race.

As if this were not enough, the civil service bureaucracy also came under assault from the political center as a system that no longer worked—that no longer effectively delivered the very expertise and public-regarding ethos the civil service reformers at the turn of the century expected it to provide. Consider this thoughtful critique of the civil service offered in *The Public Interest*. Published in the summer of 1973, it was entitled, "The Civil Service: A Meritless System?" Its authors, E. S. Savas and Sigmund G. Ginsburg, knew whereof they spoke, both having served as administrators in the New York City mayor's office from 1967 to 1972. "The low productivity of public employees and the malfunctioning of governmental bureaucracies are becoming apparent to an increasing number of frustrated and indignant taxpayers," they observe. "The problem shows up all over the country in the form of uncivil servants going through preprogrammed motions while awaiting their pensions."[19]

Anticipating by two decades the rhetoric of those who would propose to "reinvent" public bureaucracies, Savas and Ginsburg excoriate the status quo. "Too often, the result is mindless bureaucracies that appear to function for the convenience of their staffs rather than for the public whom they are supposed to serve." But the problem was not simply the preponderance of inadequate public employees. "It is the system itself . . . rather than the hapless politician who heads it or the minions toiling within it that is basically at fault."[20]

That system, they declare, "prohibits good management, frustrates able employees, inhibits productivity, lacks the confidence of the taxpayers, and fails to respond to the needs of citizens." The "worst feature of the promotion system," they continue, "is that an employee's chance of promotion bears no relationship to his performance on the job." At fault was "the rigor mortis of overdeveloped and regressive civil service systems."[21]

Interestingly this line of criticism, repeated often in subsequent years, led to what might be seen as a neo-Jacksonian call to replace parts of the civil service with political appointees, especially in city governments. The idea (it does, indeed, sound like rotation in office) was to give politicians more direct control over government—and to make governments more accountable to electorates. Arguments along this line became a staple of the neoliberals who gathered around Charles Peters and his influential magazine, *The Washington Monthly*.

Indeed, this neo-Jacksonian reaction also encompassed a certain informed nostalgia in political science for the old political machine—the very institution upon which the civil service reformers had waged war. The problem with institutionalizing social benefits in national entitlement programs, says Calvin Mackenzie in his appropriately titled book, *The Irony of Reform*, was that doing so allowed their beneficiaries "to be less attentive to politics" and less active at election time. Why? Because "government had taken over control of the benefits that had once inspired so much political activity. What had long been the game of the political machines—the provision of material benefits in exchange for political support—soon became the game of government. And when it did, the machines ran out of fuel and shut down." As a result, "the parties and the traditional politics they represented began to wither."[22] Never has patronage and "rotation in office" played as well among political scientists as it does now—after, of course, the machines (and, yes, their abuses) are gone.

But in truth, the spoils system and the political appointees who might be part of it play no better with the public than does the professional bureaucrat. Politics and government still do not enjoy the prestige they did when Caroline Kennedy Schlossberg's father was president. The tendency in both political parties, described well by Benjamin Ginsberg and Martin Shefter in their book *Politics by Other Means*, is to fight political battles through the courts, press disclosures, and congressional investigations.[23] Whatever the merit or utility of these approaches, they have had the effect of making the never-easy life of the political appointee far more difficult—and far less attractive.

It is thus striking, and not surprising, that young people devoted to public service tend less than ever to carry out that service through government—in either civil service or political posts. As Paul C. Light has pointed out, the trend among young people oriented toward service is to seek to reform institutions and change society through the nonprofit sector rather than through government itself.[24] Part of the problem, as Light points out, is the difficulty government has under current rules and practices in offering the flexibility and work opportunities available in the nonprofit sector. But it is also true that the idea of government service as an adventure, described so well by Hodgson, is about as fashionable as the now late, lamented Oldsmobile.

Another response to the discrediting of both civil servants and political nominees has been the rise in demands for the "privatization" of public services. As Light has shown, even as the formal numbers in some areas of government employment have fallen, many tasks once performed by government employees are taken on by employees of private companies—hired by the government.[25] The merits of privatization can be debated—in general, government officials tend to make pragmatic rather than ideological judgments about which services should be performed by whom. But what is noticeable in much of the privatization rhetoric is the discrediting of government servants as efficient deliverers of public wants and the elevation of the market as the preferred mechanism for introducing responsiveness and productivity.

At its best, the American tradition of tension between the political and the professional control of government is highly productive. The Jacksonian instinct that elections should matter and that there should be a significant degree of political control—meaning democratic control—over the bureaucracy is correct. But the desire for genuine expertise in the right places is also correct. The president, and the people, need military strategists, research scientists, lawyers, economists, and environmental specialists who will feel free to tell the truth as they see it and inform decisionmaking. A democratic government cannot be effective if it changes capriciously from one administration to another.

The American tradition creates a constant battle between the democratic impulse and the impulse for efficiency and predictability. This tension is not only useful but also necessary. The Jacksonian principle insists that in a democracy, there is not a bright line between "the government" on the one side and "civil society"—the array of communal institutions independent of government—on the other. If a government is not rooted in, and does not draw on, civil society, it can be neither democratic nor effective.

A Plague on Both Your Houses

It is not at all clear that the tension between our traditions is serving us well today. At most points in our history, at least one side of the government (the politicians or the professionals) enjoyed some claim on public esteem. Now it can be argued that neither does—and thus the tendency to want to farm government out as much as possible. The Jacksonians lifted up the political appointee to put a check on the arrogance of expertise. The civil service reformers lifted up expertise to put a check on political abuses. Now putting down both sides is the general rule.

The rise of a specifically presidential bureaucracy has in some ways divided the executive branch itself, aggravating its problems and the problems of those who work for it. As the political scientist Nelson Polsby has argued, one of the most interesting developments of the past half century "is the emergence of a presidential branch of government separate and apart from the executive branch." It is the presidential branch, Polsby writes, "that sits across the table from the executive branch at budgetary hearings, and that imperfectly attempts to coordinate both the executive and legislative branches in its own behalf."[26]

In *The Presidency in a Separated System*, Charles O. Jones makes a parallel point: that "the mix of career ambitions represented by presidential appointees may well bring the outside world to Washington, but there is no guarantee that these officials will cohere into a working government." Jones sees the president as "somewhat in the position of the Olympic basketball coach. He may well have talented players but lack a team."[27]

None of this means that George W. Bush or any future president will have trouble filling his (or, someday, her) government. None of it means that the country lacks the "practical idealists" of whom Al Gore liked to speak. But a government as peculiarly dependent as ours is on the willingness of citizens to interrupt the normal trajectory of their lives to devote themselves to government service needs to worry that it is not nourishing either of our great traditions of public service. When the political tradition has faltered, we have been able to call on our civil service tradition. When expertise falters, the politicos can step in to right the balance. But when both traditions fail, where do we turn?

We can privatize as much as we want, but government will never work if there is not a broadly accepted ethic that sees government service as honorable, productive, and creative—if there is not an ethic that views government service as public service. Nor will government work if young people see the independent sector as dynamic and the government sector as sterile and stolid. And, yes, it would help to have a president who drew people to public service because he asked them to do it and because he made it an adventure in which ambition and democratic idealism could coexist.

Notes

1. Caroline Kennedy Schlossberg, Remarks to the Democratic National Convention, Staples Center, Los Angeles, August 15, 2000.

2. Godfrey Hodgson, *The Gentleman from New York: Daniel Patrick Moynihan, A Biography* (Houghton Mifflin, 2000), p. 73.

3. Ibid., pp. 73, 74.

4. James Q. Wilson, *The Amateur Democrat* (University of Chicago Press, 1966), p. 200.

5. Cited in Harry L. Watson, *Liberty and Power: The Politics of Jacksonian America* (New York: Noonday Press, 1990), p. 103.

6. Ibid.

7. Robert Remini, *Martin Van Buren and the Making of the Democratic Party* (Norton, 1970), p. 194.

8. Robert Remini, *The Revolutionary Age of Andrew Jackson* (Harper and Row, 1976), p. 74.

9. Ibid.

10. Jefferson cited ibid.

11. Watson, *Liberty and Power*, p. 104.

12. Ibid.

13. Remini, *The Revolutionary Age*, p. 75.

14. Robert H. Wiebe, *The Search for Order, 1877–1920* (New York: Hill and Wang, 1967), pp. 60–61.

15. Ibid., p. 154.

16. Max Weber, "Bureaucracy," in H. H. Gerth and C. Wright Mills, eds., *From Max Weber* (New York: Oxford University Press, 1946), p. 240.

17. Mitchell quoted in Daniel Patrick Moynihan, "The Professionalization of Reform II," *Public Interest*, no. 121 (Fall 1995), p. 23. In this essay, Moynihan revisits and cites his classic essay, written thirty years earlier.

18. Moynihan, "The Professionalization of Reform II," p. 40.

19. E. S. Savas and Sigmund G. Ginsburg, "The Civil Service: A Meritless System?" *Public Interest*, no. 32 (Summer 1973), p. 71.

20. Ibid.

21. Ibid., pp. 78, 71.

22. G. Calvin Mackenzie, *The Irony of Reform: Roots of American Disenchantment* (Boulder: Westview Press, 1996), p. 64.

23. Benjamin Ginsberg and Martin Shefter, *Politics by Other Means: Politicians, Prosecutors, and the Press from Watergate to Whitewater* (New York: Basic Books, 1990).

24. Paul C. Light, *The New Public Service* (Brookings, 1999).

25. Paul C. Light, *The True Size of Government* (Brookings, 1999).

26. Quoted in Charles O. Jones, *The Presidency in a Separated System* (Brookings, 1994), p. 56.

27. Ibid., p. 60.

Contributors

Sarah A. Binder is assistant professor of political science at George Washington University and a fellow in the Brookings Governmental Studies program.

E. J. Dionne Jr. is a senior fellow in the Brookings Governmental Studies program.

George C. Edwards III is distinguished professor of political science and director of the Center for Presidential Studies in the Bush School of Government and Public Service at Texas A&M University.

Stephen Hess is a senior fellow in the Brookings Governmental Studies program.

Judith M. Labiner is deputy director of the Brookings Center for Public Service.

Paul C. Light is vice president and director of the Brookings Governmental Studies program and senior adviser to the Presidential Appointee Initiative.

Burdett Loomis is professor of political science and program coordinator at the Robert J. Dole Institute for Public Service and Public Policy at the University of Kansas.

G. Calvin Mackenzie is the Goldfarb Family Distinguished Professor of American Government at Colby College and a visiting fellow in the Brookings Governmental Studies program.

James P. Pfiffner is professor of government and public policy at George Mason University.

Terry Sullivan is a member of the Political Science Department at the University of North Carolina at Chapel Hill and holds the Edwards Chair in Democracy and Public Policy at the James A. Baker III Institute for Public Policy at Rice University.

Index